Children's Lives in an Era of Children's Rights

The Convention on the Rights of the Child (CRC), which was adopted unanimously by the United Nations General Assembly in 1989, marked a turning point in the perception of children in international law and policy. Although it was hoped that the Convention would have a significant and positive impact on the lives of all children, this has not happened in many parts of the world. This edited volume, based on empirical research and non-governmental organization project data, explores the progress of the Convention on the Rights of the Child in nine African countries in the 25 years since it was adopted by the UN General Assembly.

The book considers the implementation of the Convention both in terms of policy and practice, and its impact on the lived experiences of children in societies across the continent, focusing on specific themes such as AIDS, education and disability, child labour, witchcraft stigmatization, street children, parent–child relationships, and child participation. The book breaks new ground in blending legal and social perspectives of the experiences of children, and identifies concrete ways forward for the better implementation of the CRC in the various political contexts that exist in Africa.

Afua Twum-Danso Imoh is a Lecturer in the Sociology of Childhood at the University of Sheffield. Her research focuses on constructions of childhood, children's rights, and parent–child relationships in Africa. She is co-editor of *Childhoods at the Intersection of the Local and Global* (Palgrave, 2012).

Nicola Ansell is a Reader in Human Geography at Brunel University. Her research focuses on young people's experiences of social change in southern Africa. She is the author of *Children, Youth and Development* (Routledge, 2005) and directs an MA in 'Children, youth and international development'.

Routledge Research in Human Rights Law

Available titles in this series include:

The Right to Development in International Law
The case of Pakistan
Khurshid Iqbal

Global Health and Human Rights
Legal and philosophical perspectives
John Harrington and Maria Stuttaford

The Right to Religious Freedom in International Law
Between group rights and individual rights
Anat Scolnicov

Emerging Areas of Human Rights in the 21st Century
The role of the Universal Declaration of Human Rights
Marco Odello and Sofia Cavandoli

The Human Right to Water and its Application in the Occupied Palestinian Territories
Amanda Cahill

International Human Rights Law and Domestic Violence
The effectiveness of international human rights law
Ronagh McQuigg

Human Rights in the Asia-Pacific Region
Towards institution building
Hitoshi Nasu and Ben Saul

Human Rights Monitoring Mechanisms of the Council of Europe
Gauthier de Beco

The Positive Obligations of the State under the European Convention of Human Rights
Dimitris Xenos

Vindicating Socio-Economic Rights
International standards and comparative experiences
Paul O'Connell

The EU as a 'Global Player' in Human Rights?
Jan Wetzel

Regulating Corporate Human Rights Violations
Humanizing business
Surya Deva

The UN Committee on Economic, Social and Cultural Rights
The law, process and practice
Marco Odello and Francesco Seatzu

State Security Regimes and the Right to Freedom of Religion and Belief
Changes in Europe since 2001
Karen Murphy

The European Court of Human Rights in the Post-Cold War Era
Universality in transition
James A. Sweeney

The United Nations Human Rights Council
A critique and early assessment
Rosa Freedman

Children's Lives in an Era of Children's Rights
The progress of the Convention on the Rights of the Child in Africa
Afua Twum-Danso Imoh and Nicola Ansell

Litigating Transnational Human Rights Obligations
Alternative judgements
Mark Gibney and Wouter Vandenhole

Forthcoming titles in this series include:

Jurisdiction, Immunity and Transnational Human Rights Litigation
Xiaodong Yang

Children and International Human Rights Law
The right of the child to be heard
Aisling Parkes

Reproductive Freedom, Torture and International Human Rights
Challenging the masculinisation of torture
Ronli Noa Sifris

Applying an International Human Rights Framework to State Budget Allocations
Rights and resources
Rory O'Connell, Aoife Nolan, Colin Harvey, Mira Dutschke and Eoin Rooney

Children's Lives in an Era of Children's Rights

The Progress of the Convention on the Rights of the Child in Africa

Edited by
Afua Twum-Danso Imoh
and Nicola Ansell

 Routledge
Taylor & Francis Group

LONDON AND NEW YORK

First published 2014
by Routledge
2 Park Square, Milton Park, Abingdon, Oxon, OX14 4RN

and by Routledge
711 Third Avenue, New York, NY 10017

Routledge is an imprint of the Taylor & Francis Group, an informa business

British Library Cataloguing in Publication Data
A catalogue record for this book is available from the British Library

Library of Congress Cataloging-in-Publication Data
Children's lives in an era of children's rights : the progress of the
Convention on the Rights of the Child in Africa / edited by Afua
Twum-Danso Imoh, Nicola Ansell.
pages cm. – (Routledge research in human rights law)
ISBN 978-0-415-81607-6 (hardback) – ISBN 978-0-203-59492-6 (ebk)
1. Children's rights–Africa. 2. Children–Legal status, laws, etc.–Africa.
3. Convention on the Rights of the Child (1989 November 20)
4. African Charter on the Rights and Welfare of the Child (1990)
I. Imoh, Afua Twum-Danso, editor of compilation. II. Ansell, Nicola,
1965 – editor of compilation.
KQC145.M55C45 2014
342.08'772–dc23
2013029504

ISBN: 978-0-415-81607-6 (hbk)
ISBN: 978-0-203-59492-6 (ebk)

Typeset in Baskerville
by Cenveo Publisher Services

MIX
Paper from
responsible sources
FSC   FSC® C013604
www.fsc.org

Printed and bound in Great Britain by
CPI Group (UK) Ltd, Croydon, CR0 4YY

Contents

Notes on contributors

Dr Tatek Abebe holds a BA in geography from Addis Ababa University, an MPhil degree in development studies, and a PhD in human geography from the Norwegian University of Sciences and Technology (NTNU). He is an Associate Professor at the Norwegian Centre for Child Research (NTNU) where he teaches postgraduate courses on 'Children and development in the Global South', 'Urban children and youth in Africa', and 'Methods and ethics in childhood studies'. Abebe coordinates the Nordic Network of African Childhood and Youth Research (2011–15). He has published widely on topics related to street children, children's work, children's rights, rural and urban livelihoods, poverty, social reproduction, orphanhood, AIDS, and family collectives in Ethiopia. His co-edited anthology (with A.T. Kjørholt) on *Childhood and Local Knowledge in Ethiopia: Livelihood, Rights and Intergenerational Relationships* was published by Academika Press in the spring of 2013.

Dr Géraldine André is a Postdoctoral Researcher for the National Fund for Scientific Research in Belgium and affiliated to Pôle Sud and the Laboratoire d'Anthropologie Sociale et Culturelle at the University of Liège. Her PhD on working-class youth and vocational education in Belgium has recently been published by the French Publisher, Les Presses Universitaires de France (2012). Her postdoctoral research focuses on the case of African child workers in small-scale artisanal mining. With this focus, she aims to analyse the effects of the children's rights legislation on the evolution of processes of socialization in sub-Saharan Africa, more especially in the Democratic Republic of Congo (DRC) and Ghana.

Dr Nicola Ansell is a Reader in Human Geography at Brunel University, where she has worked for the past 14 years, since obtaining her PhD from Keele University. Her research has concerned the lives of young people living amid, and contributing to, social change in southern Africa. In particular, she has researched young people's engagements with their schooling experiences, the impacts of the AIDS pandemic, and the policies of the education sector. She has carried out extensive primary research with young people in Lesotho, Malawi, and Zimbabwe with funding from, among others, the Economic and Social Research Council, the Department for International Development, and the Royal Geographical Society. She has published more than thirty academic papers, a substantial number of book chapters, and a single-authored book entitled *Children, Youth and Development* (Routledge, 2005). She is the Director of Brunel University's MA programme in 'Children, youth, and international development'.

Professor Michael Bourdillon was born in Zambia and has lived most of his life in Zimbabwe. He acquired his doctorate in social anthropology at Oxford University and taught for many years in the Department of Sociology, University of Zimbabwe, where he now holds the post of Emeritus Professor. Apart from academic work, he has been practically involved in interventions for street children and for working children, working with both local and international NGOs. Following from this practical experience, his research and writing focused for some years on children's work and his many publications on this topic include the edited volume, *Earning a Life: Working Children in Zimbabwe* (Weaver Press, 2000); a co-authored work, *Girls on the Street* (Weaver Press, 2003); another co-authored book, *Rights and Wrongs of Children's Work* (Rutgers University Press, 2010); and a co-edited volume *African Children at Work* (LIT Verlag, 2012). He has directed two Institutes on Children and Youth in Dakar, Senegal, for CODESRIA (Council for the Development of Social Science Research in Africa). Recently he has co-edited volumes arising from the Young Lives multinational panel study situated at Oxford University: *Childhood Poverty* (Palgrave, 2012) and *Child Protection in Development* (Routledge, 2012).

Dr Kristen E. Cheney is Senior Lecturer in Children and Youth Studies for the International Institute of Social Studies, a graduate development studies institute in The Hague, Netherlands. From 2007 to 2013, she served as co-founder and advisory board chair for the American Anthropological Association's Anthropology of Children and Youth Interest Group. Her research focuses on children's survival strategies amid difficult circumstances, mainly in Eastern and Southern Africa. Her first book, *Pillars of the Nation: Child Citizens and Ugandan National Development* (2007, University of Chicago Press), looks broadly at the social intersections of childhood and nationhood in international development, while her Fulbright-funded ethnographic research with orphans and vulnerable children (OVC) examines issues of social exclusion, policy, and protection for children affected by AIDS. Her most recent research concerns the political economy of inter-country adoption and its relation to international development strategies. She is also involved in several research, consultancy, and capacity-building projects in Africa and the Middle East on issues ranging from children's rights to youth sexual and reproductive health. Her work takes an explicitly child-centred approach that considers how children experience and respond to the various hegemonic institutional and structural elements of global and local development practices.

Marie Godin is a PhD student at the University of East London (UK) affiliated to the Centre for Research on Migration, Refugees, and Belonging (CMRB) and a research associate at the Group for Research on Ethnic Relations, Migration, and Equality (GERME) at the Université Libre de Bruxelles. She holds an MA in social science from the Université Libre de Bruxelles and an MSc in forced migration from the Refugee Studies Centre, Oxford University. Her research interests lie in the fields of gender, African diasporas, peace-building, and development. She is also a research consultant for a number of international organizations in the field of migration, integration, and development.

Matemoho Khatleli has an MEd in the management of special education in developing countries and a BPhil Ed in special education (visual impairment). She is a Lecturer in the Department of Special Education at the Lesotho College of Education, Maseru, and previously worked with the Department of Education and Training as an Assistant Inspector in the Special Education Unit. She was a member of the research team on the Centre for Global Development through Education/Lesotho College of Education project on the identification and assessment of children with disabilities in Lesotho.

Stella Long is a Lecturer in Special Education at Mary Immaculate College, Limerick. She has undertaken research on special education in Lesotho and has presented nationally and internationally on this topic. Stella has co-authored (with O'Riordan, Urwick, and Campbell) 'Towards a holistic understanding of special educational needs', in R. Griffin (ed.) (2012) *Teacher Education in Sub-Saharan Africa: Closer Perspectives* (Oxford: Symposium Books). In addition to her interest in development education, Stella's expertise is in gifted education, dyspraxia, co-teaching, and teaching mathematics to pupils with special educational needs. She is currently a PhD candidate at Trinity College Dublin.

Nthabeleng Maketela is associated with deaf education in Lesotho where she has been engaged in teaching and supervising trainee teachers in special education at post-secondary institutions. She has worked at the Ministry of Education and Training as a general teacher and later on joined the Special Education Unit where she worked as an itinerant teacher. She has worked closely with teachers at early childhood centres and primary and secondary schools to support learners with disabilities/SEN in Lesotho. She has taken part in research, especially focusing on the education of learners with disabilities/SEN in Lesotho. She is also a member of the National Association of the Deaf in Lesotho (NADL) – the association of deaf persons in Lesotho.

Kate McAlpine works across disciplinary and geographic boundaries and on the intersection between scholarship, practice, and activism. Her scholarly work lies in developing a theory of altruistic social action and in applying this theory to development work in East Africa. Kate is currently an Associate Faculty at the International Health Department of Johns Hopkins University School of Public Health, USA. In addition Kate is a social entrepreneur and founder of the Caucus for Children's Rights (www.ccr-tz.org) and Mkombozi (www.mkombozi.org) NGOs in Tanzania, where she researches the situation of children affected by violence and the barriers that Tanzanians face in protecting children; designs social impact strategies that apply her integral activist approach to child protection programming; and facilitates participatory action research processes that support citizens to develop community-based child protection mechanisms. Kate is a graduate student in the Faculty of Human and Organizational Development at Fielding Graduate University, USA.

Eve Musvosvi is a Lecturer in the Faculty of Humanities and Social Sciences at Africa University in Mutare, Zimbabwe. She teaches childhood, youth, and development, among other social science modules. Currently she is a DPhil candidate in the Anthropology and Archaeology Department at the University of Pretoria in South Africa. Her thesis is entitled 'Growing up in the era of AIDS: childhood experiences in rural Zimbabwe'. Her research focuses on the complex and diverse experiences and meanings of being a child in a context of AIDS and political economic change in rural Zimbabwe. She also instructed a module called 'Culture, sex, and society' in the Anthropology and Archaeology Department at the University of Pretoria. Prior to that, she also taught at the University of Zimbabwe, where she got her MSc and honours in sociology and anthropology. Her work has been presented at various international and regional conferences and supported by the Ford Foundation, the African Population and Health Research Center (APHRC) doctoral fellowship, and the Centre for the Study of AIDS at the University of Pretoria where she was a research intern.

Dr Amy Norman is an independent researcher currently based in Pittsburgh, USA. She completed her PhD in geography at Queen Mary, University of London in 2011, exploring issues related to children's experiences in the time of AIDS in South Africa. Her research interests encompass family relationships and children's lives in southern Africa, focusing on AIDS, caregiving dynamics, household coping strategies, children's rights, and 'AIDS orphan tourism'. Over the last decade, she has worked collaboratively with the International Food Policy Research Institute (IFPRI), the Regional Network on HIV/AIDS, Rural Livelihoods and Food Security (RENEWAL), and the South African Human Sciences Research Council.

Grace Makeletso Ntaote is a Lecturer at the Lesotho College of Education in the Department of Special Education where she lectures special education courses to both in-service and pre-service educators. She has 28 years of teaching experience and has devoted her career to teaching and also has a passion for children, especially orphans and children rendered vulnerable by the HIV and AIDS pandemic. As a lecturer, she is aware that the HIV and AIDS pandemic has affected Lesotho educators at personal and professional levels. Teachers in Lesotho are overwhelmed by the pandemic. She considers that one of her duties at the Lesotho College of Education is to train student teachers on ways of better dealing with the challenges that result from having these children in their classrooms. Her PhD research explores ways of assisting Lesotho educators to offer care and support to vulnerable children orphaned by AIDS. Her research is not only topical, but also of great value as the country's education system works on its response to the crisis.

Florence Nyakudya is Lecturer in the Department of Special Education at the Lesotho College of Education, Maseru.

Dr Samuel Okyere is a child rights advocate who has recently completed his PhD at the University of Nottingham. Sam's PhD was focused on children's involvement in prohibited employment. His thesis, which was entitled 'Understanding child labour: the case of children working in artisanal gold mining at Kenyasi, Ghana', used the accounts of a group of children working in artisanal gold mining to examine the dominant representations and policy guidance on children's involvement in precarious work. Sam has also worked at the University of Sheffield, where he assisted on a research project which sought to facilitate the practice of children's participation rights within NGOs and other groups working with children in the Niger Delta region of Nigeria. Currently, Sam is a postdoctoral research fellow at the Centre for Advanced Studies at the University of Nottingham, where he supports the work of the Children and Childhood Network.

Evelyn Omoike is a doctoral researcher at the University of Warwick. She has a background in law and an MA in development from the University of Manchester. She has worked in various organizations in the public and private sectors. Her research interests include child soldiers, child domestic labour on a historical and contemporary level, the fosterage system in Africa, and the interpretation and applicability of the Convention of the Rights of the Child's (CRC) in West African societies. Her experience of growing up in a West African society where the use of children as domestic workers is commonplace gave birth to her PhD. Her current research focuses on children's experience of life as domestic workers and their interpretation of the CRC's principle of best interest. When she is not working on her thesis, Evelyn can be found cooking, watching movies, and spending time with her family.

Dr Jacqui O'Riordan lectures in the School of Applied Social Studies, University College Cork. She has extensive experience in a range of equality concerns, through her research in Tanzania in the mid-1990s, as well as number of community sector research consultancies undertaken in Ireland. Her research interests include gendered lives and livelihoods, analysis of care and caring, and, more recently, examination of aspects of childhood and children's lives. She has recently undertaken research on trafficking in children, and children living in direct provision in Ireland.

Dr Emilie Secker is the Violence, Abuse, and Neglect Programme Manager for Stepping Stones Nigeria, a UK-based charity which works with Nigerian partner organizations to support vulnerable and disadvantaged children in the Niger Delta region of Nigeria and to advocate for their rights at the local, national, and international levels. She is a former Honorary Fellow of the Law School of Lancaster University and holds a PhD in international human rights law. She has previously researched, taught, and published on children's rights, the right to participation, the right to development, and witchcraft accusations as a form of abuse of children's rights.

Tamirat Tefera holds an MA in sociology and social anthropology from Addis Ababa University (AAU). He has carried out different research and consultancies focusing on children, women, health, environment, tourism, and education in Ethiopia. Currently Tamirat is a PhD candidate at AAU, undertaking ethnographic fieldwork on the socioeconomic interaction of tourists and young tour guides in the Hamar community of south-western Ethiopia.

Dr Afua Twum-Danso Imoh is a Lecturer in the Sociology of Childhood at the University of Sheffield. She holds a PhD from the Centre of West African Studies at the University of Birmingham. Her thesis was entitled 'Searching for a middle ground in children's rights: the implementation of the Convention on the Rights of the Child in Ghana'. Since completing her PhD her research has focused on the changing nature of parent–child relationships; the impact of cultural values on universal children's rights standards; and the impact of globalization on the concept of childhood. Her work has been published in a number of edited collections as well as in peer-reviewed journals such as *Childhood: A Journal of Global Child Research, Journal of Human Rights, International Social Work, Journal of Family History, International Journal of Children's Rights, Children's Geographies,* and *Journal for the History of Childhood and Youth.* She is also the lead co-editor of another edited volume, *Childhoods at the Intersection of the Global and the Local,* which was published by Palgrave in October 2012.

Dr James Urwick is a specialist in educational policy and planning who has worked in various higher education institutions in Africa for long periods. His more recent research has focused on issues of basic education, teacher provision, and educational quality that are relevant to the achievement of the Dakar goals in low-income countries. In 2009–10 he was a research fellow in the Centre for Global Development through Education at Mary Immaculate College, Limerick, Ireland.

Dr Lorraine van Blerk is a Reader in Human Geography at the University of Dundee. She has conducted research with street-connected children and youth in sub-Saharan Africa over the past 15 years and has written more than 60 academic and policy-related publications in this area. In particular, Lorraine has a keen interest in working for the more effective participation of street children in both research and policy practices and this has featured widely in her writing. She is also a core member of the Consortium for Street Children's Research Forum which actively encourages collaboration between research, practice, and policy.

List of abbreviations

ACRWC	African Charter on the Rights and Welfare of the Child
ADHD	Attention Deficit Hyperactive Disorder
AIDS	Acquired Immunodeficiency Syndrome
ASM	artisanal and small-scale mining
BHRC	UK Bar Human Rights Committee
CCF	Christian Children's Fund
CCR	Caucus for Children's Rights (Tanzania)
CECE	Certificate in Early Childhood Education
CG	Capitation Grant (Ghana schools)
CGDE	Centre for Global Development through Education
CRA	Child Rights Act (Nigeria)
CRC	Convention on the Rights of the Child
CRIN	Child Rights Information Network
CRPD	UN Convention on the Rights of Persons with Disabilities
DCD	Development Co-ordination Disorder
DRC	Democratic Republic of the Congo
FCUBE	Free Compulsory Universal Basic Education (Ghana)
FDRE	Federal Democratic Republic of Ethiopia
FGD	focus group discussion
FGM	female genital mutilation
GO	governmental organization
HIPC	highly indebted poor country
HIV	Human Immunodeficiency Virus
HIV/AIDS	Human Immunodeficiency Virus/Acquired Immunodeficiency Syndrome
IECCD	Integrated Early Childhood Care and Development
IEP	Individual Educational Programme
ILO	International Labour Organization
IMCI	Integrated Management of Child Illnesses
IMF	International Monetary Fund
INGO	international non-governmental organization
IPEC	International Programme on the Elimination of Child Labour

LCE	Lesotho College of Education
LEAP	Livelihood Against Poverty (Ghana)
LNFOD	Lesotho National Federation of Organizations for the Disabled
MDG	Millennium Development Goal
MoET	Ministry of Education and Training (Lesotho)
MoHSW	Ministry of Health and Social Welfare (Lesotho)
MoLSA	Ministry of Labour and Social Affairs (Ethiopia)
NAPTIP	National Agency for the Prohibition and Trafficking of Persons and Other Related Matters (Ghana)
NCCL	National Committee to Combat the Worst Forms of Child Labour (Democratic Republic of the Congo)
NDCRW	Niger Delta Child Rights Watch project
NGO	non-governmental organization
OAU	Organization for African Unity
OHCHR	Office of the High Commissioner for Human Rights
OVC	orphans and vulnerable children
PTA	parent–teacher association
PTR	pupil–teacher ratio
PWDs	persons with disabilities
RDC	République démocratique du Congo (DRC)
SEN	special educational needs
SNNPR	Southern Nations, Nationalities, and People's Region (Ethiopia)
UCRNN	Uganda Child Rights NGO Network
UN	United Nations
UNAIDS	Joint United Nations Programme on HIV/AIDS
UNICEF	United Nations Children's Fund
WHO	World Health Organization

1 Realizing children's rights in Africa

An introduction

Afua Twum-Danso Imoh

Rationale and background

Two key anniversaries will soon be celebrated in the international human rights system. Both the Convention on the Rights of the Child (CRC) and the African Charter on the Rights and Welfare of the Child (ACRWC) will be marking their 25th anniversaries on 20 November 2014 and 11 July 2015 respectively. The anniversaries of these treaties are significant as they both marked a turning point in how children were perceived within international and regional human rights frameworks.

The Convention, which was the culmination of over 100 years of international discourse on children's rights and the successor to two international declarations (the 1924 Declaration on the Rights of the Child and the 1959 Declaration of the Rights of the Child), was a unique treaty within the history of the United Nations. Unlike its predecessors which were non-binding, aspirational, and paternalistic declarations focusing more on the welfare and protection of the child, the Convention, for the first time in international law, viewed children as rights holders instead of 'objects of adult charity' (Veerman, 1992: 184). As Fottrell (2000: 1) states, 'the Convention elevated the child to the status of an independent rights-holder' (see also Stahl, 2007). Additionally, the Convention was not only the first binding treaty on children's rights, but it was also the first to combine and integrate social, economic, and cultural rights with civil and political rights in a single legal instrument with equal emphasis placed on all the rights provided in its preamble and 54 articles. As a result of its focus on the whole spectrum of rights, the Convention, which is based on the underlying principles of non-discrimination, participation, survival and development, and the best interests of the child, contains articles that apply to virtually every area of children's lives regardless of their age as well as articles that relate to children in difficult circumstances. Hence, it has been called the 'most comprehensive treaty' ever to appear in the field of human rights (Stahl, 2007: 804–5). This is supported by Kilkelly and Lundy (2006: 335) who assert that:

> The coverage and scope of the UNCRC in recognising the rights of children and young people, and setting out how they are to be both

promoted and protected is unrivalled in terms of their comprehensive nature, international and national standing and relevance.

Furthermore, the role the Convention allocates to specialized agencies such as UNICEF and other civil society organizations in terms of its promotion and implementation is, again, unprecedented in the United Nations human rights framework (see also Woll, 2000). This role for civil society agencies can partly be attributed to the role they played in the drafting process. UNICEF, for example, began to play an active role in the drafting of the Convention from 1986 onwards and encouraged and facilitated the active participation of developing countries (see also Oestreich, 1998). The result of this, it is argued, is that 'more countries were prepared to accept the principles of the Convention and this explains the extraordinary widespread support, which was to be accorded this treaty in the early 1990s' (Alston, 1994: 7).

After its adoption by the United Nations General Assembly in 1989 the Convention continued to blaze the trail for international treaties. Almost 25 years after its adoption, it remains the most widely and most rapidly ratified Convention in the history of the United Nations. In under a year the required 20 states had ratified the Convention, thus bringing it into force by September 1990 – a record for any UN treaty (Viljoen, 1998). As of today all countries in the world except the United States, Somalia, and the new country of south Sudan have ratified it, thereby indicating their commitment to 'respect and ensure the children's rights provided within' this binding treaty (Spitz, 2005: 872).

Beyond the realm of the United Nations the Convention has also had an impact. As Myers (2001: 39) claims, 'its global reach is unparalleled and today it is now the prevailing general framework for most international action on children's rights'. This is supported by Stahl (2007: 805) who argues that 'the CRC has influenced the world, both in how societies regard children and in how they react to children as people'. Similar sentiments were expressed some years earlier by Veerhellen (1994) who asserted that the Convention led to the first faltering steps towards recognizing children as 'human beings' and it was supposed to mark the beginning of a new way of dealing with children.

Indeed, the Convention's impact has been felt in a number of areas. Critically, it has influenced the process of legal reform in various countries to ensure that domestic laws better protect the rights of children. Hence, since its adoption, governments have revised their national constitutions to explicitly take into account the rights of children. As Tobin (2005) notes, greater attention has been accorded to the rights of children within constitutions adopted in the years after the adoption of the Convention (see also Sloth-Nielsen, 2008b). A good example is that of the government of post-apartheid South Africa, which ratified the Convention in 1995 (Spitz, 2005; Richter and Dawes, 2008). More specifically, numerous governments have introduced child-focused laws into their legislative systems such as India (Juvenile Justice

Care and Protection of Children Act 2000), Mauritius (Children Act 2003), Goa (The Goa Children's Act 2003), Nepal (Children's Act 1992), Maldives (The Law on the Protection of the Rights of Children 1991), Indonesia (Law on Child Protection 2002), Malaysia (Child Act of 2001), Thailand (Child Protection Act 2004), Vietnam (Law on the Protection, Care, and Education of Children 2004), Venezuela (Organic Law for the Protection of the Child and Adolescent 1998), Peru (Children's and Adolescents' Code 2000), Paraguay (Code of Childhood and Adolescence 2001), Bolivia (Code of the Child and Adolescent 1999), Guatemala (The Law for the Fundamental Protection of Childhood and Adolescence 2002), Jamaica (The Child Care and Protection Act 2003), the Dominican Republic (Code for the Protection of Children and Adolescents 2004), and Antigua and Barbuda (Child Care and Protection Act 2003).

In Brazil, for example, the Brazilian Children's Act (the Statute on the Child and Adolescent), which came into force in October 1990, was inspired partly by the drafting process of the Convention and facilitated by the re-democratization of politics in the country. For the first time in Brazilian society, the concept of childhood was now associated with rights. Thus it is believed that there has been a real change in societal perceptions of children in general as well as widespread recognition of children as subjects of rights and much of this has been attributed to the influence of the Convention in the country (Rizzini and Barker, 2002, cited in Twum-Danso Imoh, 2012a).

The Convention has further been used as a key advocacy and lobbying tool by non-governmental organizations (NGOs) and international agencies seeking to both ensure governments abide by their commitments and also to sensitize local communities around the world. Thus children's rights watch-dogs, commissioners/ombudsmen, and coalitions of NGOs have been established to monitor and push forward the children's rights agenda as stipulated by the Convention. Myers (2001: 50) provides an outline of some of the key ways the Convention is used:

> Workshops, media campaigns, and other activities aimed at bringing social behaviour in line with rights guaranteed by the CRC are now common, and in some places school children now receive instruction about their rights under the CRC as part of their regular curriculum.

UNICEF, which became involved in the drafting of the Convention, continued to play a key role in its implementation. As Oestreich (1998: 187) states:

> By the mid-1990s, the CRC had become a sort of unofficial constitution of UNICEF, with almost every facet of its operations directed toward the convention's implementation, at least on the rhetorical level. UNICEF operations are now routinely justified, and progress measured, with reference to the goals of the CRC.

As a result of these developments, the concept and language of children's rights are more widespread in societies around the world today than they were 25 years ago. According to Woll (2000: 26):

> The adoption of the Convention foregrounded the concept of children as people with rights, beginning a transformation of public policy from one based on needs to one based on rights. Human rights, including child rights, are generally more visible in society than they were a decade ago. (see also Fottrell, 2000)

These are among the achievements that led Alderson and Morrow (2004: 10) to argue that 'respect for children's rights has grown since the adoption of the Convention ... [It] inspired countless new policies and projects around the world'.

With specific regards to the African continent, the Convention's influence, at least, in terms of law and policy, is also noteworthy. African governments were among the first to ratify the Convention with Ghana being the very first to do so in February 1990.[1] Subsequently, a number of governments have sought to bring their laws in line with the standards of the Convention. While some have made amendments to their constitutions, children's acts have been introduced into the legislative framework of countries such as Uganda (1997), Ghana (1998), Kenya (2001), Nigeria (2003),[2] South Africa (2005), Togo (2007), Tanzania (2009), Botswana (2009), and the Democratic Republic of Congo (2009) (see also Sloth-Nielsen, 2008b).

Despite the uptake of the Convention by African governments and the subsequent harmonization of laws with its standards, questions have remained about the relevance of the Convention to the continent as well as other non-Western regions of the world. The Convention, which was drafted mainly by the governments of Western Europe and North America, was firmly rooted in recent developments that have taken place with regards to children and their position in these societies. As a result any universality claimed by the number of governments that have ratified the Convention has been refuted by numerous commentators (Boyden, 1997; de Waal, 2002). In fact, the universality vs. relativity debate has underpinned the post-Convention years, rearing its stubborn head at key junctures in the life of this treaty.

The drafting and adoption of the African Charter on the Rights and Welfare of the Child, the first regional treaty on children's rights, partly reflects the feeling among some sectors that the Convention did not reflect the priorities and concerns relating to children on the African continent. According to Viljoen (1998: 205), African governments were frustrated with the drafting of the Convention for the following three reasons:

- Africans were underrepresented during the drafting process of the CRC;
- Potentially divisive and emotive issues were omitted in the search for consensus between states from diverse backgrounds;

- Specific provisions on aspects peculiar to Africa fell victim to the overriding aim of reaching a compromise, and were not sufficiently addressed in the UN instrument.

Thus in light of these concerns and frustrations the Charter was drafted with the aim of specifically and explicitly foregrounding the African cultural and historical heritage as made clear in its preamble:

> Taking into consideration the virtues of their cultural heritage, historical background and the values of the African civilization which should inspire and characterize their reflection on the concept of the rights and welfare of the child. (OAU, 1990: para. 6)

Beyond a desire to foreground the culture and historical traditions in the regional instrument, it also sought to address what Lee Muthoga, chair of the working group of African experts established by the then Organization of African Unity (OAU)[3] to draft the Charter, called 'certain peculiarly African problems' (Viljoen, 1998: 205). The third paragraph of the preamble sets forth what some of these issues are:

> Noting with concern that the situation of most African children, remains critical due to the unique factors of their socio-economic, cultural, traditional and developmental circumstances, natural disasters, armed conflicts, exploitation and hunger, and on account of the child's physical and mental immaturity he/she needs special safeguards and care. (OAU, 1990: para. 3)

Viljoen (1998) adds to this by pointing out:

> In many respects, children are more likely to be victims of human rights violations than adults, and African children are more likely to be victims than children on other continents. Causes of human rights violations in Africa, such as poverty, HIV/AIDS, warfare, famine and harmful cultural practices have a disproportionate impact on the continent's children. (cited in Sloth-Nielsen, 2008a: 3)

As result of its aim to reflect both historical and cultural traditions of Africa and the contemporary problems facing children on the continent today, the Charter outlines provisions which are both more flexible than the Convention and at the same time more stringent depending on the issue. Take these two examples for comparison. First, while Article 19 of the Convention stipulates that all appropriate legislative, administrative, social, and educational measures be taken to protect the child from all forms of physical or mental violence, injury or abuse, neglect or negligent treatment, maltreatment or exploitation, Article 20 (1) (c) of the Charter allows the administration of domestic discipline although it stipulates that this must be applied with humanity and be consistent with the inherent dignity of the child. Hence, while the Convention is against all forms of violence, it can be inferred from this article of the Charter that it allows for the administration of physical punishment within the context of the family, which is in line with traditional socialization practices in communities across the continent where physical punishment is perceived as a key component of the training children require to grow into the responsible adults their communities expect them to become (Twum-Danso Imoh, 2012b, 2013).

However, on other matters, it is the Convention which is flexible while the Charter remains rigid. For example, although the Convention and the Charter both define a child as every human being below the age of 18, the Convention (Article 1) adds a condition that '...unless, under the law applicable to the child, majority is attained earlier'. Thus on this issue the Convention leaves more room for manoeuvre by governments than the Charter which allows no such caveat (Article 2), possibly because of its recognition of some of the key challenges facing those under the age of 18 on the continent at a difficult point in time: the end of the Cold War had started to unleash a number of internal conflicts involving many children; IMF and World Bank structural adjustment policies which were introduced in the 1980s were continuing to impact the life chances of children across the continent; traditional practices such as child marriage remained prevalent in a number of countries at a time when many local activists were beginning to vocalize their opposition to these practices; and children in South Africa were still being discriminated against, oppressed, and killed under the apartheid regime. Such differing positions within the Charter may initially come across as a contradiction. However, any contradiction may be explained once it is taken into account that the drafters of the Charter were attempting to address the entirety of the challenges facing children on the continent. Thus it can be argued that both the flexibility and stringency inherent in the Charter can be attributed to its stated aim of foregrounding African 'peculiarities' – be they historical or contemporary.

This notwithstanding, it is important to note that while the Charter sought to explicitly take into account the peculiarities of the African context, it is not in opposition to the Convention. In fact, the Charter contains explicit acknowledgement that the Convention was a source of inspiration (Thompson, 1992; Lloyd, 2002). This is supported by its structure and contents. For example, the underlying principles of the Charter are the same as those of the Convention: non-discrimination; the best interests of the child; the right to life, survival, and development; and the participation of the child. Further, a number of articles within the Charter are striking in their similarity to those articulated in the Convention. Therefore, as Oluwu (2002: 128) states, 'the two pieces of legislation are complementary and both provide the framework within which children and their welfare are increasingly discussed in Africa' (see also Lloyd, 2008).

Despite the introduction of these two complementary legal instruments which should arguably provide a strong human rights framework for the protection and promotion of children's rights in Africa, the impact of these instruments on the lived experiences of children on the continent has remained limited. Hence, almost 25 years after the Convention and the Charter were adopted by their respective governing bodies, the lives of many children remain unchanged. In fact, in some respects conditions on the continent have worsened for some groups of children. This has implications for a continent which is not only the poorest in the world, but also the most youthful as children and young people under the age of 15 constitute 44% of its population (Ashford, 2007). Once those aged 16 and 17 are taken into account, this age group becomes the majority of the population of the continent and thus their demographic importance becomes strikingly apparent and, in fact, critical.

Aims and description of volume

It is within this context that this volume was developed. In particular, it aimed to assess the progress the Convention especially has made in the past two decades in nine countries located in four different regions of the continent (Southern, Central, East, and West) both in terms of policy and practice, and its impact on the lived experiences of children in societies across the continent. It is hoped that through these country-based in-depth studies drawing primarily on empirical fieldwork with children and the key adults in their lives as well as on the projects of child-focused NGOs, this volume will provide a critical analysis of the progress of this treaty and identify concrete ways forward for its effective implementation in the various social, cultural, and political contexts that exist in Africa. As the volume aims to explore the progress of the Convention, and to a lesser extent the Charter, vis-à-vis the lived experiences of children's lives, the chapters in this volume seek to move their analysis beyond a legalistic perspective and demonstrate how these legal instruments impact (or not as the case may be) on children's everyday lives and relationships within their families as well as elsewhere.

First, in her chapter on orphans and vulnerable children in Uganda, Kristen Cheney strongly argues that the concept of children's rights, as it is currently discussed and realized, is hindering this group of children more than helping them. She goes on to claim that rights discourses are actually disempowering children in this context as they foreground protection over participation and as a result, present an obstacle to children's survival strategies, leading to a situation whereby children have to rely on adults in order to claim their rights. In response to this infantilization, she argues, these children have adopted various strategies, including adopting the notion of victimcy imposed on them and using it to ensure their own survival. Furthermore, Cheney argues that the attention international NGOs have focused on the plight of orphans has disrupted child–adult power relations as they are singled out for attention and, in this way, are removed from the context of their families.

Also focusing on the context of HIV/AIDS, but in South Africa, Amy Norman presents an excellent case study of the ability of the Convention to reach into the most basic unit of society – the family and affect child–adult relations. Thus she shows how the Convention's influence is being currently felt in South African society. However, far from this leading to the better protection of children in this context, she found that these rights have led to new challenges in society, especially in relation to intergenerational relationships within the sphere of the family in particular. Specifically, the expansion of the rights discourse has led to frustration on the part of adults who feel that rights are eroding traditional values such as respect and reciprocity which is seen as problematic, or downright dangerous, in the era of HIV/AIDS. She outlines how parents feel that children's rights are leading to the production of children who are 'overly empowered' and 'independent from home life', the creation of a power imbalance within family dynamics, and the dissonance between parents and children, which she blames for causing the lack of engagement and communication between generations on topics such as sex and relationships. Instead, parents are surrendering their parenting rights to the state which, they believe, is imposing itself on them as co-parent without consultation or buy-in.

Similar to Norman's chapter, Tatek Abebe and Tamirat Tefera also demonstrate the extent to which the discourse of children's rights has filtered into local community contexts in Ethiopia – to the extent that it is now discussed by local governments, schools, and even community-based organizations such as burial and credit associations. However, they also show that the visibility of rights discourses at the local level does not automatically mean it is accepted by these communities. Instead, they highlight how rights are contested, rejected, and ignored as a 'passing fad'. Like Cheney, and Norman, Abebe and Tefera also argue that rights discourses, with their focus on the individual child, have been more problematic than useful in a context where interdependency, reciprocity, and the family collective is seen as paramount. The resulting outcome, in some cases, has been a dissonance between children and their families, leading some children to move on to the streets in search of self-determination. Partly as a result of the importance of interdependency and collectivity in this context, parents expressed frustration that NGOs were focusing on children's rights without considering broader issues of national development and the impact of poverty on families as a whole.

In a similar vein in their chapter on children's work in the mining industry in Katanga province, DRC, Géraldine André and Marie Godin show how children's rights and NGO narratives have combined with a neoliberal agenda to filter new values, especially around concepts such as 'responsible parenthood' and 'proper childhood', which have been accepted by some Congolese parents especially those within the middle classes. Nevertheless, they have also led to unintended consequences due to the fact that they overlook the economic and cultural context of Congolese society which continues to stress interdependencies within family relationships, the importance of the family collective, and reciprocity. The resulting outcome is that instead of protecting children, these representations of a proper childhood and proper parenthood advocated by these NGOs have 'ruptured pathways of survival' for the young and in some cases, have led to the migration of older children to other artisanal mining sites away from home. Further, they argue that these narratives promoted by NGOs are reinforcing the fears of elders about the young leading to a disruption in child–adult relations.

Samuel Okyere's chapter, which also looks at artisanal mining, but in Kenyasi, Ghana, draws on children's views to show that poverty is the key driving factor behind their work in these mines. Thus while he acknowledges that cultural factors may play a role in children's engagement in work that is seen as dangerous and hazardous, he insists that it is predominately poverty that drives children to these mines in search of work. Thus until structural issues relating to poverty are addressed, children's rights, as they relate to child labour, cannot be realized. Hence, he argues that national development and poverty reduction programmes must play a central role in any solution developed to tackle child labour. Interestingly, he also wades into the debate on children's work vs. children's schooling and shows that for these children, it is not a case of choosing between school and work. They strongly assert that in order to be able to go to school and pay for all the attendant costs, they need to work. Thus far from school and work being polar opposites in the child labour debate, they may, in fact, be more complementary than policy-makers and children's rights advocates have, hitherto, been prepared to acknowledge.

Similarly, in their chapter on children's lives in Chiweshe Communal Land in Zimbabwe in the era of AIDS as well as political and economic decline, Michael Bourdillon and Eve Musovosi point to the agency these children demonstrate in the strategies they adopt for survival, including forming survival bands and engaging in mining. This leads the authors to question the applicability of the traditional social work model to this group of children as it positions them as victims instead of supporting and empowering them in their strategies for survival. Further, they argue that the current social work model fails to consider the context in which children face risks and the need to address the issue of poverty before focusing on the issue of child protection within such contexts. Failure to do so, they argue, not only compounds the situation of these children, but it may also put them at greater risk.

That children themselves may well see work as being in their 'best interests' due to the realities of their lives also emerges in Evelyn Omoike's chapter on predominately female child domestic workers in Nigeria and Ghana. Omoike shows that although the literature on child domestic workers normally casts this group as victims, when you take their views into account some demonstrate the agency they have in decisions relating to entering and exiting domestic work. While many may not like the work they do, they are aware that that this work may present the least worst option in their lives at the current time. This chapter not only shows that the way children may determine their best interests may clash with those of the children's rights advocates and child protection experts seeking to rescue them from the conditions in which they live and work, but also it further underscores the point that has emerged in other chapters (Okyere; Bourdillon and Musovosi) that until broader structural issues such as poverty and its impact on families and communities in their entirety are addressed, child labour, whatever form it may take, will remain a viable option for families and children themselves.

In her chapter on the limited impact of children's rights on children's lived experiences in Tanzania, Kate McAlpine, like other contributors to this volume, calls for a broader, more holistic approach to the realization of children's rights. However, drawing on her work as the founder of the Caucus for Children's Rights, a network of NGOs based in Tanzania, she argues that while the government of Tanzania has focused on the technical and financial aspects of development, which have led to some progress in the areas of education and health, these are, as she puts it 'just quick fixes'. For real progress to take place she argues that there is a need to also invest in human development – especially with regards to interventions that focus on people's emotional and relational needs. In particular, she argues that there is a need to ensure that there is investment in programmes and initiatives that support behaviour and attitudinal change towards children as these will contribute significantly to the more effective protection of their rights. Not doing so, she argues, is short sighted as without this investment the progress the country has been making in terms of its development will be hampered.

The experiences of children in particularly difficult circumstances in relation to their ability to enjoy rights as stipulated in the Convention and the Charter are also addressed in this volume. In their chapter on children with special needs in Lesotho, Jacqui O'Riordan and her colleagues provide a case study which demonstrates the isolation that disabled children and their families face within their communities as well as the challenges they experience in accessing services especially in relation to early childhood care and education. These are very much intertwined as they argue that the isolation that these children experience may be minimized through medical consultations, identification of their needs, and greater awareness of these disabilities. In particular they point out that greater communication between medical staff and other professionals may contribute to improving the wellbeing of these children. In addition, in her chapter on the implementation of the Convention in the Niger Delta of Nigeria, Emilie Secker focuses on the challenges facing the country's Children's Rights Act and the implications for children whose rights have been violated in their search for justice. Specifically, she draws on a project she has managed as Violence, Abuse and Neglect Programme Manager at Stepping Stones Nigeria, a UK-based NGO working in the Niger Delta, to outline the various violations of children that this project has recorded (mainly sexual and physical abuse and witchcraft accusations), the causes behind these, and the obstacles that prevent this group of children from obtaining justice. As a result of the social and cultural factors that present real barriers to the realization of children's rights in the Niger Delta, and in fact, contribute to these violations in the first place, she concludes that for laws to be implemented in a particular context they must be meaningful to those communities. Following on from this Lorraine van Blerk examines policy representations of street children, who normally exist outside idealized conceptualizations of childhood, and argues that for this group to be able to access their rights to protection, it is critical that they are able to claim their participatory rights – otherwise strategies developed to help them will not be useful or sustainable.

Finally, drawing on a recent study on children's participation in the Niger Delta of Nigeria, Samuel Okyere and Afua Twum-Danso Imoh challenge the notion of child participation as it is defined by the international community and inspired by the Convention. Specifically, they argue that while the conventional notion of child participation is certainly worthy, it does not take into account children's own understanding of the concept in the Niger Delta and Nigeria more generally. Thus even when the children in their study were aware of the conventional definition of child participation, they insisted that their own definition, which included housework, should also apply. Thus the authors conclude that in order for this concept to be realized within this social and cultural context, there is a need to broaden the concept of child participation to allow for more local understandings as that will make it more meaningful for these children and their communities. Together these chapters provide an insight into the minutiae of family and community relations which ultimately have an impact on the enforcement of children's rights in various African countries. Such insight is critical to obtain as it will not only contribute to furthering the discourse on children's rights, but it will also be invaluable for policy-makers developing strategies for the more effective implementation of children's rights laws and policies in their national and local contexts.

Foregrounding the Convention over the Charter

It must be acknowledged that there is a distinct focus on the Convention as opposed to the Charter not only in the chapters in this volume, but also in its title. Considering that the continent of Africa has its own binding treaty on children's rights and welfare, this requires explanation. Despite its explicit aim to address African historical and contemporary peculiarities, the Charter's influence has been much more limited than the Convention within its jurisdiction. While African governments were among the very first to ratify the Convention, the uptake of the Charter by these same governments was much slower. Hence, although the Convention entered into force less than a year after its adoption by the United Nations General Assembly, the Charter did not receive the requisite number of ratifications to enable it to be enforced until November 1999, over nine years after it was adopted by the Organization of African Unity. As of May 2013, only 41 out of the 53 African Union Member States have ratified the Charter. This means that while all African governments – bar two – have ratified the Convention, 12 have still not ratified their very own regional treaty. Various reasons have been put forward to explain the slow uptake of the Charter compared to the Convention (see, for example, de Waal, 2002; Lloyd, 2003) and while it is not the remit of this introduction, nor indeed this volume, to explore these, it is sufficient to say that the resulting outcome, in real terms, has been that the influence of the Charter has been in stark contrast to that of the Convention.

While some governments have taken into account some of the articles of the Charter, especially its provisions on children's responsibilities to family and community as well as the need to respect elders (see Secker, this volume; André and Godin, this volume), it must be acknowledged that beyond law and policy, any influence the Charter may possess remains limited. Today, in countries across Africa those people who are aware of the concept of children's rights know about it in connection with the Convention, not the Charter (see Abebe and Tefera, this volume; Norman, this volume). In workshops and seminars that are held across the continent for NGOs and policymakers, the focus of attention is more often than not on the Convention, with the Charter added on as an afterthought, if at all. In feature articles and television and radio programmes aiming to sensitize children and others within their communities on children's rights, the reference point used is almost always the Convention, not the Charter. As a result, although it is a binding treaty and the first regional treaty to be adopted for the protection and promotion of children's rights, the Charter's visibility, and thus impact on children's real lives, has been limited.

Having said that, its potential as a tool for community engagement and action with local communities must be recognized. This can particularly be seen in Article 31 of the Charter which imparts duties on children: every child has responsibilities towards his/her family and society, the state, and other legally recognized communities, including the international community. In addition, it states that children should respect parents and elders at all times and to assist them in cases of need. This provision has caused some unease within human rights circles. Van Bueren (1995: 24–5) puts forward her concerns about this provision as follows: 'apart from the difficulties of creating such duties in international law, the responsibility to respect parents and elders at all times is too unquestioning and general.' Kaime (2005: 231) further adds that the relationship between children and adults in communities across the continent is characterized by enormous 'filial respect, and in turn, is reinforced by the ethic of dominance' and he calls for 'a reconsideration of the position of children vis-à-vis their parents and the development of a culture of listening on the latter's part'.

While these points have some validity, it must also be noted that this article has the potential to facilitate dialogue on children's rights on this continent. As Lloyd (2008: 33) asserts:

> The ACRWC recognizes children in Africa as direct bearers of rights, and in turn, children bear responsibilities to others. This may be considered a controversial addition by Western thinkers, but it reflects the underpinning of African society, and positive conclusions can be drawn from this addition, once one understands the African concept of human rights.

Hence, for children's rights to be realized in Africa there is a need to work with the cultural values that remain important to communities instead of work against them or overlook their existence. Thus the Charter's provisions on respect could potentially facilitate dialogue with communities about children's rights. This became apparent in a project in which I was recently involved which focused on children's participation in the Niger Delta of Nigeria and was funded by the University of Sheffield's R&D Collaborative fund (see Twum-Danso Imoh *et al.*, 2012; see also Okyere and Twum-Danso Imoh, this volume). In one of the focus groups that was organized as part of this project some participants pointed out that the principles of the Charter may be more welcomed than the Convention by local communities in their context. According to one participant:

> I will add to that by saying that sometimes, the laws do not work very well here if we practice them as they are. For instance, we used to go to schools to educate children on their rights using the UNCRC. However, we started receiving complaints that some of the children who were involved in the programme had become argumentative and disruptive in home and the school. My NGO realized that the children were not enjoying their rights responsibly or according to the values of their society because the UNCRC makes no such demands of children. Therefore, we now also refer to the ACRWC because it talks about the duties and responsibilities of African children as part of their rights and entitlements. (FGD participant Calabar, quoted in Twum-Danso Imoh *et al.*, 2012: 70)

A similar example is provided by Norman (this volume) who argues that the challenges presented by the rights discourse in South Africa have now led to the development of a Bill of Responsibilities (2010) which is now taught alongside the Convention in schools in order to emphasize that children's rights are inseparable from their duties and responsibilities to others. Thus with its focus on children's duties and the need for children to respect adults, the Charter may resonate more strongly with local communities across the continent and may be a useful tool to facilitate dialogue with such communities.

What these two examples show is that while the Convention has had more influence than the Charter at the grassroots level in some communities as demonstrated by a number of the chapters in this volume, the Convention alone is not sufficient as a human rights framework for the African continent. The Convention by itself, with its emphasis on individuality, biological parents, the nuclear family, school-based education vs. work, may not only struggle to sit easily with children and adults even if it filters through to local communities, but also it may lead to unintended outcomes such as intergenerational tensions and dissonance between adults and children. However, the Charter, with its emphasis on the peculiarities of the African context, may be more acceptable at the level of the family and local community. Thus together the Convention and Charter may provide a complementary framework within which children's rights can be protected and promoted, not just at the level of law and policy, but also at the local level where children live out their lives – within their families and communities. Hence, not only should these treaties complement each other in the international human rights framework, they must also complement, and be utilized alongside each other, in efforts to realize children's rights in the various spheres in which they actually live their lives.

Notes

1 Two years after the Convention was adopted, on 31 December 1992, 39 out of a possible 52 states in Africa had already ratified the Convention.
2 Although the 2003 Nigerian Child Rights Act was passed at the Federal level, it is only effective if state assemblies also enact it. As of February 2013, 10 of the country's 36 states had yet to pass the Act.
3 In 2002 the Organization of African Unity, established in 1963, changed its name to the African Union (AU).

References

Alderson, P. and Morrow, V. (2004) *Ethics, Social Research and Consulting with Children and Young People*, Ilford: Barnardo's.
Alston, P. (1994) 'The best interest principle: towards a reconciliation of culture and human rights', in P. Alston (ed.) *The Best Interests of the Child: Reconciling Culture and Human Rights*, Oxford: Clarendon Press.
Ashford, L. (2007) *Africa's Youthful Population: Risk or Opportunity?* Washington, DC: Population Reference Bureau.
Boyden, J. (1997) 'Childhood and the policy makers: a comparative perspective on the globalization of childhood', in A. James and A. Prout (eds) *Constructing and Reconstructing Childhood: Contemporary Issues in the Sociological Study of Childhood* (2nd edn), London and New York, NY: Routledge Falmer.

de Waal, A. (2002) 'Realising child rights in Africa: children, young people and leadership', in A. de Waal and N. Argenti (eds) *Young Africa: Realising the Rights of Children and Youth, Trenton*, NJ and Asmara: Africa World Press.

Fottrell, D. (2000) 'One step forward or two steps sideways? Assessing the first decade of the CRC', in D. Fottrell (ed.) *Revisiting Children's Rights: 10 Years of the UN Convention on the Rights of the Child*, The Hague: Kluwer.

Kaime, T. (2005) 'The Convention on the Rights of the Child and the cultural legitimacy of children's rights in Africa: some reflections', *African Human Rights Law Journal*, 5 (2): 221–38.

Kilkelly, U. and Lundy, L. (2006) 'Children's rights in action: using the UN Convention on the Rights of the Child as an auditing tool', *Child and Family Law Quarterly*, 18 (3): 333–50.

Lloyd, A. (2002) 'Evolution of the African Charter on the Rights and Welfare of the Child and the African Committee of Experts: raising the gauntlet', *The International Journal of Children's Rights*, 10: 179–98.

Lloyd, A. (2003) 'Regional developments on the rights and welfare of children in Africa: a general report on the African Charter on the Rights and Welfare of the Child and the African Committee of Experts.' Unpublished article.

Lloyd, A. (2008) 'The African regional system for the protection of children's rights', in J. Sloth-Nielsen (ed.) *Children's Rights in Africa: A Legal Perspective*, Farnham and Burlington, VT: Ashgate.

Myers, W. (2001) 'The right rights? Child labor in a globalizing world', *Annals of the American Academy of Political and Social Science*, 575 (1): 38–55.

OAU (1990) *The African Charter on the Rights and Welfare of the Child*, Addis Ababa: Organization of African Unity.

Oestreich, J. (1998) 'UNICEF and the implementation of the Convention on the Rights of the Child', *Global Governance*, 4 (2): 183–98.

Oluwu, D. (2002) 'Children's rights in Africa: a critique of the African Charter on the Rights and Welfare of the Child', *International Journal of the Rights of the Child*, 10: 127–36.

Richter, L. and Dawes, A. (2008) 'Child abuse in South Africa: rights and wrongs', *Child Abuse Review*, 17 (2): 79–93.

Sloth-Nielsen, J. (2008a) 'Children's rights and the law in African context: an introduction', in J. Sloth-Nielsen (ed.) *Children's Rights in Africa: A Legal Perspective*, Farnham and Burlington, VT: Ashgate.

Sloth-Nielsen, J. (2008b) 'Domestication of children's rights in national legal systems in African context: progress and prospects', in J. Sloth-Nielsen (ed.) *Children's Rights in Africa: A Legal Perspective*, Farnham and Burlington, VT: Ashgate.

Spitz, L. (2005) 'Implementing the UN Convention on the Rights of the Child: children's rights under the 1996 South African Constitution', *Vanderbilt Journal of Transnational Law*, 38–853.

Stahl, R. (2007) 'Don't forget about me: implementing Article 12 of the United Nations Convention on the Rights of the Child', *Arizona Journal of International and Contemporary Law*, 24 (3): 803–42.

Thompson, B. (1992) 'Africa's charter on children's rights: a normative break with cultural traditionalism', *The International and Comparative Law Quarterly*, 41 (2): 432–44.

Tobin, J. (2005) 'Increasingly seen and heard: the constitutional recognition of children's rights', *South African Journal on Human Rights*, 21 (1): 86–126.

Twum-Danso Imoh, A. (2012a) 'The Convention on the Rights of the Child: a product and facilitator of a global childhood', in A. Twum-Danso Imoh and R. Ame (eds) *Childhoods at the Intersection of the Local and Global*, Basingstoke: Palgrave.

Twum-Danso Imoh, A. (2012b) '"This is how we do it here": the persistence of cultural practices in the face of globalized ideals: the case of physical punishment of children in Ghana', in A. Twum-Danso Imoh and R. Ame (eds) *Childhoods at the Intersection of the Local and Global*, Basingstoke: Palgrave.

Twum-Danso Imoh, A. (online first edition available 18 January 2013) 'Children's perceptions of physical punishment in Ghana and the implications for children's rights', *Childhood: A Journal of Global Child Research.*

Twum-Danso Imoh, A., Okyere, S. and Secker, E. (2012) 'Facilitating children's participation in the Niger Delta of Nigeria.' Unpublished Project Report funded by the University of Sheffield R&D Collaborative Scheme.

Van Bueren, G. (1995) *The International Law on the Rights of the Child*, Dordrecht, Boston, MA, and London: Martinus Nijhoff Publishers.

Veerhellen, E. (1994) *The Convention on the Rights of the Child: Background, Motivation, Strategies, Main Themes*, Leuven and Apeldoorn: Garant Publishers.

Veerman, P. (1992) *The Rights of the Child and the Changing Image of Childhood*, Dordrecht: Martinus Nijhoff Publishers.

Viljoen, F. (1998) 'Supra-national human rights instruments for the protection of children in Africa: the Convention on the Rights of the Child and the African Charter on the Rights and Welfare of the Child', *The Comparative and International Law Journal of Southern Africa*, 31 (2): 199–212.

Woll, L. (2000) *The Convention on the Rights of the Child: Impact Study*, Stockholm: Save the Children Sweden.

2 Conflicting protectionist and participation models of children's rights

Their consequences for Uganda's orphans and vulnerable children[1]

Kristen E. Cheney

During my 2001 dissertation fieldwork at a primary school in Kampala, Uganda, I met many children living with their extended families after their parents had died, often of AIDS. Margaret was one of them. She was the tallest girl in the fifth grade, with bright eyes and a gracious smile. She lived with her uncle because both her parents had already passed away. One Monday morning at school, she accosted me. Her uncle had also passed away from AIDS complications the previous Friday. Her aunt was not her blood relative, and if Margaret stayed with her, her aunt could not guarantee that she could afford to pay Margaret's school fees. Three days after her uncle's death, Margaret was already soliciting alternative sources of support: Might I be able to find someone to sponsor her education, she asked? (from field notes, 2009)

African AIDS orphans are typically institutionally framed as particularly vulnerable children, and thus even less endowed with agency than 'normal' children. There has been ample research on governmental and non-governmental response to the African 'orphan crisis' (Guest, 2003; Singhal and Howard, 2003; Foster *et al.*, 2005), but – though it is apparent that their needs are not being met (UNICEF, 2008) – little work has been done to document children's own responses to orphanhood and their agency in ameliorating its circumstances. Yet in my research with orphans, I have noted that children like Margaret are very active in securing their perceived needs (Cheney, 2013). Ironically, rights discourse may in fact hinder their efforts more than help them: the current historical convergence of children's rights dissemination and the global aid industry's attention towards the AIDS orphan crisis in Africa has led to a paradox of social justice for orphans and vulnerable children (OVC), in which their vulnerability is pitted against their empowerment.

Drawing on anthropological fieldwork with OVC conducted in Uganda from 2007 to 2009, my aim here is to detail the parallel development of children's rights implementation and the aid industry's response to Africa's 'orphan crisis' in order to track the effects of children's rights implementation on OVC in Africa. My argument is that, despite claims that children's rights discourses emphasize participation, rights implementation remains largely protectionist and can therefore impede rather than facilitate orphans' survival strategies. I first discuss what the Convention on the Rights of the Child actually conveys about empowerment, participation, and protection of children. Next, I contextualize the debate by considering the evolution of humanitarian assistance to orphans and how this has influenced local dynamics of orphans' support. This leads to the conclusion that, due to protectionist emphases on children's rights, they tend to disempower OVC. What is needed to augment children's rights' potential to empower OVC, I will argue, is a reconceptualization of child citizenship and renewed emphasis on substantive participation in practice.

The Convention on the Rights of the Child: participatory, or protectionist?

One of the routes to empowerment of children is through participation in decisions that affect them. Children's rights scholars and practitioners alike have contended that the Convention on the Rights of the Child (CRC) is guided by principles of child participation, and/or child protection. The UNICEF website on the CRC states that 'Human rights apply to all age groups; children have the same general human rights as adults. But children are particularly vulnerable and so they also have particular rights that recognize their special need for protection' (UNICEF, 2005). Indeed, the words 'protection' and 'protect' occur not less than 47 times in the CRC (versus 19 times in the Universal Declaration of Human Rights), while the African Charter on the Rights and Welfare of the Child (ACRWC) uses the term 'protect' 33 times. Even the stated purpose of the Ugandan Government's Children Act is 'to provide for local authority support for children' (Government of Uganda, 1997: 1); it does not contain the word 'participation'. Similarly, the terms 'empowerment', 'empower', or even 'power' do not appear at all – in any of these documents.

Many scholars have endorsed UNICEF's contention that 'Participation is one of the guiding principles of the Convention...' (UNICEF, n.d.a). However, this seems a broad interpretation when 'participation' is not defined as a key term in the introduction (UNICEF, n.d.b), and the word only appears twice in the whole document (as opposed to five appearances in the Universal Declaration of Human Rights) – once in Article 23 on disability, where it says that the state should facilitate disabled children's active participation in community, and once in Article 40, where it actually refers to other witnesses in penal cases involving children. Other mentions of children's right to 'participate' are in relation to separation from family (Article 9) and play (Article 31). The ACRWC similarly refers only to participation of disabled children and in reference to cultural and leisure activities. Article 12 is often referred to as the main participation provision in the CRC, but it does not use the term, either. Rather, it states:

1. States Parties shall assure to the child who is capable of forming his or her own views *the right to express those views freely in all matters affecting the child*, the views of the child being given due weight in accordance with the age and maturity of the child.
2. For this purpose, *the child shall in particular be provided the opportunity to be heard in any judicial and administrative proceedings affecting the child*, either directly, or through a representative or an appropriate body, in a manner consistent with the procedural rules of national law. (United Nations, 1989, my emphasis)

These provisions are about the expression of views, and not participation in decision-making per se. Like 'participation', what 'being heard' means is quite open to interpretation. It also appears to refer to individual children and not to entire groups (like orphans), who are subject to policy implementation. Even UNICEF, in its generous interpretation of the CRC as guaranteeing participation, acknowledges 'Expressing an opinion is not the same as taking a decision, but it implies the ability to influence decisions' (UNICEF, n.d.b). So Article 12 and other references to children's rights to the expression of views is still, at best, a precursor to children as a social group being able to influence decision-making processes and policies that affect them.

This leaves one to wonder where people got the idea that participation is enshrined in children's rights conventions. Despite no obvious emphasis in a basic content analysis of the documents, many still insist that the CRC itself emphasizes children's participation in decisions that affect them – any discrepancies resting with implementation alone. While the CRC, as Dipak Naker (2007: 148) has shown, tends to emphasize protection over participation, I suspect that the stakes in recognizing participation as a guiding principle of the CRC may be linked to recent emphases in childhood studies on children's agency. While it has been fairly well established that children do have agency, attention must now turn to how that agency is constrained under difficult circumstances, such as orphanhood. I argue that the fact that protection and 'best interests' are emphasized so much more than participation or empowerment in these documents points to the underlying assumption of children's vulnerability and reliance on adults, and that this is what still informs practice. Take, for instance, the fact that human rights declarations generally allow adults to make direct claims for their rights while children cannot. This makes children's rights different from their inception – and perhaps to some extent they should be, as it is important to acknowledge children's age-related developmental distinctiveness by providing more protection. On the other hand, it requires adult interlocutors to intervene on children's behalves in order to make claims for their rights (Brennan, 2002). This does not necessarily help children to be empowered by rights, then, as children like Margaret must still rely on adult gatekeepers to take the first agentive steps to fulfil even her basic rights.

The new Optional Protocol 3, ratified in February 2012, allows 'children the possibility to access justice at the international level through a newly adopted complaints procedure' (Child Rights Coalition Asia, 2012). This holds promise for increasing children's participation, but it is still *optional.* Contradicting UNICEF's claim that 'children have the same general human rights as adults', Peter Newell, the chair of the non-governmental organization (NGO) coalition that pushed for the optional protocol said, 'It was high time to put children's rights on an equal footing with other human rights!... Children's rights are no longer "mini rights"' (CRIN, 2011). Whether the optional protocol will put children's rights on equal footing with adults' rights remains to be seen, however, depending on the committee's actions and the implementation of states parties. Although 20 states signed the protocol, they are not bound by it until it is actually ratified, 'and at least ten countries must ratify the Protocol before it can be used' (Child Rights Coalition Asia, 2012).

Global dynamics of orphan policy

Humanitarian attention shifted to orphans in Africa not long after the shift in attention to children's rights which drives international OVC policy. Recent scholarship on the institutional entanglements of transnational development regimes with local African AIDS orphans suggests a profound reification of the category 'orphan' (Chirwa, 2002; Henderson, 2006; Meintjes and Giese, 2006). The CRC makes no specific mention – and therefore sets no definition – of orphans.[2] UNICEF (2006: 4) defines an orphan as 'a child under 18 years of age whose mother, father, or both parents have died'. An estimated 15.7 million sub-Saharan African children have been orphaned by AIDS – 30% of the 53 million total orphans (UNICEF, 2006: iv). Uganda's orphan population is about two million, or 19% of all children in the country (Oleke *et al.*, 2006: 267). Almost half of those children were made orphans due to AIDS (UNICEF, 2006). Yet the government's response to mass orphanhood in Uganda did not come until 2004, with the penning of a national OVC policy – twelve years after peak HIV prevalence in 1992 (Cheney, 2010: 9).

UNICEF's definition of an orphan as any child whose mother or father has died puts the emphasis on static, biological definitions of kinship and orphanhood in contexts where traditionally, orphans are socially defined. Wiseman Chirwa (2002) points out that, due to strong extended-family networks, local definitions of orphanhood in Malawi and much of African society have historically been based on social delineations in which situations of actual care are emphasized: most vernacular translations of orphan mean 'left behind or abandoned'. '*Mlanda,* an orphan,' he writes, 'is conceptualized as a person who has gone astray, has lost his/her bearings because he/she is no longer in the protection of the family system' (Chirwa, 2002: 96). As with many African countries with a strong ethos of caring for children who lose their parents, Ugandan vernacular languages use similar terminology to describe orphans; children typically have to lose not only their mother and father but most of their aunts and uncles, and become essentially homeless to be considered orphans. In Luganda, the use of vernacular terms for orphans, like *mulekwa* and *enfunzi* are so rare and stigmatizing that my 23-year-old research assistant, whose first language is Luganda, had never heard some of them. The UN definition therefore distorts these definitions and inflates local orphan numbers, as it singles out the orphaned child as particularly vulnerable despite widespread extended family social safety nets (Meintjes and Giese, 2006). In efforts to raise their visibility, international NGOs have highlighted the plight of Africa's AIDS orphans, lifting them out of the family context. Thus, rather than emphasizing their social resilience, this reification creates an orphan identity that is both pathologized (Henderson, 2006: 304) and made a site for benevolent humanitarian intervention (Ferguson and Freidus, 2007). I argue that the introduction of international rights regimes, by disrupting adult–child power relations and reifying orphans in Africa, has infantilized both orphaned children and their guardians as people in need of supervision. Much of the aid to orphans in Africa is thus driven by a discourse of humanitarianism that draws upon protectionist interpretations of the CRC and a model of charity by compelling Westerners to 'save the children', with Africa more broadly as their target for intervention.

Despite this objectification, around the same time as the drafting of national OVC policies, African government CRC signatories and NGOs were widely adopting rights-based approaches in their OVC programming. According to Save the Children (2006: 14), who started implementing rights-based approaches in 1999, 'A rights-based approach to development considers the fulfillment of everyone's human rights as the end goal of development'. The development of rights-based approaches was meant to address the structural issues that needs-based approaches, which are charity- rather than policy-driven, do not. Rights-based approaches were developed to make space for the empowerment of development aid's target populations, thus opening the possibility for societal transformation (Abdelmoneium, 2008). However, the concept of empowerment was quickly co-opted by neoliberal institutions that reduced it from a mode of transformative collective action to a Foucauldian means of individual self-improvement within market-based national economies (Pease, 2002; McEwen and Bek, 2006).

In the case of aid targeting OVC, rights-based approaches have thus far failed to achieve widespread empowerment of children, nor have they addressed structural causes of the problems of orphanhood. Aid organizations targeting children took the CRC as their mandate, but this found expression mainly in the application of the 'best interests' principle enshrined in the CRC, thus operating similarly to needs-based approaches. By this principle, adults and adult institutions should make the best interests of children a primary consideration in any activities or policies that affect children. Like other key concepts mentioned above, 'best interests' themselves were intentionally left undefined by the CRC committee in order 'to provide room for contextual application, and for it to be interpreted and applied according to the detailed situation of one or more particular children, in accordance with the specific features of national and local circumstances and the nature of decisions to be made' (Arts, 2010: 14). While this intentional ephemeralism was established with respect for cultural diversity in mind, it hinders the actionability of orphaned children's rights because the convergence of the AIDS epidemic, children's rights discourses, and the international development community's intervention in traditional extended-family systems of orphan support triply disenfranchise orphaned children through constant reinstatement of their vulnerability rather than their collective empowerment through rights. Despite the acknowledgement of a full-blown orphan 'crisis' in Uganda, little is being done to empower the increasing number of children like Margaret, who are left unaccompanied by adult caregivers as a result of the AIDS pandemic. Though the Ugandan government has encouraged participatory OVC programming, it tends to clash with cultural constructions of children that demand their silence and deference to adult opinion. Further, attention to the way in which AIDS in particular is made the culprit conceals the vulnerabilities of children (not only orphans) created by the devastation of neoliberal, postcolonial state restructuring and Africa's destabilization by the global free-market economy (Englund, 2006). Children are deprived daily of food security, health care, housing, and education by the vagaries of the free market and Uganda's crippling foreign debt. Children's rights cannot be made meaningful without full acknowledgement of their very violation, especially economically and socially. The efforts of international non-governmental organizations (INGOs) to address this vulnerability through a discourse of benevolent humanitarianism enshrined in CRC-style protectionism – without directly addressing broader issues of structural poverty through a discourse of *human* rights – has serious consequences for pursuing children's rights, most especially for 'vulnerable' orphans. Due to this inherent contradiction, rather than argue for their rights, children necessarily reproduce tropes of orphan victimhood to ensure their own survivals (Cheney, 2013). In what follows, I address this dynamic and its implications for children's social justice.

Local dynamics of orphan support

The introduction of aid for OVC has shifted the dynamics of extended-family care in Uganda. This is seen, for example, in the ways in which families make decisions about how to allocate care-giving responsibilities for orphans after their parents have died. Orphans are typically reared by relatives of their extended family, who in the past rarely received material assistance from sources outside the family. While several scholars have detailed a long African tradition of child circulation and fosterage for adult self-interest (Bledsoe and Isiugo-Abanihe, 1989; Notermans, 2004), Oleke *et al.* (2005: 2628) note 'a transition over the past 30 years from a situation dominated by "Purposeful" voluntary exchange of non-orphaned children to one dominated by "crisis fostering" of orphans'.

As OVC numbers have grown past extended-family networks' capacities to absorb them, the number of children-headed households has proliferated. Yet stories like Margaret's demonstrate how children's abilities to act on their own behalves are still thwarted by systems of power that emphasize protectionist discourses of children's rights instead of participatory ones. If all rights claims necessarily require access to a public sphere that is not so much a space of rational deliberation as a site of power (Asad, 2003: 184), orphans' vulnerabilities in particular reveal how little access children actually have to their rights. Advocacy groups turn out to be a necessary intermediary in the process to claiming rights, yet children cannot even access those groups without a guardian's assistance.

This lack of accessibility does not stop children like Margaret from trying to secure NGO resources for themselves, though. Children who learn about children's rights – through schools or government/NGO 'sensitization' campaigns – may utilize the language of rights to try to operationalize them in their own interests, but they are quickly disavowed of the tactic by the very institutions that promote children's rights, as these often stress obedience to adults over assertion of rights (Cheney, 2007: 66–9). For example, I regularly received verbal and written requests like Margaret's from guardians and children, for educational sponsorship of orphans. In Margaret's instance, I suggested that she seek assistance from one of the NGOs whose offices were ubiquitous in the city of Kampala. In a 2008 survey, VIVA International found more than 500 organizations in Kampala working on OVC issues,[3] so there was certainly no shortage. Margaret replied that she had already been to Christian Children's Fund (CCF), but they told her she would have to come back with an adult to vouch for her if she wanted to be considered for CCF sponsorship.

With or without assistance, orphans have become commoditized in a chain of local and global support. Rather than demand their rights, then, OVC and their guardians tend to appropriate – and even embrace – the tropes of vulnerability placed upon them by discourses of benevolent humanitarianism. Children's innovative survival strategies also tend to capitalize more on the 'vulnerable child' discourse than on their rights as children. A clever nine-year-old boy proudly described his strategy: on weekends, he roamed from 10 a.m. to 4 p.m. (after his chores and before his grandmother required him to be home), keeping close tabs on all the neighbourhood celebrations, from birthdays to funerals. He had even ranked which families tend to have the best food at their gatherings so he could make the rounds and get fed by charming his neighbours. Few chased him away, knowing that his elderly grandmother cared for 13 more grandchildren in a dilapidated brick house with a dirt floor, no windows, and little food. Rather than declare his right to food according to Article 24 of the CRC, the boy savvily drew on his family's known vulnerability so neighbours, many of whom do not have much themselves, would be charitable towards him in light of his public admission of vulnerability.

Guardians were also clearly aware that OVC have become commoditized as NGO targets in ways that reinforce their need for protection over their empowerment. Now, where guardians would still not dare call a child *mulekwa* in her presence, they gladly parade their 'orphans' (in English, the language of international aid) before potential benefactors. This is because presenting as an 'orphan', in international aid parlance, may now literally pay. Some guardians therefore cultivate an OVC identity in children, coaching them to emphasize their deprivation in order to solicit handouts. As the codifying of OVC identities recreates orphans as sites for both local and global humanitarian intervention, children and adults alike learn how to 'work it', manipulating the powerful social categories placed upon OVC by both local and global discourses about orphans in order to procure resources in a resource-strapped environment. Rather than interpreting this appropriation of children's rights as a simple act of postcolonial mimicry (Young, 2003: 141) or fulfilling the 'script' of childhood helplessness, we might see OVC and their caregivers as translating the disempowering language of international aid in hopes of gaining entitlement to basic human rights and social justice through the back door: 'I am vulnerable, and I therefore deserve assistance.' We can discern, in these actions, examples of children's resilience and agentive skills in navigating the adverse conditions of their existence as orphans. The drawback, however, is that their own strategies tend to play into a deferred understanding of children's rights as transformatively empowering rather than simply protectionist. Is this what we want the CRC to achieve in the end?

Children's rights' disempowering role

As I have shown above, the way children's rights have been interpreted and operationalized, particularly in relation to OVC, is incommensurate with thinking of children as rights bearers because, while NGOs claim participation as a guiding principle, protectionist aspects of rights discourses strip children of their capacity to make claims on their rights. While many aid organizations have shifted to rights-based approaches, constructions of orphans as particularly vulnerable lead the aid industry to continue to emphasize protectionist aspects of children's rights discourse rather than children's empowerment through rights. It thus serves to reproduce the status quo between children and adults.

The reasons for this can be traced to the ways in which children's rights were conceptualized in the first place. The recent development of the field of childhood studies has helped situate the concept of childhood socially and historically, establishing that, while childhood as a biological stage is universal, what it means to be a child varies significantly across societies and historical periods (Aries, 1962; Alanen, 2001; Schwartzman, 2001). The concept of children's rights arose in the West in the wake of the Industrial Revolution. In the twentieth century, children came to be seen as innocent and precious (Zelizer, 1985) but incompetent and vulnerable by nature (World Bank,

2005) – and therefore in need of protection.[4] The construction of children's rights was, therefore, primarily informed by Western developmental psychology's understandings of childhood (James, 2011), whose underlying presumptions about children as people in need of protection justified the removal of children not only from the factory but from public space, hyper-surveillance of children (Katz, 2003), deferred citizenship (Cheney, 2007), and their separation from adults in specialized institutions such as schools (Fass, 2008: 34). Children came to be seen as belonging in private space, and ensconced in the bosom of the nuclear family. Yet rights discourses contradictorily lift them out of those private and family spaces by granting individual rights that they as rights bearers cannot in fact claim because they need an adult interlocutor to help claim or even fulfil their entitlements. Then they are expected to go to adults/adult institutions for redress when their rights are denied them. This is the way children's rights are universally codified in international human rights law. Addressing children as part of nuclear households as well as extended family networks is not the problem per se; children can act as rights bearers within the family. And children *are* indeed vulnerable beings, but history shows that this is a social designation as much as a natural one. Such a hegemonic notion of childhood reinforces the imperative of all adults to act as duty-bearers – even in children's rights-based approaches.

Combine this with the neoliberal influence that has led to the privatization of development in the hands of NGOs rather than government, and making claims on the state as the ultimate duty-bearer of rights to its citizens becomes even more difficult as services become more market-based and commercialized to appeal to private donors. I have written elsewhere that:

> use of children's rights mandates, especially when operationalized through identification of vulnerable child populations, reinforces the status quo of the vulnerable (child, developing nation, receiver) and the powerful (adult, industrialized nation, giver) in a symbiotic relationship of charity... This approach depoliticizes the roots of global poverty that have precipitated both the AIDS epidemic and its consequent 'orphan crisis' by training attention on micro-solutions rather than macro systems of structural violence, as it strips children and families of their agency and rights-based arguments for making claims on the neoliberal state (Farmer, 2003: 8). Yet we cannot deny that in most cases, basic needs must be met before rights can be adequately addressed. These two approaches are contradictorily wedded by constructions of OVC as children who are *both* victims *and* denied rights, yet in need of *charitable care* more than *empowerment* to act for themselves. The result is a failure to achieve an environment of actionable children's rights for OVC. (Cheney, 2010: 12–13)

Starting with the perceived needs of children conjures up Maslow's hierarchy (1943), and in a sequential sense might be seen as working towards the fulfilment of rights; some will claim that basic needs must often be met before rights can be fulfilled. Ennew (2002) refers to the 'three P's' of the CRC – provision, protection, and participation – suggesting that these also constitute a kind of hierarchy in which the first takes priority, and the rest are achieved sequentially. However, because of the ways rights-based approaches have been conceptualized and implemented in OVC programming, neither needs nor rights are adequately fulfilled. Perhaps it can, and should, happen the other way around; I would argue that we need to enable children to make claims on their rights to basic needs (provision). Because it is so easy to see orphans as especially vulnerable children, however, we have yet to see much action extending from such a rights-based premise in OVC programming.

From protectionist rights to children's citizenship

One way to reverse these alarming trends is to redouble efforts to use children's rights to promote orphans' empowerment – rather than their victim-hood – through the development of more actionable legal protections for children. The new optional protocol is a good start. Building more productive models for family, government, and NGO intervention on behalf of OVC lies not only in local and transnational discourses *about* orphans, but in rooting policy in a more nuanced understanding of AIDS-affected children's own experiences and their perceptions of their circumstances. Doing so may shift the discourse of humanitarian intervention towards augmenting children's agency, rather than ameliorating – and thereby sometimes deepening – their vulnerability. To be effective, children's rights must also move from being a rhetorical, discursive device to an everyday, indigenous language that holds its own weight in social practice to build a culture of children's rights. This may yield a greater sense of social justice for children, but it will rely on adults and adult institutions – whether local or global, rights-based or humanitarian-based – relinquishing their power over children and recognizing children's citizenship through more transformative models of assistance (Invernizzi and Milne, 2005). Effecting such a drastic shift in attitude will not be easy, of course; in 2007, UNICEF HIV Specialist for OVC Prevention in Uganda, Dorothy Oulanyan, admitted to me in an interview that UNICEF may have erred in their initial efforts to promote children's rights:

> We started by telling people what children's rights were, and children quickly picked up on it... but then we got to a point where the children were running ahead of the parents and the rest of the community. Now, when you mention child rights in a community, they will say, 'You are spoiling our children! Now we can't even discipline our children. We can't tell them what to do because you've come with this child rights message'. So now we're trying to reverse that and say that children also have a right to parental guidance and put it in context so that it is not that

children rule over you. But it's something so hard to reverse because we had such a big drive in the early 90s, really pushing the issue.

To overcome this backlash, children's rights must not only be reframed to emphasize participation in decision-making processes, but adults must come to see children's rights as beneficial to the entire community rather than as a tool that can either be manipulated or implemented at the expense of adults. Given that childhood is such a naturalized concept, however, that will likely require a significant shift in both local and global understandings of children as rights-bearers. As Allison James (2011: 167) has recently pointed out, adult's ideas about childhood limit children's agency and actions, thereby denying them status as citizens'. That today's children have rights and agency has been well established in childhood studies literature (Franklin, 1986; Stephens, 1995; Jenks, 1996; Mayall, 1999). The challenge now is to go beyond these social truths to think about how and why these concepts are or are not actionable in the everyday lives of children.

Children's citizenship is one analytical framework for this task. If children are seen as incomplete citizens-in-training, to be protected in order to foster the growth of complete (read: adult) citizens in the future, it is no wonder that rights-based approaches are not increasing children's empowerment; the cultural politics of childhood put forward in children's rights discourses tend to place children's citizenship in the future (James, 2011). This sort of protectionism in the guise of rights is thus detrimental to children's citizenship but also, in the case of OVC in Africa, it affects their very survival as more and more children like Margaret are left without adult caregivers. Yet, it should not be as hard to promote children's citizenship in Africa as international development discourse suggests: while 'traditional culture' is often framed as the barrier to the fulfilment of children's rights, I have shown here how the protectionism of children's rights actually originates in Western concepts of the 'precious child'. In Africa, by contrast, children have long been comparatively more autonomous – but are also more accountable to their communities (Whiting and Whiting, 1975). However, due to the way rights tend to be individually conceptualized (i.e. granted to sovereign individuals rather than communities), OVC aid prescriptions get applied in Africa as if the extended-family care systems are not already well established or are incapable of properly caring for children, undermining rather than bolstering their capacity to do so (Phiri and Tolfree, 2005). So while many international rights organizations talk of the need to 'sensitize' societies in the Global South to children's rights, perhaps the bigger issue is one of framing: for example, rooting children's rights discourse in indigenous knowledge so that it is not seen as alien or neocolonial but rather compatible with local understandings of children's social roles.[5] The Uganda Child Rights NGO Network (UCRNN) has tried to localize children's rights by emphasizing children's responsibilities alongside their rights (Cheney, 2007: 60). Taylor and Smith (2009: 16) note that 'The rights and duties of citizens are what make them full members of community'.

Contextualizing children's rights and responsibilities in this way makes them more compatible with local constructions of children as it supports recognition of children's contributions to family, community, and society – i.e. their citizenship.

Returning to the question of participation, standards of participation in aid and development are applied very differently in the case of children. Despite their stated goals to promote participation rights for children, many aid organizations gloss over this point in their own programming. When it comes to decision-making within the very organizations assisting children, participation efforts can be tokenistic at best. While Save the Children (2006: 33–4) argues that 'Participation transforms the power relations between children and adults, challenges authoritarian structures and supports children's capacity to influence families, communities and institutions', these are the very reasons why aid organizations tend to resist children's participation, 'because it disrupts adults' established working pattern and challenges existing norms' (West, 2007: 126). If rights are to 'hold powerful people and institutions accountable for their responsibilities to those with less power' (Save the Children, 2006: 23), as if intergenerational power relations are a zero-sum game, they apparently are not necessarily going to shift the balance of power within children's rights organizations, instead maintaining the relationship of the weak relying on the powerful to grant them their rights.

In Uganda, the OVC secretariat has tried to promote children's participation in its coordination of OVC programming by both government and NGO offices. John Okiror, Manager of the Uganda OVC National Implementation Unit, told me that this was the biggest challenge because children do not tend to express their views.[6] The Ministry of Gender, Labour, and Social Development even produced a participation handbook with UNICEF and the Uganda Child Rights NGO Network that instructs organizations on how to involve children (Uganda Ministry of Gender Labour and Social Development *et al.*, 2008). But it reproduces many prevalent stereotypes about children's inherently incompetent nature that quickly lead organizations to give up trying to respect, involve, and listen to children. It rarely occurs to them that children are taught not to express their views and that such socialization takes time, patience, and the building of rapport with children in order to undo it. This trend indicates that the deeper issues have to do with cultural presumptions (in Western and developing country contexts) about children as people who are dependent, seen but not heard, irrational, incompetent, and so on. The language of protection is then commonly used as an excuse for excluding children from participating in decision-making that affects them, easily masking the fact that adults may not really want to do the work necessary to hear what children have to say. Mary Ann Powell and Anne Smith (2009: 138) point out that:

> the nature of protection is a disputable concept, with overprotection seen as harmful... True protection of children requires all rights, including

participation rights, to be respected... A distinction has been made between the inherent and the structural vulnerability of children... The inherent vulnerability of children, as a consequence of biological imma- turity, emphasizes that researchers and significant adults in children's lives have an ethical responsibility to protect children. However, the structural vulnerability of children comes about as a consequence of, and subsequently serves to reinforce, social and political mechanisms that reduce children's power, fail to take their agency into account and disre- gard their rights.

This dynamic demonstrates a conflict between children's right to be pro- tected and their right to be heard. Accommodating children's participation may therefore involve adults learning to more effectively communicate with children, which in turn may require a greater attitude shift on the part of adults than of children. Thus, the challenge is not so much to convince chil- dren that they have something to say as to convince adults that children's opinions do indeed matter. Taylor and Smith (2009: 19) remind us that par- ticipation and citizenship go hand-in-hand: 'The more children are treated and constructed as citizens, the more likely it is that they will actively par- ticipate in society', thereby claiming what Liebel (2012) calls 'children's rights from below'.

Recognition of OVC as citizens in Uganda may ironically have been set back by humanitarian interventions that reified orphans, set them apart from family contexts, and reinforced their 'victim' status. I do not wish to claim here that participation and protection are mutually exclusive. Indeed, guar- anteeing children's citizenship also entails adults' protection of (particularly very young) children from harm for them to reach their full potential as citi- zens. Those who truly wish to protect children may thereby come to realize that participation itself may act as a means of protection by allowing children access to opportunities and resources previously denied them (Powell and Smith, 2009: 129). Further, doing this builds citizenship skills in children that will strengthen fledgling democracies such as Uganda.

Policy-makers and aid organizations would do well to be more reflexive in their authoring and implementing of children's rights approaches, to over- come their own myopia in regard to advancing children's lived citizenship rather than deferring it to the future. Save the Children (2006: 32), for instance, mentions forms of discrimination and talks of 'Enabling children and young people from discriminated against groups to speak out and engage with decision makers', going on to mention devices like children's parlia- ments. They do not, however, go so far as to suggest children's representa- tives in state parliaments. Is their assumption that governments are already watching out for children's interests, or that separate and unequal participa- tion for children is sufficient for the fulfilment of their rights? The reality is that, from a rights perspective, children generally can be seen as a marginal- ized majority that is discriminated against. But the way these policies are constructed belies that very simple fact, instead maintaining the status quo in which children may be protected but largely remain powerless to change their own circumstances by claiming their rights.

How should we deal with discrimination against children like Margaret who are trying to seek services that will in fact protect them and provide for their own best interests in the absence or diminished capacity of adult caregivers? The achievement of lived rights and citizenship for children lies not only in emphasizing social and economic rights to alleviate the widespread poverty that drives global humanitarianism, but in recognizing children's capacity to act, legally and socially, on their own behalf to secure the resources necessary for survival. Until the promise of children's rights can be used to help advance children's lived citizenship, however, orphans like Margaret will continue to embrace their vulnerabilities in order to seek care, wherever and from whomever it is available. While some orphans will gain certain entitlements this way, it will ultimately uphold their collective marginalization, thereby denying their participation rights.

Notes

1　This chapter was developed from a paper prepared for the Columbia University Human Rights Seminar (April 2011) and previous publications in *International Social Work* 56 (2012) and Cambridge University Press (2013). Reprinted with permission.
2　The CRC's Articles 20 and 21 deal with fosterage and adoption of any child 'deprived of his or her family environment' (United Nations, 1989).
3　Interview communication from VIVA officers.
4　There is a robust body of children's studies literature that takes on the issue of children's competence to act as rights bearers. The historical evolution of thinking about children's competencies and entitlements to rights bears striking resemblance to women's struggles for recognition of their humanity. Most agree that age designations are somewhat arbitrary in determining children's competence. Judith Ennew (2002) points out that the CRC, on the other hand, makes no distinction between a 17-month-old and a 17-year-old child.
5　Personal communication with colleague Auma Okwany.
6　Interview communication.

References

Abdelmoneium, A.O.A. (2008) 'Non-governmental organizations and the rights of displaced children in Sudan.' Unpublished thesis, Radboud University.
Alanen, L. (2001) 'Explorations in generational analysis', in L. Alanen and B. Mayall (eds) *Conceptualizing Child–Adult Relations*, New York, NY: Routledge/Falmer.
Aries, P. (1962) *Centuries of Childhood*, London: Cape and Penguin Books.
Arts, K. (2010) 'Coming of age in a world of diversity?' Paper presented at Inaugural Lecture, The Hague, November.
Asad, T. (2003) *Formations of the Secular: Christianity, Islam, Modernity,* Stanford, CA: Stanford University Press.

Bledsoe, C. and Isiugo-Abanihe, U. (1989) 'Strategies of child-fosterage among Mende grannies in Sierra Leone', in Lesthaeghe, R.J. (ed.) *Reproduction and Social Organization in Sub-Saharan Africa*, Berkeley, CA: University of California Press.

Brennan, S. (2002) 'Children's choices or children's interests: which do their rights protect?' in D. Archard and C.M. MacLeod (eds) *The Moral and Political Status of Children*, New York, NY: Oxford University Press.

Cheney, K.E. (2007) *Pillars of the Nation: Child Citizens and Ugandan National Development*, Chicago, IL: University of Chicago Press.

Cheney, K.E. (2010) 'Expanding vulnerability, dwindling resources: implications for orphaned futures in Uganda', *Childhood in Africa*, 2: 8–15.

Cheney, K.E. (2013) 'Malik and his three mothers: AIDS orphans' survival strategies and how children's rights translations hinder them', in K. Hanson and O. Nieuwenhuys (eds) *Reconceptualizing Children's Rights in International Development: Living Rights, Social Justice, Translations*, Cambridge: Cambridge University Press.

Child Rights Coalition Asia (2012) New Optional Protocol to the CRC officially signed by States (available online at http://www.childrightscoalitionasia.org/new-optional-protocol-to-the-crc-officially-signed-by-states/) (accessed 4 June 2013).

Child Rights International Network (CRIN) (2011) UN Adopts Complaints Mechanism for Children (available online at http://www.crin.org/resources/infodetail.asp?id=26980) (accessed 4 June 2013).

Chirwa, W. (2002) 'Social exclusion and inclusion: challenges to orphan care in Malawi', *Nordic Journal of African Studies*, 11: 93–113.

Englund, H. (2006) *Prisoners of Freedom: Human Rights and the African Poor*, Berkeley, CA: University of California Press.

Ennew, J. (2002) 'Future generations and global standards: children's rights at the start of the millennium', in J. MacClancy (ed.) *Exotic No More: Anthropology on the Front Lines*, Chicago, IL: University of Chicago Press.

Farmer, P. (2003) *Pathologies of Power: Health, Human Rights, and the New War on the Poor*, Berkeley, CA: University of California Press.

Fass, P.S. (2008) 'Childhood and youth as an American/global experience in the context of the past', in J. Cole and D. Durham (eds) *Figuring the Future: Globalization and Temporalities of Children and Youth*, Santa Fe, CA: School for Advanced Research Press.

Ferguson, A. and Freidus, A. (2007) 'Orphan care in Malawi: examining the transnational images and discourses of humanitarianism.' Paper presented at the American Anthropological Association Annual Meeting, Washington, DC, November.

Foster, G., Levine, C., and Williamson, J. (eds) (2005) *A Generation at Risk: The Global Impact of HIV/AIDS on Orphans and Vulnerable Children*, New York, NY: Cambridge University Press.

Franklin, B. (ed.) (1986) *The Rights of Children*, Oxford: Basil Blackwell.

Government of Uganda (1997) 'The Children Act', Kampala: Government of Uganda.

Guest, E. (2003) *Children of AIDS: Africa's Orphan Crisis*, London: Pluto Press.

Henderson, P.C. (2006) 'South African AIDS orphans: examining assumptions around vulnerability from the perspective of rural children and youth', *Childhood*, 13: 303–27.

Invernizzi, A. and Milne, B. (2005) 'Introduction: children's citizenship: a new discourse?' *Journal of Social Sciences*, 9: 1–6.

James, A. (2011) 'To be (come) or not to be (come): understanding children's citizenship', *The ANNALS of the American Academy of Political and Social Science*, 633: 167–79.

Jenks, C. (1996) *Childhood*, New York, NY: Routledge.

Katz, C. (2003) 'The state goes home: children, social reproduction, and the terrors of "hypervigilance".' Paper presented at the American Anthropological Association Annual Meeting, Chicago, November.

Liebel, M. (2012) *Children's Rights from Below: Cross-Cultural Perspectives*, New York, NY: Palgrave-MacMillan.

Maslow, A.H. (1943) 'A theory of human motivation', *Psychological Review*, 50: 370–96.

Mayall, B. (1999) 'Children and childhood', in S. Hood *et al.* (eds) *Critical Issues in Social Research: Power and Prejudice*, Philadelphia, PA: Open University Press.

McEwen, C. and Bek, D. (2006) '(Re)politicizing empowerment: lessons from the South African wine industry', *Geoforum*, 37: 1021–34.

Meintjes, H. and Giese, S. (2006) 'Spinning the epidemic: the making of mythologies of orphanhood in the context of AIDS', *Childhood*, 13: 407–30.

Naker, D. (2007) 'From rhetoric to practice: bridging the gap between what we believe and what we do', *Children, Youth, and Environments*, 17: 146–58.

Notermans, C. (2004) 'Fosterage and the politics of marriage and kinship in East Cameroon', in F. Bowie (ed.) *Cross-Cultural Approaches to Adoption*, New York, NY: Routledge.

Oleke, C., Blystad, A., Moland, K.M., Rekdal, O.B., and Heggenhougen, K. (2006) 'The varying vulnerability of African orphans: the case of the Langi, northern Uganda', *Childhood*, 13: 267–84.

Oleke, C., Blystad, A., and Rekdal, O.B. (2005) '"When the obvious brother is not there": political and cultural contexts of the orphan challenge in northern Uganda', *Social Science and Medicine*, 61: 2628–38.

Pease, B. (2002) 'Rethinking empowerment: a postmodern reappraisal for emancipatory practice', *British Journal of Social Work*, 32: 135–47.

Phiri, S.N. and Tolfree, D. (2005) 'Family and community-based care for children affected by HIV/AIDS: strengthening the front line response', in G. Foster et al. (eds) *A Generation at Risk: The Global Impact of HIV/AIDS on Orphans and Vulnerable Children*, New York, NY: Cambridge University Press.

Powell, M.A. and Smith, A.B. (2009) 'Children's participation rights in research', *Childhood*, 16: 124–42.

Save the Children (2006) *Child Rights Programming: How to Apply Rights-Based Approaches to Programming – A Handbook for Internationals*, London: Save the Children Alliance Members.

Schwartzman, H.B. (ed.) (2001) *Children and Anthropology: Perspectives for the 21st Century*, Westport, CT: Bergin & Garvey.

Singhal, A. and Howard, W.S. (eds) (2003) *The Children of Africa Confront AIDS: From Vulnerability to Possibility*, Athens, OH: Ohio University Press.

Stephens, S. (ed.) (1995) *Children and the Politics of Culture*, Princeton, NJ: Princeton University Press.

Taylor, N.J. and Smith, A.B. (eds) (2009) *Children as Citizens? International Voices*, Dunedin, NZ: Otago University Press.

Uganda Ministry of Gender Labour and Social Development, Uganda Child Rights NGO Network and UNICEF – Uganda Office (2008) *The National Child Participation Guide for Uganda*, Kampala: Uganda Ministry of Gender Labour and Social Development.

UNICEF (2005) Convention on the Rights of the Child: protecting and realizing children's rights (available online at http://www.unicef.org/crc/index_protecting.html) (accessed 4 June 2013).

UNICEF (2006) *Africa's Orphaned and Vulnerable Generations: Children Affected by AIDS*, New York, NY: UNICEF, UNAIDS, and PEPFAR.

UNICEF (2008) *Uganda Annual Report 2007*, Kampala: UNICEF Uganda.

UNICEF (n.d.a) 'FACT SHEET: the right to participation' (available online at http://www.unicef.org/crc/files/Right-to-Participation.pdf) (accessed 4 June 2013).

UNICEF (n.d.b) 'Introduction to the Convention on the Rights of the Child: definition of key terms' (available online at http://www.unicef.org/crc/files/Definitions.pdf) (accessed 4 June 2013).

United Nations (1989) *United Nations Convention on the Rights of the Child*, New York, NY: UN General Assembly.

West, A. (2007) 'Power relationships and adult resistance to children's participation', *Children, Youth and Environments*, 17: 123–35.

Whiting, J. and Whiting, B. (1975) *Children of Six Cultures: A Psycho-Cultural Analysis*, Cambridge, MA: Harvard University Press.

World Bank (2005) *OVC toolkit*, Washington, DC: World Bank.

Young, R.J.C. (2003) *Postcolonialism: A Very Short Introduction*, Oxford: Oxford University Press.

Zelizer, V.A. (1985) *Pricing the Priceless Child: The Changing Value of Children*, New York, NY: Basic Books.

3   Children's rights in the time of AIDS in KwaZulu-Natal, South Africa

Amy Norman

> I used to explain it like this: 'your freedom ends where my freedom starts'…
> so you can have rights, but your rights stop where my rights start. (Sfiso,
> teacher/traditional healer, 35)
> They say no child should be having rights, they say rights do not exist.
> (Nduduzo, 14)

Introduction

The nature of childhood in South Africa has changed dramatically in the decades following the end of the apartheid era. A new constitution, together with the passing of the United Nations Convention on the Rights of the Child (CRC) and the African Charter on the Rights and Welfare of the Child (ACRWC), have led to the prominent place of children within the human rights landscape. However, the parallel rise of the AIDS epidemic has presented particular challenges to the realization and furthering of children's rights, as children face increased vulnerability, poverty, and the weakening of social safety nets. Furthermore, while children's rights are utilized to protect children and promote their development, such discourses tend to neglect local realities where conflicts between generations and dissonance within the home can exacerbate child vulnerability. At the very moment when family relations are arguably most critical to child well-being, 'rights' themselves have presented new and significant challenges for constructive relationships between adults and children.

The aim of this chapter is not to evaluate the advancement of particular rights in the context of AIDS in South Africa, but to explore how hegemonic discourses and narratives surrounding children's rights have been reinterpreted and reimagined within the family setting. This chapter is based on doctoral research conducted over eight months in three locations in the highly affected province of KwaZulu-Natal, between 2007 and 2008. Sixty-four children and 65 adults participated across 28 families in both urban and rural areas. The study took an alternative approach by exploring childhood holistically, with a methodology based upon in-depth interviews and participatory methods that did not separate 'orphans' and 'other vulnerable children' from *other* and *all* children in the study communities. Further, childhood was explored generationally and historically, through the inclusion of both adults and children as research participants (Vanderbeck, 2007). Such an approach allowed for an understanding that power, resources, and rights are unevenly distributed between children and adults, and the inclusion of adults is necessary if rights are to be meaningfully realized (Mayall and Zeiher, 2003). As such, this study offers important findings for developing deeper understandings of the ways in which children and adults interact in relation to children's rights within the family sphere (Twum-Danso, 2009).

The chapter begins with a brief overview of the history of democratization and children's rights within the post-apartheid landscape, as well as an outline and understanding of the context of AIDS in South Africa. Subsequent sections explore the altering landscape of childhood in the time of rights, the significant chasms that have arisen between adults and children, and the implications for communication, risk, and relationships in the time of AIDS.

Democracy and children's rights in South Africa

The evolution of children's rights in South Africa transpired within a broader history of democratization, as the end of the repressive apartheid era brought about strong commitments to human rights generally, and in particular for children. The first step in this process was the new Constitution that came into effect on 27 April 1994, designed to radically reverse decades of institutionalized discrimination. The Constitution aimed to produce social, political, and legal structures that would recognize the injustices of the past, while depicting South Africa as an open and democratic society based on human dignity, equality, and freedom. New laws, progressive public spending, and the reorganization of administrative systems have all contributed to the acceleration of rights for all, and for children in particular. Today, the South African Constitution is one of the most progressive in the world, and it gives full recognition of children's rights at the very highest level (Moses, 2006). Within the Bill of Rights, children hold a special place in Section 28 which safeguards their rights to care and protection, over and above the rights they have in common with adults. The Constitution recognizes that children are particularly vulnerable to violations of their rights, and that they have specific and unique interests. Children are entitled to the right to education, personal autonomy, privacy, freedom of religion, freedom of expression, and freedom of association. The inclusion in the Bill of Rights of a special section on the rights of the child was an important development for South African children, as under apartheid, the vast majority had faced discrimination in healthcare, education, and housing, as well as numerous children having been detained without trial, tortured, and assaulted as a result of their participation in anti-apartheid activism (McKendrick and Hoffman, 1990; Higson-Smith and Killian, 2000).

Alongside the Constitution, South Africa ratified the United Nations Convention on the Rights of the Child (CRC) in 1995, a framework for promoting children's welfare as an issue of justice rather than one of charity (Veerman, 1992). With its passage, the CRC articulated rights of freedom of expression, a variety of protective measures, rights concerning the civil status of children, their development and welfare, and rights concerning children in special or 'especially difficult' circumstances (Freeman, 2000). South Africa also signed on to the African Charter on the Rights and Welfare of the Child which was adopted by the Organization of African Unity (OAU) Assembly in 1990 and entered into force in 1999. The ACRWC originated from the recognition by member states of particular sociocultural and economic realities that were unique to Africa, and emphasized the need to include African cultural values and experiences when dealing with the rights of the child. For example, it was distinguishable by its inclusion of duties in its provisions, recognizing that children, too, have responsibilities depending on their evolving capacities (Chirwa, 2002). The Charter also noted with concern that the situation of most African children remains critical due to sociocultural, traditional, and developmental circumstances, as well as natural disasters, armed conflicts, exploitation, and hunger (OAU, 1999).

Domestically, South Africa has further promoted the special status of children in recent years with the Children's Act of 2005 which set out more specific principles on issues relating to the care and protection of children, the definition of parental responsibilities and rights, and the provision for matters such as children's courts, adoption, and child abduction. The principles call for the prioritization of the best interests of the child, the right of the child to participate in any matter concerning that child, and a child's right of access to court. One of the major recent amendments in 2007 was a provision which granted access to HIV testing and contraception to those aged 12 years and above, despite the legal age of consent remaining at 16 (Han and Bennish, 2009).

As a nation, South Africa is at the forefront of children's rights legislation and action. However, many challenges remain, such as insufficient human and material resources to implement legislation and other policy initiatives, and a consensus among many adults that children's rights have gone too far (as will be further explored in this chapter). Indeed, after years of outcry and consultation, a national Bill of Responsibilities was developed in 2010 by the South African Interfaith Council and the Department of Basic Education, and is being taught alongside the CRC in many South African schools. The Bill aims to indoctrinate children into a new human rights culture where all rights correspond to a set of responsibilities. Within the preamble, young people accept that they 'have been privileged to inherit from the sacrifice and suffering of those who came before' them, and that the rights enshrined in the Constitution are inseparable from duties and responsibilities to others.

The creation and social acceptance of the Bill provide a recent example of the on-going resistance to the CRC in South Africa, and the importance of understanding cultural nuance. Alongside a deeper understanding of these cultural contexts, this chapter provides an exploration of the resistance to the discourses related to the CRC at the family level, and how these dynamics have shaped and are shaped by the AIDS epidemic.

The AIDS epidemic in South Africa

In the midst of transition from apartheid to a newly formed democracy, the AIDS epidemic loomed in the background of South African life. Today, modern history is invariably tied to the AIDS epidemic, as the country undergoes an unprecedented and continuing epidemic (UNAIDS, 2010). HIV first appeared in South Africa in the early 1980s, but it was not until the 1990s that it started to spread significantly. The growth of the epidemic in the last twenty years has been staggering: by the end of 2009, 29% of South African women attending prenatal clinics were testing positive for HIV (South African Department of Health, 2010). Today, there are approximately 5.6 million South Africans living with HIV and AIDS (UNAIDS, 2010). Nationally, the epidemic has entered the mature phase; the number of new infections has slowed, and HIV incidence – the number of people who are newly infected – peaked in 1998. However, the number of people dying from AIDS each year has only recently increased due to the lag time between contracting the disease and AIDS-induced morbidity. Further, because infections are most likely to occur during the reproductive years of an individual's life, and because individuals remain asymptomatic for many years, it is likely that children will be conceived and born before individuals know of their status (Barnett, 2006). For these reasons, the epidemic has been termed a 'long-wave event', where large-scale impacts have emerged gradually over decades and generations, with one of the most disconcerting consequences the growing prevalence of orphanhood (Barnett and Whiteside, 2006).

In South Africa 3.7 million children, or 20% of all children, have been classified as 'orphans', a term which includes children who have lost a biological mother *or* father, but not necessarily both parents (Meintjes and Hall, 2009). These statistics are often utilized to highlight the growing concern for both the short- and long-term impacts of AIDS on children, their development, and future life chances. Indeed, such numbers are the foundation for an entire discourse related to the 'AIDS generation', the target of various prevention campaigns, donor-funded charity, and 'child-oriented' programmes (Foster *et al.*, 2005). This discourse has been dominated by a linear trajectory: children increasingly take on 'adult' household and caring responsibilities, leading to the deprivation of educational opportunities. Children are then faced with further destitution and stigmatization as households fall deeper into poverty, families dissolve, and orphaned children are left to fend for themselves (Subbarao *et al.*, 2001; Booysen and Arntz, 2002). As with other 'crises of childhood', adversities such as AIDS are seen to completely overwhelm children; they are helpless, traumatized victims, dependent on adults for their salvation and protection (Boyden, 2003). Children are emptied of their knowledge and abilities, denying both agency and competency (Henderson, 2006). It is on this highly politicized landscape of AIDS-related concern that the advocacy of children's rights has taken place. And while such concern has justifiably led to increased interventions for children, the expansion of 'rights' discourses over recent decades has not occurred without conflict. The following sections explore a number of the complexities involved, and the importance of viewing rights through a historical and generational lens.

The altering landscape of childhood in the time of rights

In South African society, where deeply embedded social hierarchies determine the nature of childhood, many of the concepts laid out in the CRC are an import from an alien world. Within the study reported in this chapter, a clear disjuncture existed between traditionally held values of appropriate childhood behaviour and practice, and the rights (both perceived and real) granted to children in the CRC and the Constitution. Such chasms caused conflicts between young and old, and led to the erosion of positive communication and relationships between adults and children.

Underlying the anger and frustration expressed by adults in interviews was a feeling of disempowerment and imposition. Without consultation, the government was seen to have enforced a legal framework and an ensuing discourse of children's rights upon their communities and in their households. Indeed, over the last two decades, there has been a widespread advocacy effort to promote children's rights and place them within the South African consciousness. Community education and development, the training of teachers, and the development of materials and resources for children by the government and non-governmental organizations (NGOs), have all worked to enhance the implementation of children's rights, and make them 'real' in children's lives. One highly successful platform has been the *Soul Buddyz* project which specifically targets children aged 8 to 12 years old and their caregivers to address children's rights within health education and social issues. The series, which has existed for over a decade, consists of television, radio, and print materials. For example, print materials are distributed to every grade 7 school child in South Africa, with accompanying activities which allow children to assess whether their rights have been infringed upon (Goldstein *et al.*, 2001). However, many of these efforts, while mobilizing children's rights discourses and activism, have left behind a landscape of frustration and anger on the part of adults, and some confusion on the part of children.

Repeatedly broached in this study was the issue of respect, with adults insisting that this essential value had been lost on the current generation, partly as a result of these discourses and children misjudging their proper place in society. Indeed, a number of children often agreed that their peers did not exhibit appropriate deference to their elders. For example, because children in traditional society belonged to everyone, the practice of greeting elders was a common expectation, but one that seemed to have fallen by the wayside. *Sawubona*, the Zulu greeting, literally translates to 'I see you', and was both a sign of respect, as well as a demonstration of social cohesion. Its decline in everyday use had been interpreted as an attempt to marginalize elders by children who no longer respect traditional notions of respect. Although not a direct result of children's rights, issues such as declining respect were perceived by adults to be part of the 'problem of modern childhood', of which children's rights were expressed as the primary origin.

Furthermore, there existed a real concern about the 'unevenness of rights':

> children do not care about children's rights to respect their parents. They just want to be taken care of, but they do not give anything back. (Thembisile, 41)

> Children do not know how to respect... now children tell you about rights... the government is corrupting our children... why should children have rights? Just look at how rude they are! (Gladys, 70)

In this 'new' South Africa, children were deemed to be overly empowered, corrupted, and unaware of their 'proper' place within the family and community. Children's rights were seen to threaten the very essence of an ideal childhood. Nowhere was this felt more, and expressed more fiercely, than in debates surrounding the use of corporal punishment. Universally, adults felt that corporal punishment was a significant feature of traditional Zulu childhood, but one whose position was being threatened by children's rights:

> children are disrespectful... they challenge their parent's authority as a result (of the rights). These rights are destroying our children... they should be spanked... it builds respect. Corporal punishment helped us a lot because we were disciplined. (Nomvula, 40)

Adults felt that corporal punishment was a feature of their own childhoods, and resulted in a transfer of critical knowledge relating to appropriate behaviour and values. Many also expressed a fear that the government, through the police, would be called into their homes if they practised corporal punishment:

> I don't like that a parent can't hit their children. When we grew up, we got hit and that prevented us from doing wrong things. Nowadays we

fear being arrested so we don't hit children. One has to put aside R300 for a fine if they want to hit their children. This one [child] always tells us he will arrest us if we hit him. He is very rude and talks back to us adults... most parents say you must have R300 for the fine. The police also tell parents that if they did hit the child they will be arrested. If the child makes that call, the police arrive in a very short space of time. (Thoko, female, 53)

It appeared to many adults that children's knowledge of legal rights *overly* empowered them in the adult–child relationship, allowing them to make threats and ultimately an imbalance in the family power structure. Such scenarios demonstrated a viewpoint that the government had betrayed African culture, and had assumed parental rights, leaving caregivers with disrespectful children who no longer faced consequences.

However, despite this rhetoric, a number of important points must be made. First, the Constitution protects children against 'maltreatment, neglect, abuse or degradation', and as a signatory to the CRC, South Africa is compelled to pass laws and take social, educational, and administrative measures to protect children from all forms of physical and mental violence, injury or abuse, neglect or negligent treatment, maltreatment, or exploitation (Porteus *et al.*, 2001). However, although the National Education Policy Act (1996) bans corporal punishment within educational institutions, there is currently no law against the use of corporal punishment in the home. Furthermore, recent efforts to amend legislation by banning the physical punishment of children in the home have been unable to gain the political will necessary to pass through parliament (Bower, 2012).

Despite these realities, during the time of this research, debates were raging on the subject within the media as proposals were underway to amend the Children's Act, possibly leading to increased discussion within the home and among adults (Bower, 2008). Children's rights discourses, caregiver frustrations, and media rhetoric all collided to further alienate adults from the goals of the CRC, and in terms of the issue of corporal punishment, the assumption that it had already been banned was widespread. This was, and remains an important example of how adults feel alienated from the process of ensuring children's rights, and that efforts to advocate for rights have ultimately led to increased friction between adults and children. Within a history of adult disempowerment through colonial and apartheid governments, and the further indignities imposed by poverty and a lack of employment opportunities, adults expressed a universal feeling that in an effort to promote children's rights, caregivers had been left behind. The lack of consultation and 'buy-in' from adults had left behind a landscape of frustration and tension. Indeed, the majority of adults expressed an opinion that not only had they been marginalized within the process, but that through the loss of tradition and respect, rights themselves were leading children down the wrong path in life.

'Eyes wide open': do rights lead to risk?

Throughout the research, adult participants articulated an outlook that 'modern children' tended to be disobedient, demanding, and disrespectful. Such children, devoid of the character traditionally imposed upon them, were seen to face significant challenges in the new South Africa, many of which were their own doing:

> Children face much worse burdens. When we grew up we didn't have incurable diseases. There were curable ones and when we were warned about them we listened. Children nowadays don't listen when they are warned about anything... They know about the dangers out there but they put themselves in trouble with their eyes wide open. (Thoko, 53)

Adult participants correlated the perceived disconnect from an idealized traditional childhood, to consequences such as increased crime, alcohol and drug abuse, and the contraction of HIV. Many adults made the specific connection between 'rights' and the risky sexual behaviours undertaken by young people. Indeed, the scale of the AIDS epidemic among young people in South Africa is staggering, as they are now the highest risk group for HIV contraction. Although awareness and knowledge about HIV/AIDS are high, this has generally not translated into substantial behaviour change (Kalichman and Simbayi, 2004), partly because young people receive conflicting messages about sex and sexuality and lack the knowledge, confidence, and skills to discuss sexual issues, including contraception and prevention of infection (Hartell, 2005). While it is clear that young people today are not the first generation to engage in premarital sex (Burman and Preston-Whyte, 1992), adult participants explained that the cultural rituals which made it socially acceptable for young people to engage in sexual exploration are now being disregarded, much to their dismay:

> [Childhood is] very different. We were very disciplined, we respected adults. When a boy wanted to talk to you, he would wait for you at the river. But today they now use cell phones to communicate and today's children show no respect... children today are mothers, they get children prematurely... they are not disciplined... back then girls did the thigh sex, they never had penetrative sex before marriage. They don't follow instructions. Back then girls did the virginity test. (Fundiswa, 29)

The implications of this contempt were seen to threaten the very future of young people, as new risks such as AIDS collided with a more brazen generation of young people. A feeling of futility was often expressed, where adults believed that children would not listen to their perceived wisdom and experience. In many instances, this resulted in a total absence of engagement with children and young people on topics such as sex, intimacy, pleasure, and relationships, highly disconcerting considering the heightened vulnerability of young people, and particularly young women to contracting HIV (Dorrington *et al*, 2002; Lesch and Kruger, 2004). Many adults felt that 'It's difficult because when you talk to your children, they don't listen... then again if you don't say a thing they go out there and bring death' (Thokozani, 49). When caregivers did openly discuss HIV, it was often by teaching children how to protect themselves in situations where blood was present, or with general sentiments that HIV was a problem in the community and dangerous. Discussions of personal choices or the risks children may face in the future were not communicated at all, despite some children stating they would benefit from more open communication.

The story of Sihle, a young man of 18, characterizes the complex nature of sex education and communication between adults and children in the time of AIDS. Sihle lived in Umlazi, a township of Durban, with his extended family. His mother, two aunts, and female cousin were all HIV-positive and living openly within the household. Despite these realities, the women expressed an inability to communicate their experiences to the young members of their family. As Camangile, Sihle's aunt, said:

> I think youngsters are more at risk of getting the virus. They are easily influenced to not use protection... they are building their confidence. You find that history repeats itself: parents die of AIDS and so do their children.

Sihle's mother Nana also expressed a feeling of futility, although, in part, it was because she had left the responsibility to educate to external influences: 'What can I say? They are taught about it at school, the media talks about it – what more can I say?' Nana's acceptance that the school and the media were now responsible for her son's sex education is a further indication of how adults feel they have been marginalized by a 'new' South Africa where children and young people are increasingly independent from home life and traditional values. It is schools where children learn about rights and health education, and adult attempts to educate and communicate within the home are felt to be futile, and thus not worth the endeavour.

Despite the experiences of this family, including the stress of Sihle's cousin who was awaiting confirmation of the HIV status of her young baby, Sihle had not moderated his behaviour. In the six months prior to our meeting, Sihle had become a father to two babies, a few months apart in age, with two different young women. From his mother's perspective, young people 'want to see what we saw. They are very stubborn and want to see for themselves what the outcome of whatever action will be'. Despite his knowledge of testing and access to HIV treatment, Sihle himself refused to test, preferring to wait for the results of his two partners and their babies.

When we asked why he did not use condoms, he felt that they were not comfortable to use, nor were they common. He admitted to being afraid now of what might happen, but that the issue of trust between a couple was paramount:

> we mislead each other as a couple. If you love someone, then what is the use of a condom or vice versa? She would accuse you of not trusting her. To prove you do, you agree not to use the condom.

The story of Sihle demonstrates the complex world of love and intimacy that young people must navigate in the time of AIDS. However, while elders and those directly impacted would be obvious bastions of education in this context, this family also exemplifies the complicated nature of communication within a culture where open discussion has been traditionally non-existent, and where topics such as peer pressure, relationships, love, and intimacy have never been discussed. Despite the openness and experience of this family, adults expressed futility, and looked to external sources such as the education system to play the role they seemed unwilling or unable to perform.

Ultimately, across numerous interviews, adults perceived children's rights to be part of the cause of young people's loss of self-respect and risky behaviour, and not part of the solution. Despite a desire on the part of some children and young people to discuss these topics openly and with loved ones, caregivers preferred to leave this dialogue to the schools and the media. As with the perceived resulting disrespect due to children's rights, adults expressed a sense of futility in relation to negotiating altering relationships with their children. It was the government, through the schools and NGOs, who would now have to deal with 'the problem' *they* had created.

Children's rights in an era of loss

> You just convinced yourself it was something a child shouldn't know about. (Nompumela, 34)

> Children must not know the life of an elder. (Sthandwa, 12)

The chapter has thus far explored how adults perceived the issue of 'children's rights' as an affront to their position as caregivers and how this impacted communication surrounding HIV education and family relationships. This section examines the landscape related to loss and bereavement in a time when children's rights permeate family relationships, and the results for children's everyday experiences. In terms of grieving and bereavement in the context of AIDS, researchers have posited that orphaned children are often exposed to multiple stressors related to having cared for, and witnessed the death of, a parent with a debilitating illness, which all serve to compound and complicate the grieving process (Cluver and Gardner, 2006). However, within these studies, an understanding of the cultural landscape of grieving and bereavement remains absent. In the time of AIDS, a series of significant shifts have occurred: cultural practices have broken from tradition, and emerging bereavement practices have meant a renegotiation of relational and generational norms surrounding communication and death. This section historically situates the realities of bereavement, before exploring the current generational and relational nature of bereavement in the time of AIDS, and issues related to attending funerals, and taking part in cultural traditions surrounding death and mourning within the context of children's rights.

Within Zulu culture and religion, death is seen to perpetuate an impure state, with children especially vulnerable to harm from death 'pollutions' (Vilakazi, 1965; Daniels, 2006; Wood *et al.*, 2006). As such, children were not permitted near a dead body or at funerals. Within this study, adult participants universally described their lack of participation in events surrounding the passing of a family member when they were children. They often described a complete lack of knowledge, and their inability to question elders about missing family members. Many were simply told that their relative had 'gone away':

> We were never told, we were just told that so and so is gone to Joburg and we would start wondering when we saw a lot of people home… but we were never told anything more… [when people came to the funeral] we were locked up in the room. (Nomvula, female, 40)

Because of the prevalence of adult labour migration, this seemed a simple explanation, shielding children from the trauma of acknowledging death. Given that children were unable to ask questions by cultural custom, they often only realized they had lost someone when they grew old enough to figure it out on their own. As such, children were entirely excluded from the bereavement process. In cases where children were 'told' of a parent's death, it tended to occur in the traditional Zulu manner, where 'at night, an adult whispers in the child's ear and tells them "so and so" is dead and they will not see that person again' (Slindile, 32). Unsurprisingly, children were not always unwary objects of the events going on in their family homes. They often suspected that someone had passed away: 'we did suspect, but we couldn't ask questions. Children used to whisper to each other… we knew, but didn't ask' (Dorcas, 75). However, generational hierarchies within family life were extremely rigid, and prevented children from asking questions: not a single adult could remember having ever posited a direct question about the loss of a family member, even many years later.

Although research has been very limited in terms of understanding the cultural processes surrounding grief, researchers and NGOs in South Africa have suggested that traditional practices, where children are told 'untruths' about the whereabouts of the deceased, or where an elder whispers into the sleeping child's ear, have been perpetuated as the continuing norms (Marcus, 1999; Denis and Ntsimane, 2006). Even in the long term, Killian (2005) states that relatives are inclined to take in very young children and never directly reveal their orphan status. However, the following discussion demonstrates that while some norms have persisted surrounding bereavement rituals, a number of practices have been modified in response to the AIDS epidemic and children's rights discourses.

First, due to the vast and endemic nature of the AIDS epidemic, many children today not only bear witness to the loss of a family member within the home, but are also often present (and possibly acting as caregivers) during months of severe illness, and thus cannot be shielded as they might have been in the past. For Nompumelelo, 12, 'it was early in the morning and my grandmother was talking to mom. She fell silent and gran started crying, and said mom had died. She then told me to get an elder from a neighbour's house'.

In the absence of direct communication or bearing witness, as with previous generations, children in this study often had other ways of knowing. Hloniphani, a 10-year-old boy from Umlazi explains:

> My mother told me. But then again even if she had not told me, I would have known... in my family when someone dies, some rooms are cleared to make room for those who will help the family mourn the death. Relatives come over and every action they take indicates that someone has died. It makes it easier to see that they are preparing for a funeral.

Due to the sheer number of losses occurring within their homes and the community, children today are increasingly knowledgeable about death and loss. However, for many, questions continued to be unanswered, particularly around the cause of a family member's passing. Many children felt that not only would it be inappropriate to ask about the cause of the death, but that such knowledge was the domain of adults, and would be improper for children to be made aware. From the perspective of adults, the question of whether children would be inquisitive as to the nature of death in the family had 'not even crossed' their minds. It was taken as a given that children would accept the information that was presented to them, and the dialogue would end there. Indeed, many adults felt that today's generation of children displayed astute intelligence if they were able to maintain 'their place' within the generational order by *not* posing questions, and *not* speaking of the person who had passed away.

However, while children today often remain passive due to their inability to communicate about death and loss, a significant shift had occurred in the active participation of children in the grieving traditions of funeral attendance and viewing the body. A number of adult participants attributed this shift to the altering climate of children's rights: 'it's because today's children have rights. They have the right to know what is going on' (Zwelindzima, 29). There was a feeling of inevitability projected, with adults struggling to come to terms with new realities. As Zwelindzima went on to add: 'there is no use of thinking that it is bad because children of today have a right, they are aware of these rights, they will tell you they have the right to attend funerals.' Indeed, many adults felt that modern children were far more demanding of knowledge, and that active participation in funerals would subdue unnecessary dialogue: 'they are shown the parent's corpse so that they don't ask questions' (Slindile, 32).

Many children described funeral attendance as a right that was significant in their lives. One reason for this was a desire to maintain the connection between themselves and their loved ones, who were now ancestral spirits. Nombuso, 11, explains the significance:

> Yes, children should go to funerals, to look at them for the last time. Plus you need to see their graves... if you are told to consult them, where would you go? You must know their graves so you can go to pray there.

In cases where children were excluded from burials, anxieties persisted even years later, as young people grappled with the loss of this connection. Freedom, 17, had lost both his parents to AIDS, and expressed both this significance and anxiety:

> I want to go to his graveyard but I don't know the tomb number. My grandmother says I must take her with me but I want to go there alone. I have so many problems and I want to tell him in secret... it's important to me that I tell him.

While both adults and children generally agreed that funeral attendance was beneficial, necessary, and in some cases, 'a right', the process of grieving became far more fraught within the accompanying process of 'viewing the corpse'. In Zulu culture, when a person passes away, they are washed and prayed over in the family home and, for the night before the funeral, the family keeps a vigil over the body. On the morning of the funeral, family and community members say their last goodbyes before the coffin is taken to the graveyard, or buried in the yard in the case of some rural families. Historically, children would have been entirely excluded from the process of viewing. However, for today's generation of children, viewings have become a common occurrence. One of the major issues expressed was a lack of communication surrounding the process. It seemed that in a number of cases, adults felt that with participation came knowledge, rather than any discussion taking place. Thus, viewing was generally thought to be a good idea, primarily because it reiterated the point that the relative had passed away, making it clear and final in the eyes of the child.

For children, sentiments associated with this process were varied. A number of children felt that it was useful, and provided closure: 'It was good for me because I was able to see my father for the last time' (Sne, 15). Some also felt empowered by the opportunity:

> we were told to come and see him... it was scary and the process was painful. My uncle loved us very much... I chose to view him. All the family members were called and asked if they wanted to view... I was not there when he died. I was happy to see him again. (Nduduzo, 14)

However, those that found it helpful or empowering were in the minority. The majority of children experienced a general sense of confusion that marred the experience, primarily because they were not given a clear explanation for what was happening, did not have a choice in the decision, and were left with many unanswered questions:

> I saw her. They let me see her, then gran told me that she was not dead, that she was sleeping, just resting. Of course she was not telling me the truth... I knew she was dead when they buried her. I saw the coffin going into the ground and I started crying. (Freedom, 17)

It is often the case that children are simply called in to view the corpse, unaware of what they are walking into, and not consulted on the decision: 'I didn't have a choice because they just called me to come and view' (Sbonelo, 13). However, children were repeatedly told by adults that viewing would be beneficial, and expressed the sense that resisting 'family law' was an impossibility.

Beyond a lack of consultation, communication, preparation, and understanding, what further complicated the experience of loss was a general lack of support and comfort within the adult–child relationship. Communication of any kind between adults and children during this time tended to be limited. In general, it was not uncommon for relatives to say that children seemed to be coping well with the death of their parents and loved ones. Very few adults expressed concern for the psychological well-being or grieving of the children in their homes. Indeed, it was clear from many of the child participants that a desire to speak of their loved ones existed, but they rarely felt there was an outlet within their families to do so. Despite 'active' participation in rituals, children were often silenced in other ways. Many children described a continuity in the expectations of children's 'place' within the generational hierarchy in terms of an inability to pose questions, and a reality where they grieved on their own, despite a desire to speak of their loved ones with adult family members.

Ultimately, tensions remain between 'old' expectations of what children should know or be told, and what children are experiencing today. For example, a number of adults were uncomfortable with children's attendance at funerals and viewings, but felt powerless to make alternative decisions, or to prepare their children for the experience. Despite new norms surrounding loss and mourning, traditional aspects related to generational communication remained, leading many children to be caught in between, and without the support they required. It is interesting that while active participation is now a common occurrence, it has not been accompanied by other shifts in the adult–child relationship in terms of communication. Clearly there are some aspects of rigid cultural custom that will take longer to reform. And while children's rights have been at least partially responsible for children's increased knowledge and awareness of death, these same discourses have also perpetuated some of the very tensions that have made it difficult for children to grieve within a supportive family environment. It is thus paramount for those working within psychosocial fields both in research and practice, to be aware of such generational and historical realities. Psychological indicators require cultural context if they are to remain meaningful, and ultimately helpful to children in the time of AIDS. Despite prevailing assumptions, children are not excluded from bereavement practices, and they are often aware of HIV status and the reality of loss in their families. However, shifts in the generational landscape of bereavement require further action if children are to cope and remain resilient in the face of widespread HIV loss. For such shifts to occur, it is critical that activists and those working on the ground with children view bereavement within an inclusive landscape which acknowledges issues related to children's rights and generational communication in the time of AIDS.

Conclusion

When the question of children's rights emerges in the context of AIDS, it is generally within a framework which is seen to promote and protect vulnerable children. Rights are seen as tools to minimize the impact of the epidemic by reducing children's vulnerability to infection, offering protection from discrimination, and through rights-based education (for example, Goldstein *et al.*, 2001; Onyango-Ouma *et al.*, 2005; Tarantola and Gruskin, 2005). However, in the time of AIDS, the promotion of children's rights has had significant implications for adult–child relations, and the cultural practices surrounding HIV within the family. By exploring childhood in a generational perspective, this chapter has highlighted the discontent adults feel at 'the state of childhood today', and in particular the dissonance surrounding children's rights and a perceived loss of traditional aspects of childhood. Adult frustration with children, and with the government, was evident in relation to issues such as corporal punishment, and the disempowerment they feel in parenting capacity. While children have gained rights in some areas of life, these very rights have also caused new conflicts to emerge, decreasing the agency that characterizes children's rights in the first place. It is this dissonance that is renegotiated daily through adult and child interactions, demonstrating the relational and generational nature of children's rights in practice at the family level.

One of the inherent paradoxes of the Convention on the Rights of the Child is that it hinges on rights being enforced by others; children cannot entirely ensure their own rights (see also Cheney, this volume), and it is the very perpetrators of children's oppression who are charged with ensuring rights. Adults in South Africa have clearly not 'bought into' the notion of children's rights, and continue to construct rights as an affront to their parental rights. Indeed, the very nature of formal children's rights is out of tune with traditional constructions of what a proper Zulu childhood should entail, and what children's roles should be within the family and society. In the era of the AIDS epidemic, while efforts to support affected children have been imbued with rights-based discourses, children's rights themselves are at the forefront of family dissonance and are a leading cause for limited and fractious communication between adults and children.

Within this study, adults perceived an overwhelming crisis within traditional childhood, despite many children holding on to values of respect, refraining from asking questions, and not insisting on the banishment of corporal punishment. This viewpoint is critical to understanding how adults and children communicate and interact around issues such as HIV education and bereavement, and how resulting fracture and conflict exacerbate child vulnerability in the time of AIDS. In order to have meaning in the lives of children, government leaders, educators, and advocates of children's rights must be aware of the implications for the laws which they seek to promote, and work with adults and caregivers on the most appropriate means of translating these into the everyday lives of families and children.

References

Barberton, C. (2006) *The Cost of the Children's Bill: Estimates of the Cost to Government of the Services Envisaged by the Comprehensive Children's Bill for the Period 2005 to 2010.* Report for the Department of Social Development.

Barnett, T. (2006) 'A long-wave event: HIV/AIDS, politics, governance and "security": sundering the intergenerational bond?' *International Affairs*, 82: 297–313.

Barnett, T. and Whiteside, A. (2006) *AIDS in the Twenty-First Century: Disease and Globalization* (2nd edn). London: Palgrave Macmillan.

Booysen, F. and Arntz, T. (2002) 'Children of the storm: HIV/AIDS and children in South Africa', *Social Dynamics*, 28 (1): 170–92.

Bower, C. (2008) 'Banning corporal punishment: the South African experience, Cape Town' (resources aimed at the prevention of child abuse and neglect).

Bower, C. (2012) 'Can't beat violence out of society', *Daily News*, 8 February.

Boyden, J. (2003) 'Children under fire: challenging assumptions about children's resilience', *Children, Youth and Environments*, 13: 1.

Burman, S. (2003) 'The best interests of the South African child', *International Journal of Law, Policy and the Family*, 17: 28–40.

Burman, S. and Preston-Whyte, E. (1992) 'Assessing illegitimacy in South Africa', in S. Burman and E. Preston-Whyte (eds) *Questionable Issue: Illegitimacy in South Africa*, Cape Town: Oxford University Press.

Campbell, C. (1991) 'The family, socialization and rapid change: transforming notions of "respect" in the social identity of township youth', in D.R. Braude et al. (eds) *Children and Families in Distress: Working Papers from a Seminar*, Pretoria: Human Sciences Research Council, Research Program on Family and Married Life.

Chirwa, D.M. (2002) 'The merits and demerits of the African Charter on the Rights and Welfare of the Child', *International Journal of Children's Rights*, 10: 157–77.

Cluver, L. and Gardner, F. (2006) 'The psychological well-being of children orphaned by AIDS in Cape Town, South Africa', *Annals of General Psychiatry*, 5: 8.

Daniels, M. (2006) 'Hidden wounds: orphanhood, expediency and cultural silence in Botswana'. Unpublished thesis, University of East Anglia, Institute of Development Studies.

Denis, P. and Ntsimane, R. (2006) 'Absent fathers: why do men not feature in stories of families affected by HIV/AIDS in KwaZulu-Natal?' in L. Richter and R. Morrell (eds) *Baba: Men and Fatherhood in South Africa*, Cape Town: HSRC Press.

Dorrington, R. *et al.* (2002) 'HIV/AIDS profile of the provinces of South Africa – indicators for 2002.' Centre for Actuarial Research, Medical Research Council and the Actuarial Society of South Africa.

Foster, G., Levine, C., and Williamson, J. (2005) *A Generation at Risk: The Global Impact of HIV/AIDS on Orphans and Vulnerable Children*, Cambridge: Cambridge University Press.

Freeman, M. (2000) 'The future of children's rights', *Children and Society*, 14: 277–93.

Goldstein, S., Anderson, A., Usdin, S., and Japhet, G. (2001) 'Soul buddyz: a children's rights mass media campaign in South Africa', *Health and Human Rights*, 5: 163–73.

Han, J. and Bennish, M.L. (2009) 'Condom access in South African schools: law, policy and practice', *PLOS Medicine*, 6: 1371.

Hartell, C. (2005) 'HIV/AIDS in South Africa: a review of sexual behavior among adolescents', *Adolescence*, 40: 171–81.

Henderson, P.C. (2006) 'South African AIDS orphans: examining assumptions around vulnerability from the perspective of rural children and youth', *Childhood*, 13: 303–27.

Higson-Smith, C. and Killian, B. (2000) 'Caring for children in fragmented communities', in D. Donald *et al.* (eds), *Addressing Childhood Adversity*, Cape Town: David Philip Publishers.

Kalichman, S. and Simbayi, L. (2004) 'Sexual assault history and risk for sexually transmitted infections among women in an African township in Cape Town, South Africa', *AIDS CARE*, 16: 681–9.

Killian, B. (2005) 'Risk and resilience', in R. Pharoah (ed.) *A Generation at Risk? HIV/AIDS, Vulnerable Children and Security in Southern Africa*, Pretoria: Institute for Security Studies.

Lesch, E. and Kruger, L. (2004) 'Reflections on the sexual agency of young women in a low-income rural South African community', *South African Journal of Psychology*, 34: 464–86.

Longmore, L. (1959) *The Dispossessed: A Study of the Sex-Life of Bantu Women in and around Johannesburg*, London: Jonathan Cape.

Marcus, T. (1999) *Wo! Zaphela Izingane – It is Destroying the Children – Living and Dying with AIDS.* Report prepared for the Children in Distress Network (CINDI), Pietermaritzburg, South Africa: CINDI.

Mayall, B. and Zeiher, H. (2003) *Childhood in Generational Perspective*, London: Institute of Education, University of London.

McKendrick, B. and Hoffman, W. (1990) *People and Violence in South Africa*, Cape Town: Oxford University Press.

Meintjes, H. and Hall, K. (2009) 'Demography of South Africa's children', in S. Pendlebury et al. (eds) *South African Child Gauge 2008/2009*, Cape Town: Children's Institute, University of Cape Town.

Moses, S. (2006) 'An overview of children's participation in South Africa.' Paper presented at the seminar, 'Theorising children's participation', University of Edinburgh, 4–6 September.

OAU (1999) *African Charter on the Rights and Welfare of the Child*, Monrovia: Organization of African Unity.

Onyango-Ouma, W., Aargaard-Hansen, J., and Jensen, B.B. (2005) 'The potential of schoolchildren as health agents in rural western Kenya', *Social Science and Medicine*, 61: 1711–22.

Porteus, K., Vally, S., and Ruth, T. (2001) *Alternatives to Corporal Punishment – Growing Discipline and Respect in our Classrooms*, Johannesburg: Heinemann.

Smith, M.K. (2002) 'Gender, poverty, and intergenerational vulnerability to HIV/AIDS', *Gender and Development*, 10: 7.

South African Department of Health (2010) *National Antenatal Sentinel HIV and Syphilis Prevalence Survey in South Africa, 2009*, Pretoria: Department of Health.

South African Department of Health, South African Interfaith Council, and LeadSA (2010) *Building a Culture of Responsibility and Humanity in our Schools: A Guide for Teachers*, Pretoria: Department of Basic Education.

Subbarao, K., Mattimore, A., and Plangemann, K. (2001) *Social Protection of Africa's Orphans and Other Vulnerable Children: Issues and Good Practice Program Options*, Washington, DC: World Bank.

Tarantola, D and Gruskin, S. (2005) 'Children confronting HIV/AIDS: charting the convergence of rights and health', in S. Gruskin *et al.* (eds) *Perspectives on Health and Human Rights*, New York, NY: Routledge.

Thembela, L.P. (2002) 'An investigation of Zulu mothers' and caregivers' views of childhood and behaviour problems in Africa, Zulu-speaking children under the age of 5.' Unpublished thesis, University of Natal, Pietermaritzberg.

Twum-Danso, A. (2009) 'Reciprocity, respect and responsibility: the 3Rs underlying parent-child relationships in Ghana and the implications for children's rights'. *International Journal of Children's Rights*, 17: 415–32.

UNAIDS (2010) *Report on the Global HIV/AIDS Epidemic 2010*, Geneva: Joint United Nations Programme on HIV/AIDS (UNAIDS).

Vanderbeck, R.M. (2007) 'Intergenerational geographies: age relations, segregation, and reengagements', *Geography Compass*, 1/2: 200–11.

Veerman, P. (1992) *The Rights of the Child and the Changing Image of Childhood*, Dordrecht: Martinus Nijhoff Publishers.

Veerman, P., Tatsa, G., Druzin, P., and Weinstein, R. (1999) 'HIV prevention, children's rights and homosexual youth', *International Journal of Children's Rights*, 7: 83–9.

Vilakazi, A. (1965) *Zulu Transformations: A Study of the Dynamics of Social Change,* Pietermaritzberg: University of Natal Press.

Wood, K., Chase, E., and Aggleton, P. (2006) '"Telling the truth is the best thing": teenage orphans' experiences of parental AIDS-related illness and bereavement in Zimbabwe', *Social Science and Medicine,* 63: 1923–33.

Zamisa, S. (2003) 'An investigation into the understanding of childhood problems in black isiZulu speakers.' Unpublished thesis, University of KwaZulu-Natal, Pietermaritzberg.

4 Earning rights

Discourses on children's rights and proper childhood in Ethiopia

Tatek Abebe and Tamirat Tefera

Introduction

In recent years sensitization programmes linked to promoting children's rights in Ethiopia have been growing. These programmes are implemented through, among other channels, school curricula, children's clubs, and Children's Parliaments. Rights discourses are infused in the activities of *kebele* (local administration), community-based organizations like saving and credit associations, as well as burial associations that have a primary function in fostering solidarity, support, solace, and interdependent livelihoods. In addition, a rights-based approach shapes the activities of government and most donor-driven non-governmental organizations (NGOs) that target the well-being of vulnerable children and families. These processes have not only created a space where children's rights are contested, but also fuel deep controversies about the nature of childhood and child–family relations in contemporary Ethiopian society.

Despite the growing body of literature on how the United Nations Convention on the Rights of the Child (CRC) 'translates' into local realities (e.g. Twum-Danso, 2009; Snipstad *et al.*, 2010; Frankenberg *et al.*, in press), there is limited knowledge on the ways in which community members who have a stake in childhood understand and interpret discourses of children's rights in Africa. In Ethiopia, although the 'investment-based approach' shapes parents' and community members' views on childhood, the growth to prominence of rights-based interventions has led to contradictory perspectives about the role and place of children. The contradictions manifest themselves in the ways in which community members describe children's duties, emphasizing the mutually interdependent nature of life as opposed to the independent and separate rights that such discourses promote. The idea that children have special rights different from adults is an anathema to the notion of *mahiberawi nuro* (literally meaning collective life) that governs everyday life in Ethiopia (Abebe, 2013). Discourses of children's rights are met with resistance by parents and sometimes by children. As this chapter reveals, whereas some children experience rights as 'hope', others tend to perceive it as mere rhetoric that heightens unmet expectations. Yet, several aspects of the global children's rights discourses continue to be appropriated by local norms, values, and legislations in Ethiopia.

Scholars have recently highlighted the need to reconceptualize 'children's rights as a living practice shaped by children's everyday concerns' (Hanson and Nieuwenhuys, 2013: 8). They called for a paradigm shift to move away from what Snipstad *et al.* (2010: 206) call the 'right-talk', as well as from a vertical state–child axis to exploring the interdependent functions and relations of children *inside* society in order to reveal the multiple responsibilities borne by children (Roche, 1999; White, 2002; Twum-Danso, 2009; Lemessa and Kjørholt, 2013). Explaining the dissonances between the lived experiences of children and the legal frameworks of 'children's rights', Hanson and Nieuwenhuys (2013: 4) argue that 'Children do not simply discover their rights after exposure to metropolitan rights discourses, but become aware of their rights as they struggle with their families and communities to give meaning to their daily existence'.

This chapter explores how discourses about children's rights shape, and are shaped by, ideas of proper childhood, and the ways in which these ideas are congruent with, or contradict, parental and community understandings of children's rights in southern Ethiopia. Drawing on fieldwork involving interviews and focus group discussions (FGDs) with parents, children, and government and NGO workers, the chapter discusses the tensions and controversies that the introduction of children's rights discourses has created in a locality that is characterized by high levels of childhood poverty and marginalization. It does so by examining local, normative ideas of proper childhood and parenting – that is, what children should do, how children should behave, and what childhood ought to be. The chapter argues that child–family relations are mediated in, and through, parents' and children's familial, social, cultural, and economic expectations and constraints. Ethiopian children earn their rights and, unlike what the preamble of the CRC emphasizes, the rights they are entitled to are met, not because of their citizenship of the nation state, but due to their contributions to, and continued involvements in reproducing the daily lives of family collectives. The chapter further reveals how children are seen by society as members of complex family collectives to whom they owe duties and obligations in return for the securing of their rights, existence, and well-being.

Research context

The data the chapter draws on are from a larger research project on 'Children, young people and local knowledge in Ethiopia and Zambia'.[1] The Ethiopian component of the research documented how families and communities set moral, social, cultural, and economic expectations on children, and the knowledge and skills children need and use as they go about fulfilling those expectations (Abebe and Kjørholt, 2013). We undertook five months of fieldwork spanning three years (2008, 2009, and 2010) on changes and continuities in 'traditional' child socialization practices and how notions of children's rights affect parents' and children's expectations and under- standings of childhood and parenthood (Tefera *et al.*, 2013). The findings reported on here are based on in-depth interviews and focus group discus- sions examining the various meanings that 'children's rights' have, how those meanings are woven into and manifest themselves in everyday social practices thereby revealing aspects of proper childhood, and ideals inform- ing community members' perspectives about the role and place of children in Ethiopian society more broadly.

Fieldwork was carried out in Dilla, a multi-ethnic bustling town located 380 kilometres south of Addis Ababa, and 90 kilometres from Hawassa, the administrative capital of the Southern Nations, Nationalities, and People's Region (SNNPR). Dilla serves as a centre for the Gedeo Zone (composed of 12 *woreda* or districts). It is an administrative seat for Zonal-level governmen- tal and non-governmental offices, including branch offices of several interna- tionally funded NGOs. Being the only major town with several large markets for cash crops like fruits, vegetables, coffee, and chat (mild stimulant crop and main source of cash for peasants), Dilla is also a transportation hub for Ethiopia's far south. Dilla has been experiencing a high level of population growth, estimated at 3.9% annually (FDRE, 2007). Based on the 2007 Population and Housing Census (FDRE, 2007), the total population of Dilla was estimated to be 90,000 of which 64% are children and young people (i.e. below 24 years of age). However, unlike other towns in Ethiopia, the popula- tion of Dilla is increasing rapidly as the town is attracting large numbers of migrants, as well as wealthy investors, due to the various economic opportu- nities that it presents. Dilla also experiences huge seasonal influx of labour migrants especially during the harvesting and processing seasons of coffee, the mainstay of Ethiopia's economy accounting for close to 70% of export revenue. Dilla's strategic location as a trading town, bulking point for com- mercial crops, and hub of transportation has created strong social, economic, political, and cultural contacts and 'selective' integration with the outside world. As a result, it offers an interesting case study on how children and parents of different socioeconomic and ethnic backgrounds encounter dis- courses of children's rights in Ethiopia.

The chapter first provides a brief discussion on theoretical debates that link child socialization practices and children's rights. It then identifies and discusses aspects of childhood and parenting that are connected to the pro- motion and implementation of children's rights. This involves analysis of empirical material regarding a) conceptualizations of childhood and chil- dren's rights; b) the challenges of mainstreaming children's rights in institu- tions that work for, or with, children; and c) children's and community members' perspectives on parenting, education, and proper childhood. The final section conceptualizes rights as interdependence, and summarizes the implications of the research findings for understanding children's rights in Ethiopia and beyond.

Linking children's rights and parenting practices

Studies indicate that an 'authoritarian' style of parenting is common in most parts of Ethiopia. Habtamu (1995) found that the hierarchical system of social relation is the dominant childrearing style in rural northern (mostly Orthodox Christian) parts of the country. Messing (1995) argued that, during early childhood, the attitude of most Amhara parents (the main ethnic group in northern Ethiopia) towards children is 'laissez-faire' due to the view that childhood is a state of innocence and imperfection. Parents leave their children with little supervision until they are old enough (7–8 years) to perform economic tasks. At that time, parents train them in an authoritarian fashion to make them grow into adults as quickly as possible, without allowing them a period of playful adolescence. Authoritarian practices are seen as being instrumental in producing what Poluha (2004) calls the cultural schemas of subordination and conformity. Drawing on longitudinal study, Poluha (2004) conceptualized adult–child relations in Ethiopia as the same as the one between patrons and clients. Both adult–child and patron–client relationships are established between persons who have something to offer the other, although the value of what is provided by the superordinate is usually considered to be higher than that of the subordinate. Thus, relations between adults and children, teachers and pupils, and men and women are strongly authoritarian and durable (Poluha, 2004).

On the other hand, research among the diverse ethnic groups of southern Ethiopia suggests a relatively permissive and communal approach to parenting. Abbink (1996) highlighted that the inter- and intra-generational relationships between adults and children, men and women, and boys and girls in southern Ethiopia are more egalitarian and complementary and, in the case of some ethnic groups, girls and boys (as opposed to their parents) decide on a marriage partner. This is different from the situation in northern Ethiopia where arranged marriage and the practice of child bride are the norm rather than the exception (Mebratie and Aspen, 2009). Differences on the social position of children between northern and southern parts of Ethiopia are explained by, among other things, the prevalence of strong traditional values and longstanding influences of the Orthodox Church in the former.

Discourses on children's rights, proper childhood, and parenting practices are inextricably linked. Boyden (1997) argued that the CRC is inscribed with an idealized version of Western childhood that is exported to the rest of the world as a 'global model'. Ansell (2005: 23) has noted that this model has failed to describe children's experiences, 'yet as an ideal, it has had significant material impacts on the lives of the young people around the world'. The notions of 'child participation' and the 'autonomous child' are also seen as impositions exerted in the era of economic and cultural globalization, whereby the state has retreated from the delivery of basic social services and adopted a neoliberal stance on human rights (Reynolds *et al.*, 2006). This is revealed in the grounding of the CRC in both 'the superiority of the child-hood model as it evolved in the North and the need to impose this model on a global scale' (Nieuwenhuys, 1998: 270). Arguably, the CRC is seen as an instrument that governs global childhoods, giving economically wealthier nations the right to reshape non-Western childhoods in Western forms.

Moreover, as Nieuwenhuys (2001: 39–40) argues, the visions of childhood the CRC promotes and its use as a template for implementation of pro-grammes for poor children are problematic:

> When transposed to the Ethiopian situation, the issue of children's rights gives rise to an ambiguous situation: predicting their emancipation from undeniably often harsh and unjust family relations, NGOs entice chil-dren into accepting self-exploitation as the price to be paid for what they expect to be the key to a 'decent' childhood... Parents are to be made aware of their children's entitlements to nurture, protection and love, while children must themselves become aware of their rights to self-determination. Children, in contrast, argue that their parents cannot sup-port them and that the rights discourse is but a pretext to push them into earning a livelihood on the streets.

A related critique against the paradigm of children's rights is that it under-mines parental authority and structures of seniority common in societies such as Ethiopia (Snipstad *et al.*, 2010). Children's rights discourses and rights-based interventions inform, and are informed by, the notion of the universality of parenting styles across societies (Tadele, 2001). Lemessa and Kjørholt (2013: 46–7) illustrate how the activities of Children's Parliaments in remote villages of south-western Ethiopia promote 'participation rights' implying a process of individualization of children whereby children are con-nected to the state as individuals in their own right. By focusing on nation states from whom children seem to get few entitlements and by moving away from family collectives (with which children have the immediate reciprocal relationship), the CRC seems to not only raise expectations (often unmet), but also undermines the role of parents and communities in improving chil-dren's rights and lives (Abebe, 2013).

Childhood and rights in Ethiopia

Childhood

In Amharic – the lingua franca in Ethiopia – there is no one term that represents the English term 'child'. The term used in the translated Amharic booklet of the CRC produced by Save the Children Norway (2003), *hitsan* – literally meaning 'someone immature' – refers to *all* children including infants, young children, and adolescents below 18 years of age. The concept is used increasingly in formal institutions such as schools and public offices, and is striking for two reasons. First, as opposed to the CRC's hegemonic model of childhood which suggests that this phase of life should be protected, cherished, and enjoyed for quite some time, the Ethiopian notion of *hitsan* indicates that this is a stage of the life course that one ought to grow out of and leave behind. Secondly, *hitsan* illustrates how 'translation' of the CRC into local languages can result in a search for a word that represents the subject 'child' that – ironically – uses a notion which contradicts the 'progressive' visions of childhood embodied in the CRC. Indeed, *hitsan* represents an infantalization of diverse experiences during childhood. Equating a 'child' to *hitsan* obscures children's differentiated level of competence and maturity linked to class, gender, and various stages within childhood. Studies indicate that an Ethiopian child is no longer *hitsan* or 'immature' once s/he is able to distinguish between 'good' and 'bad' (6–7 years of age) (Poluha, 2004). This further reveals that, instead of chronological age, social maturity and the performance of expected roles are central in gauging the development of children.

Although children in Ethiopia can be interpreted as being 'burdened with adult-like duties and responsibilities' (Kefyalew, 1996: 209), local constructions of childhood emphasize the mutuality of a collective life, which steadily draws one from the social periphery of childhood to the central stage of adulthood, and eventually eldership in the community. It upholds the centrality of imparting duties and deference to adults. In this sense, childhood is understood *in relation* to other stages of the life course. Many Ethiopian children do not know their true chronological age, but they realize their *social* age and social position with respect to who the eldest in the community is, and what is expected of their age group (stage of childhood) in terms of rights, entitlements, duties, and responsibilities.

Family collectives are crucial to ensure the well-being of the children in Ethiopia. Abebe (2013) argued that children in Gedeo Zone[2] are seen as being 'born into families': it is often a (male) family member who mediates a child's access to, and full membership of, the clan. Unlike the state, with which children and families have limited contacts, the clan bestows upon the child his or her rights regarding the utilization of physical, social, and cultural resources (e.g. land, dowry, inheritance, social security). Children are also dutiful to seniors because an elder is vested with the power to exercise authority and control over minors. In this context, children see themselves, and are seen by society, less as individuals and more as members of extended families (Abebe, 2013).

Mainstreaming children's rights in public institutions

The 'best interests' of the child are mandated 'paramount consideration' in law in Ethiopia – a country that not only heavily relies on international relief aid but also depends on bilateral, donor-driven projects for development – which ratified the CRC in 1991. The CRC underpins important legislation, including the Constitution of the Federal Democratic Republic of Ethiopia (FDRE, 1995), the Revised Family Code (FDRE, 2000) and the Children's Act (which is currently being drafted and reviewed). The CRC is also tied to policy developments and service delivery for children. Key policy documents such as *Ethiopia's National Plan of Action for Children – 2003–2010 and beyond* (MoLSA, 2004) draw immensely on the CRC. The Revised Family Code states in its preamble that one of the purposes of revision was to 'amend the existing law in such a way that it gives priority to the well-being, upbringing, and protection of children in accordance with the Constitution and International Instruments which Ethiopia has ratified' (FDRE, 2000: 2). However, although Ethiopian laws and policies about children are often considered to be 'well ahead of time' (Tadele, 2001: 117), as we argue below, enforcing these laws and implementing them to promote children's well-being are constricted by lack of material and human resources.

The Ethiopian child protection system is jointly managed by the Ministry of Justice, the Ministry of Labour and Social Affairs (MoLSA), the Ministry of Women, Children, Youth Affairs, and the Federal HIV/AIDS Prevention and Control Office. The mandates of these ministries are wide and overlapping, but are also characterized by a 'lack of standards and uniformity in the services' (MOWA, 2010: 1) especially at lower levels (Zonal and District levels). District and Zonal level offices are underfinanced and their staff are largely untrained. This not only creates inefficiency but also confusion regarding which institution is accountable for ensuring which aspects of children's rights. At present the Children's Affairs Desk in Dilla town is subordinate to the Women's Affairs Office, but the structure of the latter changes frequently highlighting that children's issues too have no permanent structure in public institutions. In this context, international NGOs appear to be charged with the task of promoting children's rights especially in the area of creating awareness about harmful traditional practices such as early marriage and female genital cutting. Yet, as Tadele (2001: 134–5) notes, there is 'considerable lack of coordination' between NGOs and government agencies as each has different priorities and, consequently, they are 'less effective in their efforts to prevent child abuse, delinquency, and other problems facing children'.

Interviews with employees of the Women's Affairs Office suggest that the institutional framework for child protection and support in Dilla is very weak. 'Professionals' who are assigned to the various positions of the child welfare system do not provide sufficient commitment to children's issues, partly because they feel incompetent and partly because of lack of financial resources. The only two areas that receive some attention are children's access to health and education. Moreover, although the Ethiopian government signed the African Charter on the Rights and Welfare of the Child (ACRWC) – whose specific articles are meant to supplement the CRC – interviews with employees of the government and NGOs reveal that they rarely use it. During fieldwork it was noted that strategic documents like the ACRWC and *Ethiopia's National Plan of Action for Children* are not even recognized by the officials at Zonal and District levels. More attention is given to implementing the CRC, although how this international document is linked with, and translates into, local laws and realities is rarely examined. There are also significant variations in the level of commitment to implementing the CRC and achievements of organizations that work for, or on behalf of, children. Many government officials explained how the implementation of laws pertaining to children falls far short of the ideal because of institutional, manpower, and economic constraints. According to one official in the Women's Affairs Office, despite the 'severity of problems children face' and awareness of their rights as stated in the CRC, its implementation in reality is seen as a 'big challenge'.

Resistance to children's rights

The role of the CRC as a dominant framework for rights-based planning and monitoring of children's well-being continues to be a contested issue in Ethiopia. This is because children's perspectives on rights are founded on interdependence and reciprocity, where children have responsibilities and duties towards their parents and families as much as (if not more than) any rights (Laird, 2005). The idea of children's rights calls for deeper understandings of the sociocultural meanings and 'values' of childhood. Ethiopians tend to consider children's rights as a 'hot potato'. Hot potato is a concept used to describe a scenario in which government officials give directives about policies, programmes, and strategies to be implemented by district authorities (unquestioningly), whereby the latter simply dump those ideas on citizens. Yet, the Ethiopian government seems to have an ambivalent position on the idea of children's rights too. For instance, the Charities and Societies Proclamation Law, called the 'NGO's Bill' passed by the Parliament in 2009 limits local and international NGOs and civil society organizations from working in areas of conflict resolution and peace building, democratization, or human rights issues. This restriction has halted the advocacy work of rights-based child-focused NGOs. Children's rights have triggered intense debates among scholars, journalists, policy-makers, and citizens alike. A senior officer at the Ministry of Labour and Social Affairs expressed concerns about the incompatibility of the CRC with child–family relations as follows: 'Western targets for development are very idealistic, especially the stress that is continually placed on the best interest of the child' (Howell, 2006, cited in Brittingham, 2010: 15). In Ethiopia, the best interest of children is inseparable from the interests of wider family collectives (Abebe, 2013). An emphasis on the individual rights of the child in communities where separate rights are neither claimed nor recognized is questioned.

It is also important to recognize how many of the so-called 'revolutionary' ideas held by the Convention have problematic, if not irrelevant, applications in sociocultural and politico-economic settings such as Ethiopia. The moral framework of rights 'reflects and carries several... assumptions, including the premise that human beings are first of all individuals and only secondarily members of communities' (Anderson, 1996: 50). An Ethiopian journalist commented, when asked about the CRC, that 'he did not begrudge Western NGOs' influence because of the minimal resources available to Ethiopian authorities', but he objected to 'the centrality accorded to the notion of the individual child [which he finds] irrelevant to the Ethiopian context' (Howell, 2006, cited in Brittingham, 2010: 15). Like in many parts of Africa, the desire to sustain group solidarity and interdependent life in Ethiopia overshadows the needs and desires of the individual children or indeed any individual at all. This contrasts with the situation in the global north, which emphasizes the development of individuality and the guarantee of separate rights.

Ethiopian parents tend to see children's rights as something that is concerned with 'liberating' children from parental control rather than protecting and empowering them. They expressed scepticism around NGOs' periodic 'sensitization' activities on the topic of children's rights. According to one parent, NGOs have a 'hidden agenda of raising funds in the name of children' but instead of investing resources to improve children's lives, 'they teach us what we have to do to fulfil their rights'. He explained that most 'child rights NGOs' (local NGOs who get funds from international donors) are largely involved in relief activities for certain children (e.g. AIDS orphans) rather than bringing about change for disadvantaged children. The activities of rights-based NGOs are perceived as 'charity' and only temporary. Community members reported that children's rights are a fad, something that will disappear when the NGOs leave. They argued that children are supported by local NGOs not based on their needs but, as White (2002: 729) points out, 'the wish to oblige the donors and to give them what they want'.

Focus group discussions with NGO workers revealed that there have been several frustrations over efforts to teach the general public about the rights of children. As one participant stated, 'issues of children's rights are not easy to educate and be internalized and practised by the society'. A social worker explained that the communities 'do not have interest to know about the rights of children. What they want is the material assistance given to them by NGOs'. The beneficiaries of the NGOs are poor families for whom 'the issue of rights is simply a luxury' (FGD participant). Many families in Dilla do not have the ability to safeguard children's rights because there are more pressing priorities such as fulfilling children's dietary requirements or health care and school expenses. Some commentators have highlighted how the CRC ignores the rights of children to food, which is a serious concern in poor countries such as Ethiopia (Reynolds *et al.*, 2006). Protection from hunger, illness, and disease are basic human rights that often go unmet. Alluding to the irony of having rights that their children cannot enjoy, parents often attribute children's rights discourse as: '*lam alegn besemai wetetuanem alay*' (meaning 'I have a cow but I neither see nor drink her milk').

Discourses on proper childhood

Community perspectives on parenting

Community members in Dilla understand children's rights in ways that both complement and contradict the ideas of childhood embedded in the CRC. Ideals linked to the CRC (e.g. childhood innocence, vulnerability, and care) are woven through public and local discourses of childhood and child-rearing practices. Yet parents expressed how they are 'fed up' with the periodic campaigns in schools and local-level administration (*kebele*) to raise 'community awareness' about children's rights. They suggested that they are often called for meetings by *kebele* officials to discuss 'child rights', but they believe that this issue should be left to families. One participant stated that 'parents are getting into a co-parenting contract with the government' on what she thought were the 'private affairs' of families. This view is also supported by a representative of one *idir* (burial association):

> I do not understand when they [government officials] say 'Your children have the rights' and that I am responsible to keep and satisfy their needs. How can I do that when I am poor? Do I hate my children when they eat? Don't I like my children to have good education?

These questions point to the need to situate children's rights within broader questions of poverty. They underscore that meeting the needs of children and protecting their rights is not a simple issue that happens when one signs a legal document like the CRC. As Ennew and Milne (1989: 14) noted long ago:

> In a world in which it is universally recognized that 'mankind owes to the child the best it has to give', surely the only reason why children lack rights must be lack of the means to provide them with rights.

The perspectives of community members in Dilla indicate the need to move away from mere recognition of children's rights to addressing why those rights are 'far away' from them in the first place. Parents stated that eradicating acute poverty and reducing the harsh living conditions of children need to be key priorities for government and NGOs.

Resistance linked to some aspects of children's rights also surfaced in discussions on topics of disciplining children. According to the children and parents, teaching the pupils in schools about children's rights is met with challenges. Alemayehu (a father of three children) explains his ambivalence to the 'sensitization programmes' of NGOs about not disciplining children:

> Parents are responsible for the future of their children and the best way is to discipline them while they are young... I give an 'elephant's-ear' [an expression to mean 'pretend not to listen'] to this new fashion of child rights.

Similarly, an in-depth interview on ideas of proper parenting with an elderly woman led to a discussion on child–family interaction including, for example, on whether children should have a separate bedroom to offer them privacy and allow them to enjoy their rights as autonomous individuals. The woman listed several reasons why she felt it is wrong to give a child a separate room and why she thinks such a practice is 'potentially dangerous':

> The first danger is that, if the child is for instance below ten, he/she has to be cared and protected by the parent. While young children are asleep, they are incapable to protect themselves from any dangers that may befall on them. They might be hanged with bed sheet or fall off the bed… If they are teenagers, they might go out without the knowledge of the parents, and their life might be endangered. The girls might use the opportunity to 'enjoy' underage love [sex]. The boys might go to the bars and acquire abnormal behaviours, which spoil their future life.

Yet another parent argued in favour of punishment and discipline:

> Children might consider their parents' control as wrong. They do so because they are innocent – as children, they do not know much about real life. When I was a child, my parents, my father, was strict. He followed every activity I did. He beat me when I misbehaved. I am grateful for that now, for the ways he disciplined me. Had I not grown up like that, my life could have taken a different course than it is today [he is a young entrepreneur owning several businesses].

What the above quotations collectively demonstrate is that control over children's actions is seen as an important aspect of upbringing. To be a lenient parent is not acceptable as it may lead to unforeseen consequences for children – including teenage pregnancy, delinquent behaviour, and exposure to dangers. The FGD participants argued that wealthier families tend to be overprotective of their children and that they are more 'egalitarian' and more lenient in the ways they relate to their children. However, as one parent, alluding to the daily hardship of poverty that many children in Dilla endure, asked: 'How can children [brought up in a lenient way] cope when life is tough?' This view speaks to the idea of socializing children so that they are aware of the difficult social and economic conditions in which they live. Another man, a grandfather, expressed his disappointment with how his grandchildren enjoy rights they have not earned and are treated 'like kings and queens' at home:

> They [the children] present themselves as if they know more about everything. They are not respectful of old people… and even their parents. For them we know little about what is wrong and right, or is good for children. They had never been punished by simple physical punishments

like 'kunticha' [light twisting of part of the body] or 'kuta' [verbal warn-
ing]... because of that, they believe that everybody around them has the
obligation to care about them.

The above quotations indicate that parents of different generations and socioeconomic backgrounds have different expectations and ways of relating to
their children. Participants in the FGD confirmed that 'wealthy' children are
'generally spoiled' and that they tend to feel superior to their peers and ignorant of the local norms and living conditions of economically disadvantaged
children. Yet most parents feel strongly about disciplining children, and the
above quotation demonstrates how they wish to raise their children to
become 'good persons' and 'successful' adults. Many parents believe that
scolding and light physical punishments (e.g. twisting the ear) when a child
misbehaves are vital to maintaining control over their children's behaviour
and to raise them 'honest'. A common saying alluded to by many parents –
siyadeg yaltekana zaaf endetameme yikeral [a growing tree needs to be straight-
ened from infancy, otherwise it will grow deformed] – reveals the importance
of 'correcting' children starting from an early age.

Children in the FGDs claimed that their rights should not be rhetoric but
should imply *real* access to basic needs like food, schooling materials, and
information. But they also realize that their parents do not have the capacity
to realize those rights. Children believe that it is important to respect adults
and that to show deference to the elderly is valued by their communities.
However, children's views on discipline are somehow different from one
another as well as from those of adults. Although children feared curses like
'*atideg(i)*' (meaning 'Don't grow or prosper') and '*woldek eyew*' (meaning 'May
your kids be a source of disappointment in future'), some of them were more
critical of curses than others. One boy stated: 'what I detest is that more often
than not the wrongs you have done and the curses are incompatible.' A
15-year-old girl said: 'the older people curse children without understanding
the real problems faced by us.'

While children agreed that adults' punishments or curses are not intended
to harm them but keep them on 'the right track', they tended to think that
corporal punishments do not have positive influence. Kassech, a 16-year-old
girl from Dilla high school, alluded to this as follows:

My father... believes that beatings could make me into a 'nice' girl. For
example, I expect some form of punishments if I come home late from
school... I know he is doing all this with the best intentions but I don't
like it. I think all fathers should be willing to discuss their children's daily
problems, and the like, so as to get their children up to their expectation.

The above quotation demonstrates that children are expected to reproduce
aspects of the culture they live in by following the advice of their parents. It
demonstrates intergenerational differences in the conceptions about whether

and how children should be disciplined. Some parents believe in the importance of corporal punishments to instil good behaviour during childhood, yet children also like it when parents use positive rewards to encourage them. Although most children said that they love being appreciated for their activities, rewards too were valued differently. A 16-year-old boy explained: 'It does not mean much if somebody blesses me by saying "may God help you be a good student" unless that blessing is supplemented by material rewards like pens, exercise book.' Children also expressed that they are disappointed when they are not appreciated or blessed by their parents for their performance. A 14-year-old boy explained the positive rewards given to his friends and how the lack of that in his household discouraged him: 'I am better achiever in the school than my friends; I have never been rewarded materially or morally. Some of my friends are not good at school but they are well-praised by their parents.' Similarly, although some children condemned curses by elders, arguing that it is 'old fashioned', others suggested that verbal blessings reinforced by concrete material rewards helps boost their morale. These perspectives highlight that children's and community members' ideas of rewards, punishment, and what is best for children are not only shaped by gender but are also interwoven with their present material circumstances. Material conditions govern daily needs and contexts for entitlements and social relationships.

Parents' perspectives on children's education

The above differences in views on parenting mirror ideas of proper childhood which are partly explained by the social and economic positions of the parents. Parents whose socioeconomic status is high tend not only to emphasize the education of their children, but also to be concerned about the quality of the schools the children attend. They also follow up on the school performances of their children. The following excerpt from an interview with Solomon, a Dilla businessman, is a case in point:

> I am proud of the way I look after my children compared to the ways in which children in my neighbourhood grow up. They are lucky... they have better chances to enjoy the privileges of childhood. I have three children; the older child is attending a private school in Addis Ababa. I want him to be well educated and go to university. I am planning to send the rest of my kids there. There are no good quality schools here. When I grew up, there was only elementary school, which I had the chance to attend only up to grade three. My aspiration was not realized when I dropped out because of my parents' poverty. I hope my children will achieve my dream: to be educated and become the person they want.

Solomon's view is representative of those of other middle-class families in cities in Ethiopia. Because the school system and the child rearing practices in local towns, in their view, are inadequate for children to realize their potential or, as the businessman put it, to fulfil the parental dream for their children, they send their children to private boarding schools. According to Solomon, education is an important factor in the future success of children. Conversations with several parents confirmed that investment in children's education is seen as key to their future success in adulthood. Yet such an 'investment-based approach' to childhood and the ideas of good parenting are explained partly by families' socioeconomic condition and ties with places outside their local environment.

As opposed to Solomon who sends his children to schools with good 'standards', Seleshi (father of two boys whose livelihood is based on selling *chat* [a mild stimulant crop]) is just happy that his children have access to education, regardless of the quality of the education they receive or the children's achievements in school. He explained that his children support his *chat* shop after returning from school, and that they help generate income, which increases the household's income-earning capacity:

> My duty is feeding and sending them to school as long as I can. I do not want to think and worry about their destination, or what I cannot do, because it is their fate that determines who they will become.

What this suggests is that some parents may not delineate responsibilities and duties and that limited educational financial capacity may shape values related to parenting. The data from an in-depth interview with Emebet (widowed woman) reveal a similar perspective:

> While my husband was alive, it was easy to raise my daughters. My eldest daughter completed high school... she is now assisting me in running our *Shai bet* [tea shop]. I considered the accomplishment of her high school as a great success. I know almost nothing about what and how my children are doing [in school]. I believed the success of children is up to the will of God. There is little parents can do. I have given *adera* [responsibility] about my children to Saint Gabriel; he knows what is good or bad for them. If God allows, my son and daughters would join university. Everyone gets *ye'arba ken edil* [a life path that children are destined to from birth].

The above quotation demonstrates that religious values of leaving things for 'fate' and the 'will of God' are important ways of dealing with the difficulties parents face in raising children, in evaluating what is possible in children's lives in particular, and their futures in general. Similarly, Belaynesh commented on her incompetence to help her children in their school work:

> I do not have the ability to evaluate their performance in each subject [at school]. My duty is to create a conducive environment for them to study and do their assignments. I pray to the Lord for the success of my children

because I know that an uneducated person is like a ladder that people with papers [educated ones] use to climb over. I do not want my children to experience the kind of low position I have in the workplace [being a cleaning lady].

Belaynesh's comments demonstrate how parents' occupation in government offices and their exposure to the ways of life of their colleagues inspired them to dream that their children could be successful too. Belaynesh indicated that her parenting style is influenced by two important factors. The first one is her 'inferior' position in the office as compared to the educated employees of the organization she works in. Had she had a better education, she would have had a better paying job with a higher status and be better able to provide for her children. Secondly, her parenting style is based on the locally exercised style of parenting, which is highly influenced by religion. In the absence of control over the future, adhering to certain belief systems gives her the power to carry on with challenging responsibilities.

Conclusion

This chapter has explored the perspectives of children, parents, and community members regarding childhood, children's rights, and parenting practices. Although research participants' views on childhood are in part shaped by the 'investment-based approach', the rights-based approach that uses the CRC as the benchmark for promoting ideas of child–parent relations is becoming increasingly grounded in the work of government and NGOs. The chapter reveals that the socioeconomic background of parents is not only the basis for the realization of children's needs and entitlements, but also for knowledge of children's entitlement to certain rights. This is demonstrated by the views of children who stated that although they know that they have rights, they think that realization of these rights is a fantasy or vain hope as long as their parents are poor. As Montgomery *et al.* (2003: 36) argued, upholding the rights of 'childhood is a privilege of the rich and practically nonexistent for the poor'.

Juxtaposing children's and community members' perspectives on childhood and parenting to the global discourses of children's rights reveals differences between children's lives on the one hand and, on the other, the rhetoric of rights that misplaces the role and 'value' of children in Ethiopian society. White (2002) suggests that while the rights language, in particular the 'universal rights of the child', sounds clear within the global community it resonates very little with children's daily lives in many local contexts. Nor does it transfer directly into the everyday contexts of children and their families. This is not because Ethiopians believe that children have no rights, but due to the fact that their rights are interdependent with those of the wider family networks with whom they collaborate and in which mutual and long-term livelihoods strategies are set (Abebe, 2013). The lives of children presented here further reveal the inherent tension emanating from an individualistic language of rights for children growing up in societies where collective duties are valued most. As Ansell (2009) points out, the emphasis on children's individual rights, as well as viewing them as subjects of rights (agents capable of independently exercising rights), potentially limits the analysis of structural constraints and the wider fields of power in which their everyday lives unfold.

The discourses on proper childhood and children's rights presented here reveal that a focus on children's individual rights in societies like Ethiopia where communal styles of raising children are predominant have many unintended outcomes. First, in localities like Dilla, such a reading sets children apart and in isolation from the family and community networks on which they depend for survival, well-being, and protection. Many children underscored that there is great gap between the rights they know they (should) have and their everyday lives. Some children commented that this knowledge about what they lack has created frustration in them, while other children blamed their parents for not meeting their basic needs. Secondly, in order to muster resources needed for viable livelihoods, children depend critically on family collectives and social networks of support and not on the state. Family collectives are, in other words, those who shape the dominant way in which children's rights and entitlements are realized. By focusing on nation states from whom children seem to get few entitlements and by moving away from family collectives (with which children have the immediate reciprocal relationship), the CRC not only detaches from but also undermines the role of families and communities in improving children's lives (Abebe, 2013). Thirdly, rights discourses have a patronizing effect. This is because they ignore the meaningful roles and contributions the children themselves make to their families and the wider society more generally. Fourthly, universal values of parenting – the core assumptions of which draw on universal ideals of family and childhood, the CRC – may have problematic policy implications. This is because on the one hand the CRC reflects neoliberal ideology of human rights and on the other promotes a particular model of childhood grounded in what Stephens (1995) argues is a once localized Western construction of children's innocence, dependence, and vulnerability. As Hart (2006: 6) points out, a failure to meet the standards set by this model is 'often attributed to misguided attitudes on part of state authorities or parents' and presents them as failures and backwards. Fifthly, the emphasis on the role of state parties in safeguarding children's wellbeing and protection raises expectations (often unmet) while simultaneously downplaying the impact of structural, economic, and political forces that sharpen poverty and hit children disproportionately. Finally, by failing to open up spaces for incorporating collectivistic understandings of children's rights and duties, there is a risk that policies that aim at implementing the CRC not only obscure the existing collective rights of children (often unwritten) but also negate the very entitlements they already have within society (Abebe, 2013).

The empirical material in this research reveals the significance of the African Charter on the Right and Welfare of the Child which emphasizes 'the need to include African cultural values and experience in considering issues pertaining to the rights of the child in Africa' (Olowu, 2002: 128). Since the Charter considers the obligations of children in tandem with their rights, it has important implications for placing children within the context of their families and communities as well as for exploring rights from the perspective of duties and responsibilities. By focusing on protection and provision, the Charter provides the global children's rights framework a useful correction, namely to re-conceptualize rights as interdependent. Article 31 states that:

> Every child shall have responsibilities towards... family and society, the state and other legally recognized communities... the child, subject to his age and ability shall have the duty... to respect his parents, superiors and elders at all times and to assist them in case of need.

By acknowledging the significance of children's responsibilities, the Article shifts attention away from the vocal, global, and participating child (as articulated in the UNCRC) to the local, dutiful, and cultural child that views its life as being closely tied together with the lives of families and communities.

In conclusion, mainstreaming children's rights issues needs to be contextualized in light of the potential and constraints of local communities. It requires building on the capacity of institutions to incorporate aspects of children's rights that are valued most by society. As participants in this research stated, implementing the CRC through GOs and NGOs is a one-way process that considers the local community and institutions as lacking and being mere recipients of rights conceived as charity/welfare. There is a need to seek out the local, cultural resources that may be mobilized in the interest of safeguarding children's entitlements (White, 2002). Attention needs to be given to poverty, inequality, and social exclusion that impede the implementation and realization of children's rights to a dignified life.

Notes

1 'Children, Young People, and Local Knowledge in Ethiopia and Zambia' is a five-year collaborative, capacity-building project (2007–11) funded by the Norwegian Council for Collaboration in Research and Higher Education (SIU-2007/10084). The authors are grateful to the SIU for the financial support to undertake the fieldwork on which this chapter is based.
2 The Gedeo are the dominant ethnic group in and around Dilla town.

References

Abbink, J. (1996) 'The challenge of education in Ethiopian agro-pastoral societies. Surma childhood in crisis', in H. Wondimu (ed.) *Research Papers on the Situation of Children and Adolescents in Ethiopia*, Addis Ababa: Addis Ababa University Press.

Abebe, T. (2013) 'Interdependent agency and rights: the role of children in collective livelihood strategies in Ethiopia', in K. Hanson and O. Nieuwenhuys (eds.)

Reconceptualizing Children's Rights in International Development: Living Rights, Social Justice and Translations, Cambridge: Cambridge University Press.

Abebe, T. and Kjørholt, A.T. (eds) (2013) *Childhood and Local Knowledge in Ethiopia: Livelihoods, Rights and Intergenerational Relationships,* Oslo/Trondheim: Akademika Press.

Anderson, T.R. (1996) 'Child and family in Christianity', in H. Coward and P. Cook (eds) *Religious Dimensions of Child and Family Life: Reflections on the UN Convention on the Rights of the Child,* Victoria, BC: Wilfrid Laurier University Press.

Ansell, N. (2005) *Children, Youth and Development,* London: Routledge.

Ansell, N. (2009) 'Producing interventions for AIDS-affected young people in Lesotho's schools: scalar relations and power differentials', *Geoforum,* 40: 674–85.

Boyden, J. (1997) 'Childhood and the policy makers: a comparative perspective on the globalization of childhood', in A. James and A. Prout (eds.) *Constructing and Reconstructing Childhood: Contemporary Issues in the Sociological Study of Childhood,* London: Falmer.

Brittingham, S. (2010) 'Birth families and intercountry adoption in Addis Ababa, Ethiopia.' Unpublished master's thesis, The Hague, Netherlands' Institute of Social Studies.

Ennew, J. and Milne, B. (1989) *The Next Generation: Lives of Third World Children,* London: Zed Books.

FDRE (1995) *Constitution of the Federal Democratic Republic of Ethiopia,* FDRE: Addis Ababa (available online at http://asareca.org/PAAP/Policy%20Instruments/Ethiopia%20Constitution%201994.pdf) (accessed on 12 June 2012).

FDRE (2000) The revised family code (213/2000) (available online at http://www.unhcr.org/refworld/docid/4c0ccc052.html) (accessed 12 June 2012).

FDRE (2007) *The 2007 Population and Housing Census of Ethiopia Statistical Report at National Level,* Addis Ababa: Population Commission Census of Ethiopia.

Frankenberg, S.J., Holmquist, R., and Rubenson, H. (in press) 'In earlier days everyone could discipline children, now they have rights – notions of responsibility in focus group discussions about care giving in urban Tanzania', *Journal of Applied Social Psychology.*

Habtamu, W. (1995) 'Dominant values and parenting styles: major limiting factors on the development of entrepreneurship in Ethiopia', in A. Zegeye and H. Hagos (eds) *Proceedings of the First Annual conference on Management in Ethiopia,* Addis Ababa: AAU.

Hanson, K. and Nieuwenhuys, O. (2013) 'Introduction: living rights, social justice and translations', in K. Hansen and O. Nieuwenhuys (eds) *Reconceptualizing Children's Rights in International Development: Living Rights, Social Justice and Translations,* Cambridge: Cambridge University Press.

Hart, J. (2006) 'Saving children: what role for anthropology?' *Anthropology Today,* 22: 5–8.

Kefyalew, F. (1996) 'The reality of child participation in research', *Childhood,* 3: 203–13.

Laird, S.E. (2005) 'International child welfare: deconstructing UNICEF's country programmes', *Social Policy and Society,* 4: 457–66.

Lemessa, A. and Kjørholt, A.T. (2013) 'Children's Parliament: a case study in Konso', in T. Abebe and A.T. Kjørholt (eds) *Childhood and Local Knowledge in Ethiopia: Livelihoods, Rights and Intergenerational Relationships,* Oslo/Trondheim: Akademika Press.

Mebratie, B. and Aspen, H. (2009) 'Early marriage and the campaign against it in Ethiopia', in *Proceedings of the 16th International Conference of Ethiopian Studies (ICES 16),* Trondheim.

Messing, S.D. (1995) *Highland Plateau Amhara of Ethiopia. Vol. 2*, New Haven, CT: Human Relations Area Files Inc.

MoLSA (2004) *Ethiopia's National Plan of Action for Children – 2003–2010*. Addis Ababa: Ministry of Labour and Social Affairs.

Montgomery, H., Burr, R., and Woodhead, M. (2003) *Changing Childhoods: Local and Global*, Chichester: Wiley/Open University.

MOWA (2010) *Standard Service Delivery Guidelines for Orphans and Vulnerable Children's Care and Support Programs*, Addis Ababa: Federal Democratic Republic of Ethiopia, Ministry of Women's Affairs.

Nieuwenhuys, O. (1998) 'Global childhood and the politics of contempt', *Alternatives*, 23: 267–89.

Nieuwenhuys, O. (2001) 'By the sweat of their brow? "Street children", NGOs and children's rights in Addis Ababa', *Africa*, 71: 539–57.

Olowu, D. (2002) 'Protecting children's rights in Africa: a critique of the African Charter on the Rights and Welfare of the Child', *International Journal of Children's Rights*, 10: 127–36.

Poluha, E. (2004) *The Power of Continuity: Ethiopia through the Eyes of its Children*, Uppsala: Nordic Africa Institute.

Reynolds, P., Nieuwenhuys, O., and Hanson, K. (2006) 'Refractions of children's rights in development practice: a view from anthropology', *Childhood*, 13: 291–302.

Roche, J. (1999) 'Children: rights, participation and citizenship', *Childhood*, 6: 475–93.

Save the Children Norway (2003) *The United Nations Convention on the Rights of the Child (in Amharic)*, Addis Ababa: Save the Children Norway.

Snipstad, M.B., Lie, G.T., and Winje, D. (2010) 'Children's rights and wrongs: dilemmas in implementing support for children in the Kilimanjaro Region, Tanzania', in T. Thelen and H. Haukanes (eds) *Parenting after the Century of the Child: Travelling Ideals, Institutional Negotiations and Individual Responses*, Aldershot: Ashgate.

Stephens, S. (1995) 'Children and the politics of culture in "late capitalism"', in S. Stephens (ed.) *Children and the Politics of Culture*, Princeton, NJ: Princeton University Press.

Tadele, G. (2001) 'Obstacles, controversies, and prospects surrounding child abuse management in Addis Ababa', *Northeast African Studies*, 8: 115–41.

Tefera, T., Abebe, T., and Elefachew, T. (2013) 'Childhood, socialization and parenting practices in Dilla Town', in T. Abebe and A.T. Kjørholt (eds) *Childhood and Local Knowledge in Ethiopia: Livelihoods, Rights and Intergenerational Relationships*, Oslo/Trondheim: Akademika Press.

Twum-Danso, A. (2009) 'Situating participatory methodologies in context: the impact of culture on adult–child interactions in research and other projects', *Children's Geographies*, 7: 379–89.

White, S. (2002) 'From the politics of poverty to the politics of identity? Child rights and working children in Bangladesh', *Journal of International Development*, 14: 725–35.

5 Children's rights in the Democratic Republic of Congo and neoliberal reforms

The case of mines in the province of Katanga

Géraldine André and Marie Godin

The Democratic Republic of Congo (DRC) has been shaken by a very long and unprecedented crisis and, despite widespread international aid spent in the country since the end of the transition period in 2006, Congo has officially become[1] one of the least developed countries on earth. Analysis and interpretations of the Congolese state vary among scholars but all of them view the Congolese case as an 'ideal-type' of the African post-colonial crisis (Peemans, 1998; Lemarchand, 2003; Poncelet *et al.*, 2010; De Herdt and Poncelet, 2011; Trefon, 2011; André and Poncelet, 2013).

Shortly after independence from Belgium, Joseph-Désiré Mobutu organized a military *coup d'état* in 1965 and established a dictatorship for three decades. The economic model of 'Zaïrianisation', based on privatization and the personalization of the state (Nzongola-Ntalaja, 2004: 10), led to the sustained informalization of the Congolese economy (MacGaffey *et al.*, 1991; Dibwe, 2001) and the collapse of the most important public institutions and services. Since that period, one of the main children's rights, the right to education, has been harshly compromised in the DRC as public investment in primary education started to disappear (Poncelet *et al.*, 2010; De Herdt, 2011). By the end of the Cold War, donors' assistance to Mobutu's regime stopped abruptly in conjunction with a 'delegitimization' of the state's power (Bongeli, 2008: 119) by Western donors. The imposition of economic reforms (also known as 'structural adjustment programmes') by international institutions such as the World Bank was then carried out and at the same time the collapsing Congolese Government was forced to adopt a juridical package rooted in a human rights framework. Indeed, it is in the context of this political and economic crisis that the Mobutu regime signed (20 March 1990) and ratified (27 October 1990) the Convention on the Rights of the Child (CRC). When the state began to become isolated from the rest of the world, Mobutu Sese Seko adopted the Convention, as well as other international treaties, in order to comply with 'new' Western and neoliberal standards.

The first war (1996–7), also called the 'war of liberation', saw Laurent Desire Kabila (supported by Rwanda and Uganda) in conflict with Mobutu, and led to the fall of the authoritarian regime and the renaming of the country as the 'Democratic Republic of Congo'. This first Congolese war was followed by a second war that lasted for a longer period (1998–2002).[2] After the assassination of President Laurent-Désiré Kabila in 2001, his son, Joseph Kabila, became President, and took measures to liberalize the Congolese economy and to re-establish a dialogue with the International Monetary Fund (IMF) as well as with the World Bank. Concomitantly, during that period of political turmoil and change, a new set of regulations and laws related to children's rights were adopted in order to prevent children from becoming involved in the worst forms of child labour.[3] After a period of transition from 2003 to 2006, the first presidential election since independence was organized with the support of the international community and led to the election of Joseph Kabila, but since that time peace has remained very fragile.[4]

Therefore, the process of adopting a children's rights legal framework in the DRC has occurred within a paradigmatic postcolonial crisis marked by, among other aspects, neoliberal reforms compensating for – as well as undermining – the very weak capacity of the Congolese State. This original coalescing between neoliberal reforms and children's rights is especially visible in the mining sector. Indeed, despite the tumultuous context in which the newly adopted legislation related to children's rights has taken place, this chapter will show that they have been concretely implemented and practised within the mining sector through the form of the fight against child labour. After having analysed issues in the mining sector between the legality of neoliberal policies and the legality of children's rights, we then analyse how children's rights are shaping subjectivities and consequently intergenerational relationships in Katanga province, whose mineral diversity and concentration are among the highest in the world. Secondly, relying on an ethnographic study on children's mining activities in the city of Lubumbashi (Province of Katanga), our aim is to highlight the continuities between the worlds of the artisanal mines and of the children's families; both are worlds where similar strategies of survival as well as processes of children's and parents' identity construction are taking place. On the basis of the analysis of how children live and experience child labour, we will be able to look at how narratives on childhood and parenthood from a children's rights perspective resonate in the lives of Congolese children and their families according to their respective social backgrounds.

Children's rights and neoliberal reforms in the mining context

Conflicts between the multinationals and the artisanal miners

As in many African countries in which the mining sector has been liberalized due to pressure from international financial institutions, the Congolese mining industry started to be privatized from the 1980s on (Rubbers, 2006; Cuvelier, 2011). However, the new Mining Code (2002)[5] was drafted by the Kabila administration in 2002 under the guidance of the World Bank and the IMF, underlining the revival of business in a country that had endured several years of conflict and, in particular, the reconnection of Katanga province to the flows of legal international investment. The mining law outlines the legal framework for the acquisition of mining titles and exploitation permits according to three modes of production: industrial mining, small-scale mining, and artisanal mining (Geenen, 2011a). While in the past the industrial mining sector was especially dominated by state-owned enterprises, the new mining code redefines the role of the state, restricting its intervention as a regulator rather than an operator; and aims at developing the private sector, and especially the large-scale companies, by promoting the most attractive tax and imposition rates for the latter (Mazalto, 2008; Geenen, 2011a). In both Katanga and Kasaï, important mining contracts were signed with multinationals which receive, in 'the form of business agreement (*joint venture*)' the most part of the mining capacity and infrastructure of the former state-owned companies (Verbruggen, 2006; Mazalto, 2008: 59).

The liberalization of the Congolese mining sector has, as in many other African countries, engendered or accentuated the conflicts between the industrial private sector and the artisanal and small-scale mining (ASM) sector (Hilson *et al.*, 2007; Geenen and Claessens, 2013). Indeed, the mining law is not as favourable to small-scale and artisanal mining as it is to the large-scale private enterprises (Geenen, 2011b), while the former sector generates 90% of mining production in the DRC (Mazalto, 2008). Beyond the legal advantages granted to the multinationals, their modes of operating have been decried as especially harmful for the environment, as well as for social life. Indeed, their mode of exploitation has caused displacements and resettlements of that sector of the population who were mainly artisanal miners. The number of artisanal miners varies according to the ups and downs of the Congolese local economy, which in turn is tied to fluctuations in the prices of raw materials in international financial markets (Ferguson, 1999; Cuvelier, 2009). According to the World Bank, in the DRC 10 million people, that is to say 16% of the population, depend on small-scale mining activities for their survival. Artisanal and small-scale mining are also crucial for securing local livelihoods in the country (Geenen, 2013). In the context of the liberalization of the mining sector, but also the parallel reforms encouraged by the World Bank and the IMF,[6] the most important national mining company in Katanga, the Gecamines (*Générale des carrières et des mines*) – created during the colonial period as the *Union minière du Haut-Katanga* and subsequently nationalized – broke down (Rubbers, 2004, 2006). Many workers from this state enterprise came to swell the ranks of artisanal miners (Mazalto, 2008) and contributed to diversifying the social profile of the artisanal workers, many of whom have more middle-class backgrounds (Cuvelier, 2011; André and Godin, 2013). In addition, the period of unprecedented social, political, and economic crises in the 1990s has contributed to the importance of the artisanal mining sector and its high rate of children's participation. Despite the fact that the Congolese constitution establishes access to free education for all children of primary school age (cf. art. 45), Congolese families often need to pay for the teachers' wages in order for their child to be educated (Poncelet *et al.*, 2010). In these circumstances, children are obliged to take economic initiatives to provide for the needs of their households (Dibwe, 2001; Petit, 2003; see also Okyere, this volume).

Despite the importance and contribution of the small-scale and artisanal mining sector in the DRC, as well as more broadly in other African countries, it is stigmatized, criminalized, and deemed illegal by the mining companies, the African governments, and a plurality of other actors in the media, development, and humanitarian fields (Hilson *et al.*, 2007; Tschakert and Singha, 2007; Aubynn, 2009). Indeed, at the legal level, the mining code recognizes the existence of artisanal small-scale miners but the sector is still sub-legal (Geenen, 2012) and the awarding of concessions has been directed to foreign private investors. Thus the liberalization of the Congolese mining sector has, as in many other African countries, engendered conflicts between the industrial private sector and its artisanal and small-scale mining counterpart (Hilson *et al.*, 2007; Geenen and Claessens, 2013). These conflicts concern issues of land, as artisanal miners are generally expropriated by large-scale companies, as well as involving very different conceptions of rights, as artisanal diggers claim advantages through customary law while the multinationals emphasize that they have legally acquired their exploitation title.

It is in the context of these oppositions and conflicts between the multinationals and the artisanal miners that we set the emerging fight against child labour and the promotion by non-governmental organizations (NGOs) of narratives of 'legal childhood' and 'responsible parenthood'[7] that have been analysed through collective field research.

The fight against child labour in the artisanal and small-scale mining sector: the field research

Our field research was carried out within the framework of a collective[8] research project on 'child labour' in small-scale mining. For funding reasons, the results had to be useful for an NGO. Hence, in addition to our socio-anthropological approach which focused on the trajectories of children and young people into small-scale mining, we analysed a development programme carried out by the Belgian NGO Group One in collaboration with the ILO and UNICEF, which aimed to end child labour in the mines, helping them to reintegrate into school.[9]

This fieldwork took place in two socioeconomically different neighbourhoods of a district of Lubumbashi known as *La Ruashi*, which was developed in the 1950s in response to demographic pressures. The work of Hilgers (2009, 2011), on the one hand, and the distance between each neighbourhood and the mines on the other, help account for the contrasts between them. In his research on the principles that establish and structure hierarchies, social divisions, and legitimacies in African secondary cities, Hilgers shows that two factors are at play in addition to cultural and economic capital. The first is the 'degree of urbanity', that is, the ability to manipulate codes, representations, and practices proper to the city, the ability to appear and to be recognized by other residents of an urban area as being more or less 'urban' oneself (Hilgers, 2009: 135–79). The second is 'capital of autochthony', which refers to a set of advantages and networks that benefit groups who claim precedence in a city's territory (Hilgers, 2011). Using this conceptual orientation and taking into account the distance which separates each site from the mines, one can distinguish Matoléo from Kalukuluku. In Matoléo, a central area of La Ruashi which is relatively far from the mines, the population is generally older and more at ease in manipulating urban codes and styles. People there have had direct experience with the wage-based culture of the *Gécamines* or another company, or engaged in occupations that led them to adhere to representations of the nuclear family. The population of Kalukuluku, located closer to the quarries and characterized by hastily built mud residences, is relatively recent, as is its experience of urban codes. It has also less cultural and economic capital than Matoléo. While such a contrast between the two neighbourhoods must be relativized given the many combined variables evident at the family level (economic and cultural capital, 'capital of autochthony', 'degree of urbanity'), it nonetheless allows us to distinguish analytically families from lower-class and middle-class backgrounds.

The fieldwork was carried out during the schools' summer vacation in 2007. Most school-going children thus had free time and were devoting it to a range of economic activities, including collecting rocks around artisanal mining locations. But at the time of our investigations, in the wake of the new Mining Code (*Code minier*[10]) and foreign investor privileges, small-scale and artisanal mining sites previously occupied by the local population were closed, the rights to use them were sold to international companies, and children and artisanal diggers were expelled. The reconfiguration of the local mining sector (from artisanal to industrial production) proved to be a favourable context in which to collect and analyse the justificatory discourses of both parents and children towards previous and more intense child mining-related activities. The method of cross-generational interviewing which seeks to interview members of a single family from different generations appeared to be an appropriate technique to analyse the effects of the development project (Cole, 2004; Cole and Durham, 2007; Alber *et al.*, 2008). Indeed, the juxtaposition and confrontation of the different viewpoints have enabled us to identify old and new interpretations of the mining experience. Besides mining, most children engaged in other types of activities, which we also observed, like creating adobe bricks (bricks made of uncooked clay), selling tomatoes, and so on. We conducted comprehensive interviews with them, as well as observations and informal discussions in their places of work and play. Finally, we conducted group discussions that included various members of the community (neighbourhood leaders, teachers, school principals) or representatives of the NGO Group One.

This fieldwork was rather tense because two types of actors, with whom participants in the fieldwork were associated, were exercising social control in the district of *la Ruashi* towards local families and children in order to legalize the artisanal and small-scale mining sector. On the one hand, the mining police were regularly making rounds to 'secure' the mining sites, preventing miners and children from penetrating them illegally for the benefit of the new mining corporations. On the other hand, the development actors (from Group One) were regularly visiting the local communities living in the area, not only to prevent children from going to the mines, but also in order to show that their financial support was somehow conditional to the long-term removal of children from the mining sites. To persuade parents to join the development programme, normative discourses about what we termed 'legal childhood' and 'responsible parenthood' were portrayed extensively. As will be shown, such normative discourses resonate differently among Congolese families whose representations of 'childhood' and 'parenthood' are shaped differently by their social trajectory.

The NGOs' narratives: 'responsible parenthood' and 'legal childhood'

As observed in similar development projects related to child-miners in West African countries, the first step of a programme such as the one carried out by Group One is the re-enrolment of child miners within the school system. Quite often the first phase of such programmes positions and tasks family members in relation to the principles and representations of what we call responsible parenthood. Following the work of different authors (Donzelot, 1977; Rose, 1989; Wells, 2009), who link discourses on responsible and autonomous children and parents to the discourses of (neo)liberal governmentality in Western countries, we suggest that this aspect of the programme diffuses a representation of the family which is derived from a neoliberal perspective. This is also the case for Hibou (2012), who places emphasis on the management structures which have been progressively set up as the new knowledge whose norms, rules, and formalities have spread beyond the world of enterprise and into all fields of activities and existence.

Indeed, this narrative tends to hold parents as the only ones accountable for the schooling of their children, and the discourses aim at making parents aware of their responsibilities regarding their children. They are urged to be the heads of the household whose duty is to provide everything for their family through their labour. Moreover, many NGOs and development projects spread dispositions and representations of the market (Elyachar, 2005; Hibou, 2012: 73–8) which attempt to turn people into active entrepreneurs in their community, household, etc., and parents received an 'economic kit' (as a form of compensation for the loss of revenues from the mining sector) and special training in order to be able to produce income-generating activities. For example, some mothers received seeds for cultivation as well as training to manage their stocks and benefits. In addition, for each child successfully reintegrated, a school kit made up of money for the payment of school fees and school furniture is provided. The school kit was planned to be given only during the first year of the programme: after one year of transition (from the child-miner to the re-enrolled child), parents were supposed to become self-sufficient and be able to pursue their 'family duties'. A local committee made up of local chiefs, teachers, headmasters, and parents was also established for the purpose of ensuring the proper functioning of the programme. At the time of fieldwork, five hundred children were part of the programme, but most of them were worried about not receiving the school kit in the future.

The second step of the programme is a phase of sensitization against the so-called 'worst forms of child labour', such as child mining activities. At the time of our inquiry and parallel to the process of reforming the mining sector, the DRC had signed ILO Convention no. 182 that defines the 'worst forms of child labour' as well as the ILO Convention no. 138 on the 'minimum age for employment'. Consequently, the DRC had modified its Labour Code[11] establishing 15 years old as the minimum of age for employment[12] and prohibiting the worst forms of child labour such as mining (Law no. 015/2002: art. 4[13]). In addition, in the Labour Code of 2002 a 'National Committee to Combat the Worst Forms of Child Labour' (NCCL) was instituted in order to set up a national strategy for eradicating this phenomenon. This committee was more concretely established in 2006 in order to gather data on child labour and implement prevention as well as reintegration programmes for children, but in the absence of public funding the prevention programmes were essentially carried out with the support of NGOs and international institutions. In Katanga Province, in collaboration with a local NGO, Youth Work Protector, and under the supervision of UNICEF, the Belgian NGO Group One aims to enforce the laws and measures on the protection of the child linked to the Convention on the Rights of the Child in order to prohibit child labour in the mining sector across the territory of Katanga.

Beyond the Western dimension of its representations of childhood (Boyden, 1990; Nieuwenhuys, 1994, 1996; Invernizzi, 2003; Twum-Danso, 2008), the campaign against the 'worst forms of child labour' in Katanga was structured around key notions which tend to stigmatize parents as one of the main causes. In that perspective, children are considered to be exploited by adults. Secondly, the campaign focused on the so-called dramatic side-effects of this form of labour: behavioural risks related to drug abuse, precocious emancipation, lack of respect shown to the elders, and loss of authority of adults over the young. By doing this, the campaign strategically activated and reinforced the fears of the elders vis-à-vis the young (Meillassoux, 1975; Elson, 1982; Nieuwenhuys, 1994) which are central in contemporary Congolese society (Honwana and De Boeck, 2005).

The Group One campaign focused on the difficult working conditions of children who were, in their view, 'forced' to undertake mining-related activities. In this regard, children are only perceived as in need of protection and the only context valued as providing such protection is the household. The campaign mainly stressed the family ruptures induced by child labour:

> The child is not responsible. Responsibility is maturity. Giving an economic kit to them, it would strengthen the exploitation that we try to fight. At the mines, they had 20 dollars a day. But what did they do with that? Nothing! But the child is not accountable for its schooling. It's parents who are accountable for schooling! That is why we give the money to the parents and not to the child! (Group One agent)

NGOs' justifying narrative for acting against child labour in the DRC relies mainly on a legal representation of childhood based on a human rights approach and more specifically, on a children's rights approach, as well as on what 'parenting' should be in the wake of neoliberal categories. Parents' social role is thus defined within the children's rights framework and, following some neoliberal norms on rules and formalities (Hibou, 2012), it tends to be limited to the role of protection and duties, such as being held accountable for the schooling of their children. In that respect, children are perceived as passive social agents who need to be protected by responsible adults. This simplistic vision of the 'passive-child' versus the 'active-parent' annihilates the complex understanding of social relationships where children's production activities take place within a set of reciprocal duties, gifts, and responsibilities towards their elders (Richards, 1939; Fortes, 1978; Schildkrout, 1978; Goody, 1982; Katz, 1996). As will be shown in the next section, children are far from 'passive social agents'. Although their work may be categorized as illegal (in regard to national and international legislation), it takes place within specific family configurations and social interdependence relations.

The 'illegal' social agency of childhood[14]

While the school reintegration programme and the associated campaign depict child mining-related activities as the result of exploitation, and as causing ruptures between elders and the young, between communities and children, our fieldwork shows that a continuum exists between the social order observed inside the mine and outside. Indeed, similar dispositions of work and representations of childhood and parenthood underpin the work and tasks that children carried out both inside the artisanal mines and outside. In fact, the mining-related activities performed by children generally displayed a certain continuity with other tasks like household chores, selling tomatoes, or brickmaking that they undertook in order to help their parents or the larger group (relatives, neighbours, members of the community). As such, tasks were divided along generational lines, just as they are outside the mine: diggers (*batshimba madini*), usually older children or adults, extracted ore from underground mine roads, while young boys gathered it on the ground's surface (*salakate*).

Our fieldwork has also shown how the division of work is gendered. While rock-sifting may be performed by both boys and girls, trash collecting (*salakate*) on mining sites is reserved to boys. Digging is essentially the work of older boys and adult men. Since the pre-colonial period, mining-related tasks have typically been masculine activities in Katanga (Cuvelier, 2011: 36), as in many other areas of sub-Saharan Africa (Herbert, 1993). Representations of the connections between mines, gender, and death (Cuvelier, 2011: 178) have led societies to bar women and girls from access to mining sites. Women and girls may work near quarries or outside mines, where they perform, alongside small children, other tasks such as sifting, crushing, and cleaning rocks or bags, and engage in petty commerce, usually with their mothers or their elder in charge of their education. These activities are less lucrative than those undertaken by men and older boys, and establish for them a subordinate role as compared to that of diggers.

In addition, Africanists have shown how 'traditional self-subsistence societies... assign children a regular share of work early on' (Lallemand, 2002: 12) as a form of socialization, constructing the child as a non-negligible workforce. Recent studies highlight the persistence of this perception of children in various sub-Saharan African countries (Berry, 1985; Schlemmer, 1996; Jézéquel, 2006; Wouango, 2011).[15] In fact, most of the families that we encountered, but especially the ones from a more lower-class background, see children as a workforce in the service of the group – at the family or community level – and this representation structures children's trajectories and experiences in artisanal mines as it is outside the mining world. In that perspective, we observed that children did not work alone in the mines. In some cases, in a similar way to rural agricultural work that emphasizes social relations of both production and socialization, all members of a family worked side by side. We also deducted that some parents encouraged their children to go and work in the mines without working there themselves. In such cases children learned tasks specific to artisanal mining by working alongside other figures of authority, such as neighbours, relatives, or men from the neighbourhood. This situation allows us to interpret the positive image that children could have of the 'traders', who hang around mining sites waiting to buy material in order to resell it later. Whereas the discourses of NGOs and middle-class parents were vehemently against these traders and construed them as scammers, children thought that some traders could play a positive role by sharing their know-how with them.

However, not all children follow adults into the mine. In fact, many children were led there by the influence of their peers or other children close in age. Even so, adults do not have to be present in order for children's mining activities to contribute to collective dynamics within the realm of the family and community. Indeed, while the children's experience of the mine could be largely the result of their own initiative, it did not challenge any relations of duty, obligation, or gift towards their relative elders. Rather, the initiatives of many children we met were made possible by collective dimensions related to the organization of families and communities and their roles within these organizations. In the same way that the children perform household chores or other small activities because it is their duty to do so, they have made the decision to go to the mines in order to help their elders – their parents or the community. In fact, the same logic of the child as worker underpins both forms of activity, that is, domestic work and work at the mines. Children respect the moral obligation to put their earnings back into the circuit of domestic relations at the same time as they acquire decision-making power in the home – by planning meals, for example. Furthermore, earnings could be interpreted by children as a problem when they were not integrated into relations of dependence, duty, and gift towards members of the household.

Not all children who go to the mines do so with similar social representations and dispositions. Middle-class families adopt an understanding of child mining activities that is more in line with notion of 'child labour' as it is understood by the development agents. The discourses of middle-class fathers rely mainly on an ideal of social roles (particularly sensitive to idea of the nuclear family, the breadwinning father, and the school-going child), which somehow prevent their children from coping with these children's economic activities. Nevertheless and paradoxically, some individualistic social values from middle-class families are pushing certain children to go to work in the mines, but more for themselves than for their parents. Even through the social figure of the mothers, who are generally driven by responsibilities for the survival of the family, which includes providing food, children from middle-class families could be led to work into the mining sites in order to develop skills and abilities related to a system of rights and obligations between children and their elders.

The neoliberal effect?

The development programme for legalizing childhood and holding parents accountable for what their children are doing has effects on families, children, and young people according to their social background. While being interviewed by researchers who enjoyed relatively strong cultural capital or who were sometimes associated with NGO agents, lower-class families expressed some embarrassment about their children's mining-related activities. Nevertheless, contact with the development programmes did not change the representations of childhood and parenthood underlying their strategies for survival and their processes of identity construction, as one can observe in the following account from a lower-class family headed by a single mother of eight children:

> I had a small kiosk and the children helped me to sell; but it was harsh to survive with that and it went bankrupt. When the mines started, my children were obliged to come to my assistance because I was not in a position to feed them by myself and their father was not anymore... Seeing the poverty at home, my children decided to go to the quarries... they felt sorry for me and they wanted to support me... When they worked at the quarries, they could not help me in my kiosk. Now they can help me because they know that it's because of the trading that we can get by... During the school period, I leave them enough time to revise. It is especially during the holiday that they help me in my business. I send them, for example, to sell the small bread that we make together at home or they guard the kiosk when I go shopping for stocking the shop (storekeeper, widow, and mother of eight children).

In addition to their schooling (when they became beneficiaries of the school-reintegration programme), the youngest children of this family have taken up again the activities that they did before the opening of the mining sites, such as selling small breads made by their mother at the roadside. Consequently, while children have stopped supporting their mother by going to the mines, they continue to help her, but at her kiosk. In lower-class families the closing of the artisanal mining site, combined with the NGO programme, has frequently caused the migration of the oldest children to other artisanal mining sites. Young people have generally decided to go away (to near Kipushi, for instance) to find new artisanal and small-scale mining sites and could thereby continue providing for their families. Indeed, as has been shown for artisanal miners in other countries, artisanal diggers have so many skills and abilities for searching and finding other mining sites, when they have been expelled from former sites by the multinationals, that some scholars have interpreted it as an act of resistance (Bush, 2007, 2009).

Concerning the most-privileged families in this area, the reverse situation appeared to be the case: despite sometimes having worked for several years in the quarries, parents and children (to a lesser extent) have re-evaluated their social trajectories in line with the NGO-dominant discourse about 'legal childhood' and the 'responsible parent', which led them to put themselves down and depreciate what they did in the small-scale mining sector – that is to say their unique job opportunity in the locality. Indeed, although child work in, and around, mines includes a collective aspect related to the organization of families and the community, parents from the most privileged sections of the population from *la Ruashi* decry the mining-related activities of their children. Their discourse is in fact ambivalent. Since living conditions had become extremely difficult, parents felt obliged to accept this additional income from their children's work. Nevertheless, while their children were working in the quarries, they were afraid of losing control over their offspring. This fear was common in those families with a more middle-class background from *la Ruashi*, who were particularly sensitive to representations of the nuclear family and the school-going child.

The *Union Minière du Haut-Katanga*, created during the colonial period and subsequently nationalized as the *Gécamines*, and more broadly the colonial administration and the railway company, had a decisive impact on representations of work, masculinity, and the family (Cuvelier, 2011). This state enterprise was organized on an ultra-paternalist model, guaranteeing all social services to its employees and their families, including school fees for children (Petit, 2003). It thus promoted ideals about the school and the nuclear family, including the image of the male breadwinner (Dibwe, 2001). Although the current context is profoundly challenging this model, with new strategies for survival contributing to processes of identity reinvention (Cuvelier, 2011), the figure of the father as the main figure in the family still has significant force in Katanga, especially among more privileged families. In this sense, local representations of childhood and the family maintain close affinities with the principles on which NGO school reintegration programmes are based. Because of these symbolic affinities, more privileged parents strongly adopted the categories spread by the NGOs which concerned child labour. Parents often denied all forms of responsibility concerning the work experience of their children in the mining sector; they were often beset with feelings of guilt, shame, and embarrassment. Papa Samuel, former miner at the *Gécamines*, explained to us how his social representations of childhood and parenthood are undermined by the choices of his children to go working in the mines:

Papa Samuel:	When the mine started, the situation has been disrupted.
Q:	Disrupted?
Papa Samuel:	That's the word because when children have started to work in the mines, it has been difficult to withdraw them from the mines… as every good parent [should]!
Q:	But why withdraw them?

Papa Samuel: To bring them back on the straight path! Working in the quarry is a temporary situation… We had to forbid them going there but at that time the quarry stimulated the young to leave the household… The children told lies, they said: 'we go to school' while they were in fact going to the quarry… if it was not the boys who contested the authority of their fathers, it was the girls becoming mothers at 9 or 10 years old and now with babies who are the charge of the grandparents!… the problem was not only that they earned money, but that they were very young to touch [deal with] money.

Q: Isn't it too difficult now to ensure alone the payment of the school fees?

Papa Samuel: With a bit of will and sacrifice, it's parents' duty!… In the mines, there is no training or supervision of children… The quarries are not a good space for children, but sewing, that's a good activity for children, it's training, education, it's through the relations with adults, with training and transmission that children become intelligent!

The discourse of Papa Samuel shows the entangled nature of discourses concerning the responsible/accountable parent (as 'every good parent'); the legal discourse of childhood ('education and training as good activities for children') in line with the children's rights regime; and, finally, a patriarchal vision of the family with men as the main breadwinners (mainly implemented during the colonial period). This interconnectedness contributes to exacerbating the fears of the elders vis-à-vis the young and generating conflicts between generations. Such interconnectedness between different normative discourses on what childhood and parenthood should be is also present in the self-perceptions of the youngest generation, which does not want to continue working in the artisanal and small-scale mining sector. For instance, Guy, 17 years old and who is the son of a teacher, explains to us why he does not want to come back to the mines while many young men of his age from the lower class have gone to other mining sites:

At my age, I cannot work to feed my family. For each one there is a role. The quarries deprave because there is bad company… At the time the mines were opened, I laughed at children who were going to school… But it's not a good job that I did. Actually, a good work for me it is, for example, staying at home, helping parents. I prefer studying and learning a trade! (Guy)

The representations of childhood and parenthood in families with a more middle-class background contribute to the young man adopting the narratives spread by the NGOs; they lead them to consider the world of the mines as a place that is not valuable for children and the young and as a place where they cannot work in the future.

Conclusion

The scope and the scale of the Congolese crisis are incommensurable. Therefore, since the beginning of the twenty-first century, a set of reforms have been forced to take place and are not easily absorbed by Congolese society (Trefon, 2011), especially since conflict is still on-going in the eastern part of the country. Moreover, the adoption of a children's rights legal framework in the DRC, and especially in the case of the mining sector, has been taking place at the same time as neoliberal reforms which promote the role of private actors and undermine the capacity of the Congolese State. Consequently, this chapter focused on child labour in the mining sector by analysing a complex form of entanglement between two forms of legalities, the new mining code and the legislation of child rights, and their mutual influence in terms of representations of childhood, parenthood, and the state.

In that perspective, representations of both the legal child and the responsible parent, which are at the core of the NGOs' justification narrative, resonate quite well with the new legal order of the mining sector in favour of multinationals. The approach that consists of labelling children's mining activities as the worst form of child labour tend to stigmatize ordinary Congolese families that struggle to survive while trying to keep a sense of community, belonging, and identity. In doing so, the development sector at large takes part in a process of stigmatization of the elders towards the young, which tends to reinforce the normative discourse behind the implementation of neoliberal policies. This neoliberal discourse positions parents and adults as the only ones responsible for the education and the economic survival of the family. But Congolese families, while forced to live in hard conditions, are still involved in an exchange of rights and obligations between the youngest and the elders, a framework within which children play an important role, even while working in the mines. Furthermore, although it is not the intention of the development agents, these representations nevertheless contribute to the expulsion of local miners and to the rupturing of pathways of survival for the youngest generation. This chapter has shown that, especially in the lower-class families, they have caused the migration of the oldest children to other artisanal mining sites. Parents and children from middle-class families have re-evaluated their social trajectories in line with the NGO-dominant discourse about 'legal childhood' and the 'responsible parent' which in the end leads them to put themselves down and devalue their only job opportunity in their locality. Consequently, through this entanglement, the children's rights framework has helped achieved a different purpose: the removal of miners from the ASM without any compensation.

Since this collective research was conducted the Congolese Government, in the wake of the CRC and the African Charter on the Rights and Welfare of the Child, adopted the Law on the Protection of the Child in 2009 (Law 09/001).[16] As this legislation regarding the well-being of the child has been adopted later than in other African countries, the influence of the African version of the CRC is more visible. Indeed, there is a specific section concerning the duties and responsibilities of children regarding their elders. Nevertheless, it is too early to analyse how these recent inflections in the law are shaping the dynamics of exchanges between generations in current Congolese society, especially as populations have been shaken by a very long-term crisis as well as powerful symbolic influences from a globalized neoliberal agenda.

Notes

1 In 2006 Congo dropped twenty places (from 167 to 187) in the Index of Human Development (UN Development Program 'Human Development Index', UNDP, New York, 2006 and 2011).

2 This second war is often considered as Africa's first continental war because of the intensity of the conflict and the number of countries involved. According to a survey by International Rescue Committee – published in 2007, 5.4 million people have died since 1998.

3 In its last report on the application of Convention no.182, the committee of experts noted that the government had planned to strengthen the capacities of the labour inspectorate in the context of the formulation and implementation of the National Plan of Action (PAN) for the elimination of child labour by 2020. However, this plan is subject to external funding that is still to materialize.

4 Since 2006, the country can be described as having experienced a post-conflict situation in the western parts while at the same time having endured a protracted conflict situation in the eastern part of the country.

5 Law no. 007/2002 of 11 July 2002.

6 For Rubbers (2006), the collapse of the *Gécamines* is not only the result of the liberalization of the sector but also linked to internal processes and the dynamics of privatization.

7 The human rights legislation officially accompanies the liberalization of the sector and is linked to the objective of a better governance of the country (Mazalto, 2009).

8 Three Belgian researchers as well as three Congolese researchers from the Urban Change Observatory and several students from the University of Lubumbashi (UNILU) were involved in this research project. The fieldwork was conducted in four teams of three researchers following the practical principles of the ECRIS methodology of Jean-Pierre Olivier de Sardan (1995).

9 The results of our research project led to improvements in their programmes of action, which were to be extended to other parts of the province, such as in Kolwezi, another mining city where many children are also involved in ASM.

10 Law no. 007/2002 of 11 July 2002.

11 Loi n 015/2002 portant Code de Travail.

12 In fact, children aged 15 years and younger are not allowed to carry out any type of labour, until their majority, when they can do work considered as 'light'.

13 The worst forms of child labour appearing in the Congolese Labour Code of 2002 are the following: the use of children in armed conflicts; for prostitution or illicit gains; for the production and trafficking of drugs; works that, because of

their nature or the conditions in which they are carried out, are liable to harm the health, security, dignity or the morality of the child.

14 This section of the chapter is based on a paper published by *Childhood* (André and Godin, 2013).

15 Some studies indicate that a function of exploitation is at play alongside that of socialization in the context of child labour (Nieuwenhuys, 1994; Schlemmer *et al.*, 1996). As Nieuwenhuys (1996) has stated, this exploitative dimension was often de-emphasized by earlier anthropologists, who tended to see rural child labour in a bucolic light.

16 Government of the Democratic Republic of the Congo, Protection de L'Enfant, Public Law no. 09/001, enacted January 2009 (http://www.leganet.cd/ Legislation/ JO/2009/L.09.001.10.01.09.htm).

References

Alber, E., van der Geest, S., and Whyte, S.R. (2008) *Generations in Africa: Connections and Conflicts*, Berlin: Lit Verlag.

André, G. and Godin, M. (2013) 'Child labour, agency and family dynamics: the case of mining in Katanga (DRC)', *Childhood* (first published online).

André, G. and Poncelet, M. (2013) 'Héritage colonial et appropriation du "pouvoir d'éduquer"', *Cahiers de la recherche sur l'éducation et les savoirs*, 12: 271–95.

Aubynn, A. (2009) 'Sustainable solution or a marriage of inconvenience? The coexistence of large-scale mining and artisanal and small-scale mining on the Abosso Gold-fields concession in western Ghana', *Resources Policy*, (34): 64–70.

Benedict, R. (1935) *Patterns of Culture*, London: Routledge & Kegan Paul.

Berry, S. (1985) *Fathers Work for their Sons: Accumulation, Mobility, and Class Formation in an Extended Yoruba Community*, Berkeley, CA, and Los Angeles, CA: University of California Press.

Bongeli, Y.Y.A.E. (2008) *D'un Etat-bébé à un Etat congolais responsible*, Paris: L'Harmattan.

Bourdieu, P. (1994) *Raisons pratiques: sur la théorie de l'action*, Paris: Seuil.

Boyden, J. (1990) 'Childhood and the policy makers: a comparative perspective on the globalization of childhood', in A. James and A. Prout (eds) *Constructing and Reconstructing Childhood: Contemporary Issues in the Sociological Study of Childhood*, London and Washington, DC: Falmer Press.

Bush, R.C. (2007) *Poverty and Neoliberalism: Persistence and Reproduction in the Global South*, London: Pluto Press.

Bush, R.C. (2009) '"Soon there will be no-one left to take the corpse to the morgue": accumulation and abjection in Ghana's mining communities', *Resources Policy*, 34: 57–63.

Cole, J. (2004) 'Fresh contact in Tamatave, Madagascar: sex, money, and intergenerational transformation', *American Ethnologist*, 31: 573–88.

Cole, J. and Durham, D. (2007) *Generations and Globalization: Youth, Age, and Family in the New World Economy*, Bloomington, ID: Indiana University Press.

Comaroff, J. and Comaroff, J. (2000) 'Réflexions sur la jeunesse: du passé à la post-colonie', *Politique africaine*, 80: 90–110.

Cuvelier, J. (2009) *The Impact of the Global Financial Crisis on Mining in Katanga*, Antwerp: IPIS.

Cuvelier, J. (2011) 'Men, mines and masculinities: the lives and practices of artisanal miners in Lwambo (Katanga province, DR Congo).' Unpublished thesis, KUL.

De Boeck, F. and Honwana, A. (2000) 'Enfants, jeunes et politique', *Politique africaine (special issue)*, 80.

De Herdt, T. (ed.) (2011) *A la recherche de l'Etat en R-D Congo; acteurs et enjeux d'une reconstruction post-conflit*, Paris: L'Harmattan.

De Herdt, T. and Poncelet, M. (2011) 'La reconstruction entre l'Etat et la société', in T. De Herdt (ed.) *A la recherche de l'Etat en R-D Congo. Collection Afrique des grands Lacs*, Paris, l'Harmattan.

Delcroix, C. (1995) 'Des récits de vie croisés aux histoires de familles', *Current Sociology/La sociologie contemporaine*, 43: 61–7.

Dibwe, D.M. (2001) *Bana Shaba abandonnés par leur père: structures de l'autorité et histoire sociale de la famille ouvrière au Katanga, 1910–1997*, Paris: l'Harmattan.

Donzelot, J. (1977) *La police des familles*, Paris: Editions de Minuit.

Elson, D. (1982) 'The differentiation of children's labour in the capitalist labour market', *Development and Change*, 13: 479–97.

Elyachar, J. (2005) *Markets of Dispossession: NGOs, Economic Development, and the State in Cairo*, Durham, NC: Duke University Press.

Ferguson, J. (1999) *Expectations of Modernity: Myths and Meanings of Urban Life on the Zambian Copperbelt*, Berkeley, CA, Los Angeles, CA, and London: University of California Press.

Fortes, M. (1978) 'Family, marriage and fertility in West Africa', in C. Oppong (ed.) *Marriage, Fertility, and Parenthood in West Africa*, Canberra: Australian National University Press.

Gallo, C.J. (2011) 'The informal economy and resource exploitation in the Democratic Republic of Congo', *St Antony's International Review*, 7 (1): 8–31

Geenen, S. (2011a) 'Constraints, opportunities and hope: artisanal gold mining and trade in South Kivu (DRC)', in A. Ansoms and S. Marysse (eds.) *Natural Resources and Local Livelihoods in the Great Lakes Region of Africa: A Political Economy Perspective*, Basingstoke: Palgrave Macmillan.

Geenen, S. (2011b) 'Relations and regulations in local gold trade networks in South-Kivu, Democratic Republic of Congo', *Journal of Eastern African Studies*, 5 (3): 427–46.

Geenen, S. (2012) 'A dangerous bet: the challenges of formalizing artisanal mining in the Democratic Republic of Congo', *Resources Policy*, 37 (3): 322–30.

Geenen, S. (2013) '"Who seeks, finds": how artisanal miners and traders benefit from gold in the eastern Democratic Republic of Congo', *European Journal of Development Research*, 25 (2): 197–212.

Geenen, S. and Claessens, K. (2013) 'Disputed access to the gold sites in Luhwindja, eastern Democratic Republic of Congo', *Journal of Modern African Studies*, 51: 85–108.

Goody, E. (1982) *Parenthood and Social Reproduction: Fostering and Occupational Roles in West Africa*, Cambridge: Cambridge University Press.

Grätz, T. (2003) 'Les chercheurs d'or et la construction d'identités de migrants en Afrique de l'Ouest', *Politique africaine*, 91: 155–69.

Herbert, E. (1993) *Iron, Gender, and Power: Rituals of Transformation in African Societies*, Bloomington, ID: Indiana University Press.

Hibou, B. (2012) *La bureaucratisation du monde à l'ère néolibérale*, Paris: La Découverte.

Hilgers, M. (2009) *Une ethnographie à l'échelle de la ville. Urbanité, histoire et reconnaissance à Koudougou (Burkina Faso)*, Paris: Karthala.

Hilgers, M. (2011) 'Autochtony as capital in a global age', *Theory, Culture and Society*, 28 (1): 34–54.

Hilson, G., Yakovleva, N., and Banchirigah, S.M. (2007) 'To move or not to move: reflections on the resettlement of artisanal miners in the Western region of Ghana', *African Affairs*, 106 (424): 413–36.

Honwana, A. and De Boeck, F. (eds) (2005) *Makers and Breakers*, Oxford, Trenton, and Dakar: James Currey, Africa World Press, and Codesria.

Invernizzi, A. (2001) *La vie quotidienne des enfants travailleurs: Stratégies de survie et socialisation dans les rues de Lima*, Paris: l'Harmattan.

Invernizzi, A. (2003) 'Des enfants libérés de l'exploitation ou des enfants travailleurs doublement discriminés? Positions et oppositions sur le travail des enfants', *Déviance et Société*, 27 (4): 459–81.

Jacquemin, M. (2002) '"Petites nieces" et petites bonnes, le travail des fillettes en milieu urbain de Côte d'Ivoire', *Journal des Africanistes*, 70: 105–22.

Jacquemin, M. (2006) 'Can the language of rights get hold of the complex realities of child domestic work? The case of young domestic workers in Abidjan, Ivory Coast', *Childhood*, 13: 389–406.

James, A. and Prout, A. (1990) *Constructing and Reconstructing Childhood*, London: Falmer Press.

Jézéquel, J.-H. (2006) 'Les enfants soldats d'Afrique, un phénomène singulier?', *Vingtième Siècle*, 89 (http://www.diplomatie.gouv.fr/fr/IMG/pdf/0605-JEZEQUEL-FR-2.pdf) (Accessed on 25 November, 2010).

Katz, C. (1996) 'On the back of children: children and work in Africa', *Anthropology of Work Review*, 17: 31–8.

Lahire, B. (1995) *Tableaux de famille: Heurs et malheurs scolaires en milieux populaires*, Paris: Gallimard.

Lallemand, S. (1993) *Circulation des enfants en société traditionnelle: Prêt, don, échange*, Paris: l'Harmattan.

Lallemand, S. (2002) 'Esquisse de la courte histoire de l'anthropologie de l'enfance: ainsi que de certains de ses thèmes électifs', *Journal des Africanistes*, 71 (1): 9–18.

Lemarchand, R. (2003) 'The DRC: from failure to potential reconstruction', in R.I. Rotberg (ed.) *State Failure and State Weakness in a Time of Terror*, Washington, DC: World Peace Foundation/Brooking Institute Press.

Le Vine, R. (2007) 'Ethnographic studies of childhood: a historical overview', *American Anthropologist*, 109: 247–60.

MacGaffey, J. et al. (1991) *The Real Economy of Zaïre: The Contribution of Smuggling and other Unofficial Activities to National Wealth*, Philadelphia, PA: University of Philadelphia Press.

Mauger, G. (1990) 'Postface', in K. Mannheim, *Le problème des générations*, Paris: Nathan.

Mazalto, M. (2008) 'La réforme du secteur minier en République démocratique du Congo: enjeux de gouvernance et perspectives de reconstruction', *Afrique contemporaine*, 227: 53–80.

Mazalto, M. (2009) 'Governance, human rights and mining in the Democratic Republic of Congo', in B. Campbell (ed.) *Mining in Africa: Regulation and Development*, London and New York, NY: Pluto Press.

Mead, M. (1928) *Coming of Age in Samoa*, New York. NY: William Morrow.

Meillassoux, C. (1975) *Femmes, greniers et capitaux*, Paris: Maspero.

Nieuwenhuys, O. (1994) *Children's Lifeworlds: Gender, Welfare and Labour in the Developing World*, London: Routledge.

Nieuwenhuys, O. (1996) 'The paradox of child labour and anthropology', *Annual Review of Anthropology*, 25: 237–51.

Nzongola-Ntalaja, G. (2004) *From Zaïre to the Democratic Republic of the Congo. Current African Issues* 28 (2nd revised edn). Uppsala: Nordiska Afrikainstitutet.

Observatoire du changement urbain (2006) *Le travail des enfants dans les mines et carrières de Lubumbashi (Sud Katanga). Enquête sur les caractéristiques socio-économiques des enfants et des familles d'enfants mineurs* (Report for Group One).

Okyere, S. (2012) 'Understanding child labour: the case of children working in artisanal gold mining at Kenyasi.' Unpublished thesis, University of Nottingham.

Olivier de Sardan, J.-P. (1995) *Anthropologie et développement: essai en socio-anthropologie du changement social,* Paris: Karthala.

Peemans, J.-P. (1997) *Crise de la modernité et pratiques populaires au Zaïre et en Afrique,* Paris: l'Harmattan.

Peemans, J-.P. (1998) *Le Congo-Zaïre au gré du XXe siècle: Etat, économie, société 1880–1990,* Paris: l'Harmattan.

Petit, P. (2003) *Ménages de Lubumbashi entre précarité et recomposition,* Paris: l'Harmattan.

Poncelet, M., André, G., and De Herdt, T. (2010) 'La survie de l'école primaire congolaise (RDC): héritage colonial, hybridité et résilience', *Autrepart,* 54: 23–42.

Rabain, J. (1979) *L'enfant du lignage,* Paris: Payot.

Reynolds, P. (1991) *Dance Civet Cat: Child Labour in the Zambesi Valley,* London: Zed Books.

Richards, A. (1939) *Land, Labour, and Diet in Northern Rhodesia: An Economic Study of the Bemba Tribe,* London: Oxford University Press.

Rose, N. (1989) *Governing the Soul: The Shaping of the Private Self,* London and New York, NY: Free Association Books.

Rubbers, B. (2004) 'La dislocation du secteur minier au Katanga (DRC). Pillage ou recomposition?' *Politique africaine,* 93: 21–41.

Rubbers, B. (2006) 'L'effondrement de la Générale des Carrières et des Mines. Chronique d'un processus de privatisation informelle', *Cahiers d'études Africaines,* 181: 115–34.

Rubbers, B. (2009) *Faire fortune en Afrique: Anthropologie des derniers colons du Katanga,* Paris: Karthala.

Schildkrout, E. 2002 (1978) 'Recommended readings: age and gender in Hausa society. Socioeconomic roles of children in urban Kano', *Childhood,* 9: 342–68.

Schlemmer, B. (1996) *L'enfant exploité: Oppression, mise au travail, prolétarisation,* Paris: Karthala.

Spindler, G. (1997) *Education and Cultural Process: Anthropological Approaches* (3rd edn), Prospect Heights, IL: Waveland Press.

Trefon, T. (2011) *Congo Masquerade: The Political Culture of Aid Inefficiency and Reform Failure. African Arguments series,* London: Zed Books and Royal Africa Society.

Tschakert, P. and Singha, K. (2007) 'Contaminated identities: mercury and marginalization in Ghana's artisanal mining sector', *Geoforum,* 38: 1304–21.

Twum-Danso, A. (2008) 'A cultural bridge, not an imposition: legitimizing children's rights in the eyes of local communities', *Journal of the History of Childhood and Youth,* 1 (3): 391–413.

Verbruggen, D. (2006) *The State Versus the People: Governance, Mining and the Transitional Regime in the Democratic Republic of Congo,* Amsterdam: Netherlands Institute for Southern Africa/Antwerp: International Peace Information Service.

Verlet, M. (2005) *Grandir à Nima (Ghana): Les figures du travail dans un faubourg populaire d'Accra,* Paris: Karthala.

Walsh, A. (2003) 'Hot money and daring consumption in a northern Malagasy sapphire-mining town', *American Ethnologist,* 30: 290–305.

Wells, K. (2009) *Childhood in Global Perspective*, Cambridge and Malden: Polity Press.

Werthmann, K. (2003) 'Cowries, gold and "bitter money": gold, mining and notions of ill-gotten wealth in Burkina Faso', *Paideuma*, 49: 105–24.

Willis, P. (1977) *Learning to Labour: How Working-Class Kids get Working-Class Jobs.* Farnborough: Saxon House.

Wouango, J. (2011) 'Travail des enfants et droit à l'éducation au Burkina. L'exemple de la carrière de Pissy', *Cahiers de la recherche sur l'éducation et les savoirs (Revue internationale de sciences sociales)*, 10: 127–41.

6 Children's participation in prohibited work in Ghana and its implications for the Convention on the Rights of the Child

Samuel Okyere

Countries which ratify the Convention on the Rights of the Child (CRC) agree to put in place new legislation and structures, or strengthen existing ones, to promote children's social, health, educational, and economic well-being, among other things. Child labour prevention or abolition is one of the main children's rights issues for which governments are called upon by the CRC to put in place new measures. Debates on child labour feature prominently in children's rights discussions in developing world contexts especially, and many argue that regardless of its format, child labour should have no place in childhood because it is inimical to children's well-being (UNICEF, 2007b). Proponents of this view point out that child labour can physically and psychologically harm children, prevent them from attaining education, and hamper their development in other ways (UNICEF, 2001). It is mainly in view of these potential risks that the CRC deems child labour a violation of human or children's rights, and in Article 32, calls on governments to put measures in place to protect children from work which carries such risks.

In spite of this clear position on child labour and the Convention's widespread ratification, recent estimates show that 150–215 million children are still found in prohibited engagements across the world (ILO, 2010; UNICEF, 2011). In sub-Saharan Africa, which has long had the highest incidence of child labour in the world, the data show that the number of children in such forms of work is actually on the ascendency (ILO, 2010). These trends raise questions about the extent to which the CRC or its guidance on child labour is being implemented by countries in this part of the world. In this chapter, the narratives of a group of children working in artisanal gold mining in Ghana are used to explore this issue. The discussion explores the children's reasons for such work, and by extension, the challenges which have impeded implementation of the CRC's guidance on child labour in that country. At the end, the chapter offers suggestions on how the situation may be improved.

The discussion is organized as follows: after briefly introducing the research with children working in artisanal gold mining, focus will be placed on the state of the CRC's implementation in Ghana and the obstacles which have impeded the progress of this process. The third and final section will then offer suggestions as to how these obstacles may be addressed.

Research with children working in artisanal gold mining

This research was conducted as part of my PhD which sought to examine how the accounts and lived experiences of children found in prohibited occupations fit with dominant debates and policy guidance on their participation. Fieldwork was undertaken over a 15-week period in Kenyasi, a rural district in Ghana. Ethnographic methodology was employed within the Kenyasi town and a burgeoning artisanal gold-mining site which is located on the outskirts of the town. The methodology employed in this study has been described by Knoblauch (2005: 2) as 'focused ethnography', in the sense that the researcher spends a comparatively shorter period of time in the field than the traditional anthropological ethnography which may last over a year. To compensate for its relative brevity, focused ethnography is characterized by a rapid and intensive data collection approach (Knoblauch, 2005).

Following on from the above, at the very onset of the fieldwork, I endeavoured to record every conversation and minute piece of information. Records were made of all events and occurrences as soon as possible. Long hours were spent, often deep into the night, playing back the day's recordings, transcribing them, and searching for follow-up information for the next day's inquiries. Save for a few weekends when I travelled outside the research setting, I was fully immersed in the town and the artisanal gold mining site for the entire duration of the fieldwork. Like many other workers, particularly migrants, I lived in rented accommodation in the Kenyasi town, joined in most communal activities, and commuted to and from the artisanal gold-mining site with other workers daily. On numerous occasions, I slept at the site overnight so as to observe what transpired there after normal working hours. Essentially, as characteristic of ethnography, I was intimately immersed into the setting within which the study was conducted.

A purposive sampling approach was used to identify the first few research participants. In a snowball process, from then on, they introduced me to their friends and acquaintances willing to provide information for the research. Altogether, a total of 57 children (30 girls and 27 boys) aged 14 to 17 were selected as core participants for the research. Many of these children were from Kenyasi and surrounding villages, but a large number were independent child migrants who had travelled from places further afield to work at the artisanal gold-mining site. Data was collected from participants primarily through observation and unstructured interviews. The interviews were conducted in a style which is quite comparable to an everyday conversation. By adopting such an informal approach, the research participants were accordingly relaxed and therefore shared their experiences in a more vivid and open manner than may otherwise have been the case. This corroborated Zhang's and Wildemuth's (2009) assertion that unstructured interviews or informal conversational methods may enable research participants to offer the researcher a lot more information than structured or formal-type interviews.

In terms of the children's work at the site, a highly gendered pattern was observed. Girls were mainly involved in fetching sand, stones, and water or carrying items on their heads from one point on the site to another for a fee. They also worked as hawkers, kitchen and shop assistants, and food sellers and were found in other roles traditionally seen as females' work. It is worth noting, however, that although some reports have suggested that girls and women commonly engage in prostitution at such places (Javia and Siop, 2010), there was no evidence of this at Kenyasi. For boys, the most common work available was to be taken on to break extracted gold ore into smaller pieces using hammers, metal pestles, and other implements. Occasionally, relatively older boys worked as machine operators who transformed the cracked rocks into a powdery form to be mixed with water for processing. Others mixed up the slurry and heaped it on to wooden trestles to sift out the gold particles. Some boys also worked in general roles such as running errands for people at the site.

The next section explores the reasons why these boys and girls took up such work at the site, arguing that their participation is symptomatic of the constraints facing the CRC's implementation in Ghana.

The CRC's implementation and working children's experiences

The children who participated in this research cited a range of reasons to explain their involvement in artisanal gold mining, an occupation counted among the worst forms of child labour by the International Labour Organization (ILO, 2010). To a considerable degree, the explanations cited by the children, which are explored shortly, underscore the comparatively limited extent to which Ghana has been able to implement aspects of the CRC. Ironically, not only was Ghana the first country to ratify the CRC (UNICEF, 2012), but also, the country did not raise any concerns or point out any limitations about its capacity to implement the Convention. And yet, almost 25 years later, the realities confronting many Ghanaian children fall painfully short of the ideals enshrined for them in the CRC. With regards to child labour in particular, it has been noted by the ILO/IPEC (2008) that Ghana has a comparatively high incidence of the phenomenon. According to the ILO/IPEC (2008) data, about 1,408,352 Ghanaian children, almost 25% of the country's child population, can be found in situations which contravene international conventions and guidance on children's work. Although some of these children combine their work with school, about 570,000 do not attend school at all. Many of these children can be observed in transport terminals and markets across the country, working in head-porterage, shoe-shining, hawking, and a range of other jobs at all times of the day and also in the night.

Arguably however, the high incidence of child labour in Ghana is not necessarily for lack of attempt by the country to meet its obligations to children as defined by the CRC. Ghana has established the Ministry of Gender, Children, and Social Protection, formerly Ministry for Women's and Children's Affairs, with the specific aim of promoting the welfare of women and children. From a legislative perspective, the Labour Act 2003, the National Gender and Children Policy 2004, and the country's flagship children's rights legislation, the Children's Act 1998, have sections specifically targeted at addressing child labour in the country. Besides the CRC itself, Ghana's commitment to promoting children's rights and addressing child labour is further evidenced by the fact that the country has ratified and entered all ILO child labour Conventions into force. It has equally ratified the African Charter on the Rights and Welfare of the Child (ACRWC), which aimed to promote the rights of children with respect to the African values. Beyond the ratification of Conventions, and in consonance with Articles 28, 29, and 32 of the CRC, the country has instituted a range of practical measures to promote educational access and retention for children. Central among these was the Free Compulsory Universal Basic Education (FCUBE) policy, which ran from 1995 to 2005. The FCUBE programme offered tuition-free attendance for children in public primary or basic schools, and when it ended in 2005, the Capitation Grant (CG) was also established to extend this ambition.

The above support the earlier assertion that the high child labour incidence in Ghana is not necessarily for lack of action by country. Rather, it is because the FCUBE, CG, and other measures which have been implemented thus far have failed to meet the educational and other welfare needs of many working children. This is precisely the point Akyeampong (2009) makes, when he notes that although theoretically all Ghanaian children should be able to attend school because it is free, a range of constraints prevent many from doing so. Ananga (2011) buttresses this observation with the argument that the CG and other programmes do not go far enough for many Ghanaian children for whom educational access still remains a challenge, if not a total mirage.

The above accurately reflect the situation of 50 of the children involved in this research, who intimated that they had taken up work in artisanal gold mining in order to be able to pursue their education. As some of them explained in our interactions, access to their rights to education, at the time of the fieldwork, was possible only by virtue of income-earning opportunities, despite the CG:

> Everybody here knows this... if you want to go, [to school] then you must be prepared to work. They say everyday on the TV that education is the future... but if you don't work, then no school for you. (Oppong, 16)

sometimes I ask myself why I am doing this, but I always say to myself that if I don't come here and hustle, then I will become like those boys who roam about in the town during the school time. (Addai, 16)

I know it is difficult and dangerous work but if someone tells me to stop working, then the person must give me money to go to school too. (Evelyn, 14)

Similar findings have also been highlighted in research with other Ghanaian children working in equally prohibited jobs such as cocoa farming, fishing, stone quarrying, head-porterage and a range of others over the country (Hashim, 2005; de Lange, 2007; Hilson, 2010). This continued reliance on work by some children as a means of accessing education, in spite of the country's free education policies, is an issue which Osei *et al.* (2009: 4–5) have subjected to much more deeper analysis, arriving at this conclusion:

School fee abolition is not just about 'tuition fees' (which do not necessarily constitute the main bulk of fees). School fee abolition must take into consideration the wide range of the costs of schooling to families and households. This means any direct and indirect costs/charges (tuition fees, costs of text books, supplies and uniforms, PTA contributions, costs related to sports and other school activities, costs related to transportation, contributions to teachers' salaries, etc) making education accessible.

Despite having 'free' access to education, substantial costs still remain for children and their families. Often, the situation comes down to two stark choices: families have to find a means of catering for these extra costs or their children have to drop out of school. The children who participated in this research had found themselves in the latter option. However, rather than drop out, they had decided to secure the necessary funds themselves:

My father cannot give us school chop money and my elder sister has already stopped school because of this. I came here with some girls to see if I can get some money by myself and continue school next term. (Mercy, 14)

It is true that we don't pay school fees, but that is not the only problem… there is no money at home, there is even nothing to eat… that is also a problem because if there is nothing at home, you can't go. (Eugene, 17)

Sometimes I need money urgently and my mother cannot afford. That day I don't go to school, or maybe I don't do extra classes that day and I come here to work to find the money. (Albert, 17)

I have been coming for three vacations now… there is nobody to help me and that is why I do this. (Rocky, 16)

Besides education, others also hoped that work at the artisanal gold-mining site would help with their efforts of saving money for apprenticeships and vocational training and would cater for other needs. Indeed, the research found that although the children primarily spent their earnings on their own needs, over 40 also supported their families and friends. They helped by paying for food, utility bills, school supplies, healthcare, and other household provisions. A few, such as Kofi (15), were actually the main breadwinners of their households:

> I live alone with my grandmother who took care of me since I lost my parents as a child. She fell very ill last year and is now bedridden so I have been taking care of her since then. I work here and use the money I earn to provide for both of us.

In effect, from the children's accounts, it was evident that work in artisanal gold mining was the means by which they could attempt to access their rights to education, healthcare and other welfare needs, assist their families, and so on. It was for this reason that all of them expressed dismay and opposition when the discussion moved on to the demand by international children's rights policy-makers that they should be prohibited from working at the mining site. Policy-makers' primary focus is on the potential harms of such jobs when deciding whether children can participate, but it was clear that for the children themselves, the opportunities which were created by their participation ranked higher than other factors:

> people say this work is bad and so we should stop and go to school… but if I can't buy books, shoes and other things I need, how can I go to school?… I will go to school but I can't eat school if I am hungry. (James, 15)

> I am in JS3[1] at the moment and I take care of myself, I also help my mother when she needs money and I give my younger sister money too. I swear to God if it was not for this work I have been coming here to do, I don't know what my life will have become by now… I think I will have been part of those boys doing armed robbery in Kumasi and Sunyani… if you tell me to stop today then I am finished. (Adu, 17)

In spite of the strong views they expressed about being denied their work at the site, it was also evident that the research participants harboured a degree of ambivalence about their participation. For some, the benefits of working at the site were not unalloyed. They were dissatisfied with the site's dirty surroundings, the difficult nature of their work, and the potential injuries they could sustain while performing it:

> This is very dirty work. The sand and the dust get in your face, your mouth and everywhere, even your eyes. Every time I have to come here and find money, I am not happy about it. (Jude, 15)

> After work, you feel like somebody has beaten you up. Your whole body pains you. Sometimes, you are so tired you just want someone to carry you home but you know everybody is also tired. (Esi, 15)

> I don't like this work because you can get injured at any time here if you are not careful. I have not been injured before, but I have seen a man who smashed his hand with a hammer when he was working. (Ebo, 16)

To conclude this section, although the CRC proposes that children should be provided their educational (Article 28), healthcare (Article 24), developmental (Article 29), and social welfare needs (Article 26), among others, this had not been the case for the participants. Not only were they attempting to provide these for themselves, but actually, some were helping to provide these for their loved ones. In the next section, the chapter argues that this situation, which is not only widespread in sub-Saharan Africa, but many other parts of the world, cast doubts as to whether the standards set out within the CRC are attainable by countries such as Ghana

Poverty and the rhetoric of rights: challenges to the CRC's implementation for working children in Ghana

Nearly three decades after the CRC was created, no country has fully implemented its provisions. However, implementation in sub-Saharan Africa is notably poor in comparison to countries in Western Europe and North America. The reasons which account for the involvement of children in artisanal gold mining work in Ghana offer pointers as to why implementation of the CRC has been relatively poor in that country and others in the wider region.

Ghana is a particularly interesting case because it is often hailed as a beacon of development and progress in the region (Accord, 2012; Awal, 2012, World Bank; 2012). With respect to the status of the CRC in Ghana, although as Twum-Danso (2009) rightly observes, aspects such as participation face opposition due to socio-cultural beliefs about childhood, the Convention broadly enjoys support in the country. This is not only among children's rights activists, civil society, and non-governmental organisations, but also, successive governments have attempted to fulfil the Convention in diverse ways. For instance, besides the free education initiatives discussed earlier, Ghana also has a free school-feeding programme for about 1 million children in the most deprived areas, the Livelihood Against Poverty (LEAP) programme, the National Health Insurance Scheme, the National Action Plan for Orphans and Vulnerable Children, and a host of other initiatives intended to meet the social welfare, health, nutrition, and protection needs of children and their families.

The reality remains, however, that a massive gap exists between the lived experiences of many Ghanaian children and many of the ideals held up for them by the CRC. A range of explanations have been put forward to account for this state of affairs, but the findings of this research strongly support the observation that in terms of child labour, Ghana's challenging economic position is the most debilitating among these (Laird, 2002; UNICEF, 2007a). The country has hovered on the brink of economic ruin since 1982 when it called upon the IMF and World Bank for financial assistance (Aryee, 2001). Much needed funds have been pumped into the economy over the years, but Ghana has remained in dire financial straits as Aryeetey *et al.* (2000) and Opare (2003) have shown. Indeed, it was the persistent economic slump which saw Ghana sign up as a highly indebted poor country (HIPC) in 2001.

The disabling impact of the country's economic challenges with regards to the implementation of many aspects of the CRC is acknowledged in both the 2006 and 2012 UNICEF periodic reports. Specialist departments are established and appealing social welfare programmes announced, with the aim of meeting the CRC's and the country's own children's rights guidance. However, the country's limited access to funds means that often these initiatives lack the requisite resources for their proper implementation. Programmes such as the FCUBE, CG, and others are therefore rendered ineffective if not entirely meaningless for those children who ironically need such initiatives the most. Ghanaian professionals such as social workers and others who deliver services to children continuously hold up the woefully limited funds and resources as one of the biggest impediments to their work (Avendal, 2012). Indeed, it is quite instructive to note that although the Ghana Children's Act (1998) tasks the department of social welfare with responsibility for vulnerable children, in rural areas such as where this research was undertaken, this department has no offices or representatives.

Economic hardships at the state level tend to trickle down into individual homes and families, and consequently, almost 30% of Ghanaians have access to less than $1.25 a day (World Bank, 2012). Massive unemployment has plagued swathes of the population since the IMF-led structural adjustment programmes in the 1980s led to massive redundancies in the public sector. Many of the parents and guardians of the children who were involved in the research were without work or a reliable source of income. Some parents were themselves hustling at the artisanal gold-mining site with their children. Others were 'by day' workers, people who roam around markets, farms, building sites, and other locations in search of poorly paid odd jobs. A substantial number of the children who had travelled from northern Ghana to seek work at Kenyasi stated that their families were mainly reliant on subsistence farming for food and income. With farming being a seasonal activity, in a lean year or in case of natural disasters such as bush fires, food, money, and other resources are truly scarce.

In sum, the chapter posits that poor implementation of the CRC in Ghana is attributable to the dire financial status of both the state and families across the country. This shortcoming, particularly at the state level, serves to question whether countries like Ghana can actually fulfil some aspects of the CRC anytime soon. This statement may appear to be overly pessimistic, but it is evident that in spite of what can arguably be deemed to be the country's best efforts, it still fails to guarantee even the most basic access to education, healthcare, nutrition, and other rights for all Ghanaian children. As such, while I agree with Bonnet (2009) that the Western cultural bias inherent in the CRC has also been an obstacle to its implementation in Africa, I insist nonetheless that the economic argument represents the biggest difference between the Convention's implementation in developed economies and developing ones, especially in terms of child labour. Britain and other Western nations have controlled children's work in coal mines and industries not just because perceptions changed about the place of the child in these societies (Heywood, 2010), but mainly because economic prosperity allowed these countries to put in place provisions which eroded children's continued need to rely on work to fund their own education, healthcare, and apprenticeships (Cunningham, 2000).

From the above, although developed economies also face challenges in implementing the CRC, economic clout is nevertheless a crucial factor in a state's capacity to implement the CRC, or at least, many aspects of it. For this reason, I remain unconvinced that in the foreseeable future, the pace at which the CRC is being implemented in poor countries such as Ghana will change in any significant fashion. However, there is cause to be slightly optimistic. This lies in the fact that although Ghana's economic standing is realistically not going to change overnight, as it improves with time, so too may conditions change such that Ghanaian children will not be compelled to make a decision between taking up potentially dangerous work or forgoing access to food, healthcare, education, and other necessities. Until then, there must be continued and increased financial and technical assistance from UNICEF and other donor partners to countries like Ghana as it attempts to improve living conditions for the 57 children who took part in this research and the thousands of their peers involved in work across the country.

Discussion and conclusion: working children's rights and the CRC

Countries cannot pick or choose aspects of the CRC which they wish to implement and others which they do not. Hence, to put it bluntly, only one ideal solution exists to address the dilemma presently faced by working children. Ghana and other countries which have ratified the CRC, but are barely able to meet the Convention's standards must therefore be supported and encouraged by UNICEF and other development partners to do so.

Having established the above point, the chapter also suggests that the conventional position on child labour itself requires re-examination. With no doubt, it is far from ideal that some children are compelled to rely on work as a means of accessing education and other rights provisions which their peers elsewhere simply take for granted. Besides the potential health threats linked to their work, working children's educational access may still be adversely affected because they may not be able to complete their studies or do very poorly in final exams due to inadequate revision and preparation time (Canagarajah and Coulombe, 1997). And yet, judging from the accounts and lived experiences of the children who were involved in this research, it can also be deemed problematic that children are pulled out of their work when the intervening measures cited in Articles 24, 25, 26, 27, 28, and 32 of the CRC have not been put in place. The potential that such action may push them into further distress, rather than help them, was amply demonstrated in the often-cited case of the Harkin Bill and Bangladeshi children working in garment factories (Rahman *et al.*, 1999).

The children who participated in this research gave a very clear indication of what they expected to happen in such situation. As noted in the second section of the chapter, in spite of the difficulties they faced in their work, they were adamant that being cast out of the site was potentially much more detrimental to them than the hardships they were already enduring. The contrast between their own views and the position adopted by children's rights policy-makers is itself telling of another challenge faced by working children. The requirement by Article 12 of the CRC that children must be given a say in matters which concern them has gained support in recent years. Yet, working children's views are seldom elicited when solutions to child labour are being discussed. It is in view of their marginalization that this chapter ends by reiterating their position on the matter. The child research participants were adamant that unless the guarantees offered them by the CRC are made readily accessible to them, they must not be denied access to their work, regardless of the potential dangers and risks associated with it.

Note

1 Equivalent to 9th grade in the US education system or Year 10 in the UK education system.

References

Accord (2012) *Ghana: A Beacon of Hope in Africa*, issue 018 (available online at http://goo.gl/O04Cs) (Accessed on 4 April 2012).

Akabzaa, T. and Darimani, A. (2001) *Impact of Mining Sector Investment in Ghana: A Study of the Tarkwa Mining Region.* Report prepared for SAPRI (available online at http://goo.gl/WZcjA) (accessed on 3 March 2011).

Akyeampong, K. (2009) 'Revisiting free compulsory universal basic education (FCUBE) in Ghana', *Comparative Education*, 45 (2): 175–95.

Amnesty International (2012) *Amnesty International Report 2012: The State of the World's Human Rights* (available online at http://goo.gl/7JgBr) (accessed on 2 February 2012).

Ananga, E.D. (2011) 'The drop out experience of basic school children in rural Ghana: implications for universal basic education policy.' Doctoral thesis, University of Sussex (available online at http://sro.sussex.ac.uk/6937/) (accessed on 14 March 2013).

Anti-Slavery International (2010) *Ending Child Trafficking in West Africa: Lessons from the Ivorian Cocoa Sector* (available online at http://goo.gl/ZXwib) (accessed 1 April 2011).

Armstrong, A.T. (2008) *Gold Strike in the Breadbasket: Indigenous Livelihoods, the World Bank and Territorial Restructuring in Western Ghana.* A report for the Institute for Food and Development Policy Development (IFDPD) (available online at http://goo.gl/VXqEZ) (accessed on 1 June 2010).

Aryee, B.N.A. (2001) 'Ghana's mining sector: its contribution to the national economy', *Resources Policy*, 27 (2): 61–75.

Aryee, B.N.A. (2003) 'Small-scale mining in Ghana as a sustainable development activity: its development and a review of the contemporary issues and challenges,' in G. Hilson (ed.) *The Socioeconomic Impacts of Artisanal and Small-Scale Mining in Developing Countries*, Rotterdam: A.A. Balkema.

Aryeetey, E., Harrigan, J., and Nissanke, M. (2000) *Economic Reforms in Ghana: The Miracle and the Mirage*, London: James Currey & Woeli Publishers.

Avendal, C. (2012) 'Social work in Ghana: engaging traditional actors in professional practices', *Journal of Comparative Social Work* (available online at http://goo.gl/iPYkh) (accessed on 12 January 2012).

Awal, M. (2012) 'Ghana: democracy, economic reform and development, 1993–2008,' *Journal of Sustainable Development in Africa*, 14 (1): 97–118.

Berg, M. and Hudson, P. (1992) 'Rehabilitating the industrial revolution,' *Economic History Review*, 45 (1): 24–50.

Betcherman, G., Fares, J., Luinstra, A., and Prouty, R. (2005) 'Child labor, education, and children's rights,' in P. Alston and M. Robinson (eds) *Human Rights and Development: Towards Mutual Reinforcement*, New York, NY: Oxford University Press.

Bhukuth, A. (2005) 'Child labour and debt bondage: a case study of brick kiln workers in Southeast India,' *Journal of Asian and African Studies*, 40 (4): 287–302.

Bonnet, M. (2009) 'Child labour in post-colonial Africa,' in H.D. Hindman (ed.) *The World of Child Labour: An Historical and Regional Survey*, Armonk, NY: M.E. Sharpe.

Bourdillon, M.F.C, Levison, D., Myers, W.E, and White, B. (2010) *Rights and Wrongs of Children's Work*, New Brunswick, NJ: Rutgers University Press.

Canagarajah, S. and Coulombe, H. (1997) *Child Labour and Schooling in Ghana. World Bank Policy Research Working Paper 1844* (available online at http://bit.ly/12i3fVy) (accessed on 2 May 2013).

Cunningham, H. (2000) 'The decline of child labour: labour markets and family economies in Europe and North America since 1830,' *Economic History Review*, LIII (3): 409–28.

Cunningham, H. (2003) 'Children's changing lives from 1800 to 2000,' in J. Maybin and M. Woodhead (eds) *Childhoods in Context*, Chichester: Wiley.

De Lange, A. (2007) *Deprived Children and Education in Ghana*, Amsterdam: IREWOC.

Fyfe, A. (2007) *The Worldwide Movement against Child Labour: Progress and Future Directions*, Geneva: ILO.

Fyfe, A. and Jankanish, M. (1997) *Trade Unions and Child Labour: A Guide to Action*, Geneva: ILO.

Ghana Statistical Service (2003) *Ghana Child Labour Survey*, Accra: Ghana Statistical Service.

Grier, B. (2004) 'Child labour and Africanist scholarship: a critical overview,' *African Studies Review*, 47 (2): 1–25.

Hashim, I. (2005) 'Exploring the Linkages between Children's Independent Migration and Education: Evidence from Ghana'. *Migration DRC Working Paper* WP-T12. Brighton: Migration DRC, University of Sussex.

Heywood, C. (2010) 'Centuries of childhood: an anniversary – and an epitaph?' *Journal of the History of Childhood and Youth*, 3 (3): 341–65.

Hilson, G. (2010) 'Child labour in African artisanal mining communities: Experiences from Northern Ghana', *Development and Change*, 41(3): 445–73.

Hinton, J.J., Veiga, M.M., and Beinhoff, C. (2003) 'Women and artisanal mining: gender roles and the road ahead', in G. Hilson (ed.) *The Socio-Economic Impacts of Artisanal and Small-Scale Mining in Developing Countries*, London: Taylor & Francis.

Human Rights Watch (2003) 'Small change bonded child labour in India's silk industry', *Human Rights Report*, 15 (2): 1–8.

Human Rights Watch (2012) *Lonely Servitude* (available online at http://goo.gl/YZdPM) (accessed on 2 February 2012).

Hussey, S. and Fletcher, A. (1999) *Childhood in Question: Children, Parents and the State*, Manchester: Manchester University Press.

ILO (2010) *Global Child Labour Developments: Measuring Trends from 2004 to 2008*, Geneva: ILO.

ILO (2011) *Children in Hazardous Work: What we Know, What we Need to Do*, Geneva: ILO.

ILO/IPEC (2008) *Ghana Child Labour Country Brief*, Geneva: ILO.

Javia, I. and Siop, P. (2010) Paper on 'Challenges and achievements on small scale mining and gender. Papua New Guinea' (available online at http://goo.gl/2QHSu) (accessed on 10 March 2012).

Jennings, N.S. (1999) *Small-Scale Gold Mining: Examples from Bolivia, Philippines and Zimbabwe. Sectoral Activities Programme Working Paper* SAP 2.76/WP.130, Geneva: ILO.

Khan, A. (2010) 'Peshgi without bondage: reconsidering the links between debt and Peshgi and bonded labour', *Cultural Dynamics*, 22 (3): 247–66.

Knoblauch, H. (2005) 'Focused ethnography', *Forum: Qualitative Social Research*, 6 (3) article 44 (available online at http://goo.gl/0zGRs) (accessed on 11 May 2011).

Laird, S. (2002) 'The 1998 Children's Act: problems of enforcement in Ghana', *British Journal of Social Work*, 32 (7): 893–905.

Liebel, M. (2003) 'Working children as social subjects', *Childhood*, 10 (3): 265–85.

Miljeteig, P. (2000) *Creating Partnerships with Working Children and Youth. World Bank Social Protection Discussion Paper Series* 21.

Montgomery, H. (2009) 'Are child prostitutes child workers? A case study', *International Journal of Sociology and Social Policy*, 29 (3/4): 130–40.

Nardinelli, C. (1980) 'Child labor and the Factory Acts', *Journal of Economic History*, 40 (04): 739–55.

O'Connell Davidson, J. (2005) *Children in the Global Sex Trade*, Cambridge: Polity Press.

Okyere, S. (2013) 'Are working children's rights and child labour abolition complementary or opposing realms?' *International Social Work*, 56 (1): 80–91.

Opare, J.A. (2003) 'Kayayei: the women head porters of southern Ghana', *Journal of Social Development in Africa*, 18 (2): 33–48.

Osei, R.D., Owusu, G.A., Asem, F.E., and Afutu-Kotey, R.L. (2009) *Effects of Capitation on Education Outcomes in Ghana, Accra: The Institute of Statistical and Economic Research*, University of Ghana (available online at http://goo.gl/E4BL6) (accessed on 3 August 2012).

Rahman, M.M., Khanam, R., and Nur-Uddin, A. (1999) 'Child labour in Bangladesh: a critical appraisal of Harkin's Bill and the MOU-type schooling program', *Journal of Economic Issues*, 33 (4): 985–1003.

Slavery to Freedom (2010) Project Report (available online at http://goo.gl/UzAaS) (accessed on 31 March 2011).

Stambler, M. (1968) 'The effect of compulsory education and child labour laws on high school attendance in New York City, 1898–1917', *History of Education Quarterly*, 8 (2): 189–214.

Teerink, M.B. and Weston, B.H. (2009) *Child Labor through a Human Rights Glass Brightly, Human Rights and Human Welfare*. Working paper 35, October 2006. (available online at http://goo.gl/gd9iy) (accessed on 2 June 2012).

Thompson, E.P. (1963) *The Making of the English Working Class*, New York. NY: Vintage Books.

Twum-Danso, A. (2009) 'The construction of childhood and the socialization of children: the implications for the implementation of Article 12 of the Convention on the Rights of the Child in Ghana', in N. Thomas and B. Percy-Smith (eds) *Participation: Theory and Practice*, Oxford: Routledge.

UN (2006) *Consideration of Reports Submitted by States Parties under Article 44 of the Convention. Concluding Observations: Ghana* (CRC/C/GHA/CO/2) (available online at http://goo.gl/sWc47) (accessed on 1 March 2012).

UNICEF (2001) *Beyond Child Labour, Affirming Rights*, New York, NY: UNICEF.

UNICEF (2007a) *Social Protection to Tackle Child Poverty in Ghana*, New York, NY: UNICEF.

UNICEF (2007b) *Child Labour, Education, and Policy Options. Division of Policy and Planning* (working papers), New York, NY: UNICEF.

UNICEF (2011) *The State of the World's Children: Adolescence – an Age of Opportunity*, New York, NY: UNICEF.

UNICEF (2012) *Submission by the United Nations Children's Fund (UNICEF) to the Office of the Human Rights Council on the Universal Periodic Review*, Accra: UNICEF (available online at http://goo.gl/nxVEDq) (accessed on 14 March 2013).

Weiner, M. (1991) *The Child and the State in India: Child Labour and Education Policy in Comparative Perspective*, Princeton, NJ: Princeton University Press.

World Bank (2012) *World Development Indicators 2012*, Washington, DC: World Bank.

World Vision (2007) *Letting the Future in: World Vision and Child Labour in India* (available online at http://goo.gl/8erF) (accessed on 2 February 2012).

Yakovleva, N. (2007) 'Perspective on female participation in artisanal and small-scale mining: a case study of Birim North District of Ghana', *Resources Policy*, 32 (1–2): 29–41.

Zelizer, V.A.R. (1994) *Pricing the Priceless Child: The Changing Social Value of Children*, Princeton, NJ: Princeton University Press.

Zhang, Y. and Wildemuth, B. (2009) 'Unstructured interview', in B. Wildemuth (ed.) *Applications of Social Research Methods to Questions in Information and Library Science*, Westport, CT: Libraries Unlimited.

7 What can children's rights mean when children are struggling to survive?

The case of Chiweshe, Zimbabwe

Michael Bourdillon and Eve Musvosvi

What rights apply?

The United Nations Convention on the Rights of the Child (CRC) is supposed to apply to all children everywhere; nevertheless, the preamble supposes an ideal childhood within a supporting formal family structure. Ten years after the adoption of the CRC, Judith Ennew (2000) noted that the Convention makes no explicit reference to street children, who commonly live without a supporting family and are frequently regarded as children out of place; consequently, their special needs are not addressed (see also Pare, 2003). The African Charter on the Rights and Welfare of the Child also bases children's rights on the model of growing up in a supporting family, even to the extent of declaring responsibilities of children to their families and communities that are commonly accepted in African cultures. Apart from children on city streets, Ennew's argument applies to many others who do not fit conventional ideas of childhood.

This chapter considers experiences of children growing up in Chiweshe Communal Lands in Zimbabwe in the context of AIDS and political-economic decline, where life chances were bleak. Most of these children had limited access to nutrition, health care, education, and few options for livelihood. They were concerned about surviving in a context of deprivation and inequality, in ways that often challenged adult ideas of maintaining traditional values on gender and age-appropriate work. From an early age, the children responded to their situation by supporting each other in hunting, gathering, gold mining, trading, providing services, and other survival tactics to meet their daily needs. While their lives were harsh and far from the ideal childhood envisaged by international treaties on children's rights and welfare, their responses revealed a degree of agency that shows the inadequacy of perceiving them simply as vulnerable victims.

Their children's rights to provision and protection as internationally conceived were clearly not being adequately realized. On the other hand, they were making many of their own decisions about how to respond to the challenges of life: it could be argued that they asserted their right to participation. It is not clear – either in terms of theoretical thinking or with respect to practical intervention – how documents like the CRC or the African Charter should be applied to these children. Although human rights are said to be indivisible, in situations like this there is need to prioritize in consultation with the children, building on what they have done for themselves, in order to improve their situation without further disrupting their lives and their families.

There is also need to consider precisely what must be involved in protecting children in this kind of situation. How is their right to protection to be conceived? Protection from hazards and exploitation in the workplace commonly take the form of preventing children from working. Such an approach would be unlikely to improve the wellbeing and prospects of the children we describe, and in our discussion at the end of this chapter, we argue for a more positive view of protection that looks to support the development of children.

The chapter draws on a wider ethnographic study that Eve Musvosvi carried out in Chiweshe Communal Lands from January 2007 to March 2008.[1] The study explored what it was like to be a child in the context of multiple crises, and how children learned and experienced growing up amid crises. It focused on 50 children aged 4–16 years, stratified according to age but otherwise picked randomly from groups of children in the villages. Their participation in the research was voluntary throughout. Musvosvi was a participant observer in the community and used a variety of techniques to ensure that the children's perspectives received due prominence, including drawing pictures (by the younger children), writing stories and keeping diaries (by the older ones), and a variety of individual and group discussions. The child-centred nature of the study also ensured due attention to the agency of children in dealing with the problems they faced.

In this chapter, we first outline the status of child rights and child protection in Zimbabwe, and provide background information on the situation in Chiweshe, where the children lived. We then describe some of the ways in which children responded to the situation and their tactics for survival. Finally, we discuss how their tactics and their agency impinge on how we think about children's rights, and particularly their right to protection.

Child rights and child protection in Zimbabwe

In 1980, Zimbabwe gained its independence from a regime of the White minority, which discriminated racially against the majority in access to secondary education, government services, and the economy in general. The first decade after independence saw radical improvement in services, particularly in health and education, to the majority of the population, who live in rural areas. By the 1990s, the economy was coming under strain, resulting in pressure to adopt the economic structural adjustment programmes that were espoused by international bodies at the time. These involved attempts to retrieve costs of services such as health and education, thus impeding access by the poorer members of the society (for discussions of Zimbabwe's changing economic experiences, see Harold-Barry, 2004; Maphosa *et al.*, 2007).

In spite of diminished services, there has been some attention to children's rights. In 1990, Zimbabwe was one of the early countries to ratify the CRC. In 1996, the 12th session of the UN Committee on the Rights of the Child noted some areas of progress towards these rights in Zimbabwe (as well as a number of areas of concern – CRC/15Add. 55, 7 June 1996; see also Chinyangara *et al.*, 1997). The Government of Zimbabwe, sometimes under pressure from international child-protection agencies, has continued to establish legislation and policies for the protection of children's rights, but has rarely provided funds to support these policies. In 1999, it published its *Zimbabwe National Orphan Care Policy* (Government of Zimbabwe, 1999) to establish a six-tier safety net particularly for the growing number of HIV/AIDS orphans in the country; the principles (Section 3) of this policy document follow several articles of the CRC and the African Charter. In December of 2001, laws on children were amended and consolidated in the *Children's Act* (Chap. 5: 06), again, largely in conformity with the international treaties, and in particular declaring that the best interests of the child shall be paramount in matters concerning them, but largely silent on children's right to a say on matters that affect them. The Children's Act established a Council for the Welfare of Children, which has achieved little.

After a change of government in 2008, there were improvements in welfare services. The number of occupied government posts for social workers has increased, but remains at around 120 for the whole country (some of which are financed by donors). Parallel child protection committees, comprising adults and children respectively, have developed in many parts of the country, producing a greater awareness of child rights, particularly among children.

In 2010, the Ministry of Labour and Social Services promulgated the National Residential Child Care Standards, in compliance with Article 3 (3) of the CRC. The standards of accommodation comply with international standards, but not necessarily with standards of accommodation for children in the country nor with the resources available to those providing care for homeless children in Zimbabwe. The demand, for example, that each child has his or her own private space of at least 3.5 square metres exceeds what is available to children in many crowded family homes in urban areas, or indeed in traditional child accommodation in rural areas. In the same year, the ministry produced Phase II of the National Action Plan for Orphans and Vulnerable children, developed in consultation with a variety of stakeholders, including children, and paying attention to issues of poverty as well as more traditional protection (Government of Zimbabwe, 2010).

With regard to children's work, Zimbabwe has formally accepted international standards. In 1997, the government amended its Labour Relations Act to forbid the employment of children under 12, while those aged 12 to 17 were permitted a maximum of six hours a day of light work during school holidays. In 1999, Zimbabwe ratified ILO Convention 138 (1973) on Minimum Age for Entry to Employment and raised the minimum age to 15. In 2000, the country ratified ILO Convention 182 on Worst Forms of Child Labour. Many consider, however, the debate about child labour to be a problem imported from the West and inappropriate to the culture and economy of Zimbabwe. Minimum-age legislation is only occasionally enforced (although there have been no prosecutions – IRIN, 2012 – children have occasionally been stopped from working). Nevertheless, the demands on children to work in many situations remain problematic (see Chinyangara *et al.*, 1997: chap. 3).

Children expect, and are expected, to undertake a variety of tasks in their homes (which can be especially problematic for girls with heavy obligations of schoolwork), on family farms, and in a variety of family enterprises (see examples in Bourdillon, 2000). A report from 2004 (Government of Zimbabwe, 2006: 26) indicated that 99% of children aged 5–14 years undertook unpaid domestic work for their families, and 42% were involved in economic activities. Such expectations conform with the responsibilities of children outlined in Article 31 of the African Charter; they also fit traditional patriarchal ideas according to which the father of the family owns, controls, and provides for his children (see Holleman, 1952: 242–58).

Formally, then, Zimbabwe has accepted international standards of child protection and has taken steps to support them in law and policy. Save the Children and Childline[2] report improved children's awareness of their rights. The question remains about how formal laws and policies serve or fail the interests of deprived children outside the centres of services and power: organizations such as Save the Children and Childline remain (early in 2013) virtually unknown in the community we consider.

The state of politics and the economy is of more relevance to the lives of the children described in this chapter. Although Zimbabwe is rich in agricultural and mineral resources, these have always been unequally distributed. The government has attempted to redress the colonial racial discrimination in favour of Whites, but differentials between rich and poor appear to be increasing, and the country has very high levels of poverty:[3] a National Nutrition Survey by the Zimbabwe Ministry of Health and Child Welfare in 2010 showed 34% of children under five to be chronically malnourished. In the first decade of the twenty-first century, massive inflation (reaching over 2,000,000% p.a. by 2007) accompanied a collapsing economy. Only around 6% of the potential workforce were estimated to be in formal employment at the end of 2008 (*Mail and Guardian*, 2009). At the same time, political tensions resulted in the discourse of rights being treated with suspicion on the part of government.[4] There are some indications of improvement since the stabilization of the economy in 2009, but poverty remains widespread.

The HIV/AIDS epidemic has compounded the situation. Zimbabwe has been one of the worst-hit countries. UNAIDS estimated the prevalence rate among 15–49-year-olds in the country to be about 27% in 1997, dropping to just over 14% in 2010 (UNAIDS, 2012). According to World Bank estimates, life expectancy at birth in Zimbabwe fell from 58 years in 1992 to 43 years in 2003, but it has since risen to 51 years in 2011 (World Bank, 2013) as the epidemic declined slightly in recent years (UNAIDS, 2010: 18). UNICEF reported in 2010 that one in four children had lost one or both parents, and there were over 100,000 child-headed households in the country. These ills in the social environment, together with mass migration to neighbouring countries like South Africa for economic reasons,[5] have left many children without effective or adequate adult support.

Chiweshe

The children presented in this chapter lived in Ward 10 of Chiweshe Communal Lands, just over 100 kilometres northeast of Harare. The soils in much of Chiweshe and the rainfall patterns are normally suitable for intensive agriculture and livestock production, and the district has mineral resources (particularly gold) and wildlife. Historically, the racial distribution of land by settler governments meant that communal lands tended to be less suitable for agriculture than nearby commercial farms, which used to be reserved for Whites. In some parts of Chiweshe, the granitic soil is thin and prone to erosion, and rainfall has become erratic in recent years compounded by problems of overgrazing and deforestation (Chiweshe, 2011), to the extent that agriculture is not a reliable source of livelihood for many people. Moreover, complex webs of gendered and generational inequalities have combined with the HIV/AIDS pandemic and the declining political economy to make the lives of children extremely precarious.

The population in Chiweshe is no exception to the incidence of poverty in the country as a whole, leaving many children without adequate adult support. The number of men out of employment was compounded by those who had lost their jobs and homes on previously White-owned farms in the rapid land reform process of the early 2000s, and who were searching for any way to make a living, including informal mining. Such people were often referred to as *makorokoza*: the verb, *kukorokoza*, is a vernacular term referring to various informal forms of legal and illegal self-employment tactics to provide a livelihood.

Ward 10 has a population of around 5,500, but only two primary schools with a total enrolment of around 1,500 pupils.[6] Both schools are short of resources, especially classroom space, and one of the schools practises 'hot seating' to cater for separate cohorts of children in the mornings and afternoons. A scarcity of teachers means that many continue to be employed past retirement age. The ward also has a secondary school, taking around 600 pupils for four years up to 'o-level'. Although fees are low, enrolment is reported to have dropped as a result of the current financial crisis. For the final two years of secondary schooling, which are necessary for local university entrance, the nearest government schools are 20 and more kilometres away (there is a girls' private school only nine kilometres away).

There are no health facilities within the ward, but there is a clinic staffed by nurses a few kilometres away and the Salvation Army's Howard Hospital some 20 kilometres away. The work of the clinic is hampered by the inadequacy of its government grants and by erratic supplies of drugs, which also affect the hospital. These problems, together with difficulties of transport, result in children frequently resorting to traditional sources of treatment.

Of the 50 children in the sample, 12 were orphaned. Some 19 were staying with grandparents, and nine were heads of their households; 37 indicated that they had to supplement inadequate food in their homes through foraging; and only three reported regularly having three meals a day. More than half the dream recollections were about hunger and lack of food.

The research was conducted before the national improvements in social services, described in the previous section. Questions remain about the rights of children living in conditions such as those of Ward 10, who are not always reached by improvements at the national level. We now consider strategies of children to provide for themselves in this situation of dire poverty when provision by adults was inadequate.

The responses of the children

Survival bands

One strategy was to band together in a way similar to the 'survival bands' described by Turnbull (1972: 134) – groups of friends cooperating and working hard for their survival. About 70% of the 50 children in our sample were regular members of such bands, with others joining occasionally. Membership was flexible and based on an ability to contribute, taking on a variety of tasks, and learning a variety of skills. The groups obtained food, medication, raw materials, and gold from their environment, though some children also grew vegetables in home gardens. The bands shared experiences, enhanced knowledge, and pooled labour. They adopted names, some of which were descriptive of the groups (such as *masista* – sisters) or their occupation (such as *gee dees* for gold diggers). Informal leadership of the bands was based on personal charisma, interpersonal skills, mastery of survival-enhancing knowledge, and social connections. Gender roles in the gangs were flexible and could be interchanged provided they enhanced one's survival chances, although all the girls still had to perform their gendered tasks when they returned home.

The children in these bands took on a variety of roles and referred to their activities as *kukorokoza* or 'doing business'. Their activities were largely child-led, although extracting gold required dealing with adults: children could not acquire mining rights, and outside traders did not deal with children.

The more roles and the more hours one could put in, the more one earned. Earnings were based directly on ability to work and on cooperation. Those absent would receive nothing.

Two main reasons for participating in the bands kept recurring in the stories of the children: hunger, and the need to survive in a harsh economic climate. The groups included children who had been orphaned, as well as children whose parents had migrated out of the district for work. One girl who had joined a band said that both her parents were alive but had poorly paying jobs in the city: they could rarely afford the bus fare home and often could not pay her school fees on time. Her work in the band ensured that she could meet school and examination expenses. Bands also included children from large polygamous families and children whose parents had divorced. Some children stayed with kin who had fostered them but made heavy demands on them to work.

One shopkeeper's daughter said she had joined a group on the invitation of a friend. Subsequent information indicated that she was included because her father's shop was sometimes used for gold exchanges with unknown strangers whom the villagers did not want to take to their homes. This shop served as the storage place for the substantial monthly rations of groceries that the children acquired in payment for regular work. Due to food shortages and high inflation, children generally preferred to be paid in kind.

Some boys joined to establish their status. When they were staying with relatively distant kin, they undertook domestic work at home to negotiate kinship relations. This they regarded as girl's work. Boys stated that going back home to their kin or grandmothers carrying a live chicken made them feel like 'real men'. Their material contributions to the households in which they lived made them feel they had retained their manhood in other spheres of life.

Mining bands

The most lucrative work was the extraction of gold. Riverbank gold mining had been legal since 1991, but was again declared illegal in 2006, partly due to fears of uncontrolled mining damaging the environment. The subsequent clampdown on illegal mining primarily targeted stereotypical adult males. By 2008, bands of adult miners had become less visible, partly because they employed children, who were less likely to be suspected by the police. Girls were preferred, since gangs of boys were more likely to attract the attention of the authorities; nevertheless, the children remained at risk of trouble with authorities. The initial groups of child miners were established under the partial supervision of adults, who controlled the marketing of gold, although the children considered themselves as self-employed *makarokoza* rather than employees. Subsequently girls established groups comprising only girls, and working with elderly women, who offered a higher price for gold 'points' (a 'point' is a tenth of a gram, worth locally at the time about US$2) than did adult males, partly because some women were involved in cross-border trading and could sell gold where the price was higher.

Those involved in extracting gold were characterized as 'owls' or 'chameleons'. The owls earned more, partly because their work was seen as more dangerous. The girls of this group worked at night, usually from 7 to 10. They worked underground, digging shafts to find the 'gold belt', and hauling and transporting rubble and gold on their own. The leader of one such group, Matriq[7] (aged 15), acquired her status partly through her skill in both underground gold mining and alluvial gold panning; we shall present her story later in this chapter.

The chameleons did not go underground but specialized in gold panning during the day. Girls in this group often aspired to become owls for greater income and expanded options for survival, notwithstanding the greater danger in underground mining. As their name suggests, chameleons were able to blend into the forest and not be seen even during the day. To join a band of chameleons one needed the ability to adopt multiple roles. The invisibility of the chameleons was aided by close networks with 'connectors', who always made them aware of the activities of the police.

The bands pooled their labour to roast and crush gold-bearing stones. They used pole and mortar or conventional grindstones for crushing. These are tools used every day by women to process grains for food. Crushing stones and processing the gold took place at the homesteads of the women who were referred to as 'mothers'; these women supervised the activities, bought the gold, and allowed flexible working hours.

The children were well aware of the risks of mining, particularly underground mining, but they did not wish to be prevented from earning money in this way. Rather they wanted to be independent of exploiting adults. They sometimes attempted to break the exclusion of children from trading the gold by making their own contacts with buyers and thus to retain a larger share of income. They complained that the government did not treat them as 'people' (*vanhu*), since they were not allowed to stake their own mining claims, which forced them to work for others and for low wages. They felt that they were being excluded from a 'serious business of survival', a new form of entrepreneurial development that seemed to have, more than schooling, attainable goals in a context of high unemployment and uncertainty.

Foraging

Foraging was part of the daily lives of the children. On their way to, and from, school, they often collected vegetables, fruit, edible insects, herbs for infusions, and firewood, thus contributing to the requirements of their households. In the bands, these activities became more intensive, and what they learned in the bands contributed to their daily activities. Matriq shared her herbal knowledge with, and learned about wild vegetables from, other band members and by experiment: Matriq said she sometimes first fed a new food to her dog to test if it were toxic. The children ate more fruit and knew more varieties than most adults, who sometimes learned from the survival-enhancing knowledge of the children.

Mutsa, an eleven-year-old girl, proudly displayed her knowledge of four types of mushroom that come out at different seasons, and continued:

> The mushrooms can be eaten fresh, boiled, or dried and are a good substitute for meat. At times we sell them to raise income, but because our *zim-kwacha*[8] is now useless, we prefer to exchange our mushrooms for food, chickens, or anything else of value.

Children below the age of 10 mainly participated in foraging, a widespread activity that took place at any time from five in the morning to midnight; working hours of individual children or groups depended on their needs and their other activities, including school. The groups shared the food they collected. They talked about *kudya tese* (to eat together), a phrase that normally applies to close family relations and now referred to sharing the resources of the band. One group leader (Dhevhi, whose story also appears later in this chapter) was well known for his skill in cooking wild vegetables and mice, probably because he also cooked at home. Being in charge of food supplies as leader of the band provided a manipulative advantage, and might enable a child to provide for siblings and other family members.

Young girls sometimes learned foraging skills by accompanying older women who combined foraging with looking for gold and gold-mining activities. Girls and boys as young as four years old could join a band. The main task of these was gathering edible insects like chafer beetles, grasshoppers, and termites, which come out in the rainy season and, if plentiful, could be shared by the group, or dried and later exchanged for vegetables.

Insects are low-status food and hunting mice is considered appropriate only for small boys. In Chiweshe, however, the issue for the children was finding the only food available for the next meal, or the only available option to raise school fees for next term. Dhevhi's foraging group also made artefacts for sale. The members belonged to a particular church and called themselves 'Young Fathers'. They practised crafts for which their church has a reputation, using natural products like reeds, grass, sisal, cattle and goat hides, rabbit skin, and natural dyes derived from indigenous trees, to make wall hangings, baskets, mats, shoe straps, shawls, blankets, and various wooden utensils and musical instruments. Dhevhi said that his band took the idea from a women's cooperative group in their village, but that his band had better 'contacts' due to their links with gold buyers from the city. He claimed that the adult women's cooperative was suggesting that the young boys used the church as a cover for illegal dealing in marijuana.

Matriq confided that when things are tough economically, certain fruits could be fermented quickly with the aid of yeast and heat, to produce a popular, cheap, but illegal alcoholic brew for sale.

Makonekts (connectors)

In the survival bands, the *makonekts* (those who connect) served as middle-men between involved parties, which could be two children's groups, children and adults, the producers and the market, the police and child work-ers. While some children were working at the mining site, those on duty as *makonekts* would be strategically placed along the roads that the police motor-bikes used. Sometimes they set up stalls at the village market and sold vari-ous household utensils, fruits, and vegetables from their foraging activities; at the same time they would look out for the police, and warn their bands whenever the police might be coming – their main role under the front of trading.

Both boys and girls took up this role from the age of 10 upwards, often on a rotating basis. *Makonekts* usually worked in pairs, learnt through observing others, and then they would improvise. For their information, they would sometimes receive monetary or other rewards from villagers, other child groups, and even the police (who sometimes paid with gold confiscated from illegal miners).

Pimping

The role of young girls as 'pimps' was not part of the prescribed duties in the band, but something on which certain children decided to capitalize. This role was open to anyone with appropriate interpersonal skills and connec-tions. The girls generally claimed that they did not have sexual relations with the adult men they dealt with. Rather than putting themselves at risk, the girls establish 'friendships' for boys in their group, and for adult male miners, by linking them to widows, to women in the village with absentee husbands, and to prostitutes. Sometimes they would even facilitate booking a room at the shops. For such activity on a good day, a girl could go home with a live chicken or pocket the equivalent, which is 'two points' of gold.

Case studies

We present accounts of two children to illustrate how their work can be inte-gral to their lives.

Matriq's story

Matriq was a fifteen-year-old girl, whose parents both died of AIDS in 1998. She lived with her twin sisters (seven years old) and four male cousins, aged nine, seven, six, and four, all under the care of their elderly grandmother until her death in 2007. Two of the boys are also AIDS orphans, and the youngest is the child of a young unmarried (at the time) mother, who subse-quently married and left the home. The grandmother was in poor health, had few resources (assets had been used on food, health care, and burials), and no stable income; Matriq, the eldest child, became responsible for the provision, production, and consumption of food; organizing work within the household; and the health needs of all, including her grandmother until she died. She was the de facto head of household: this is a common pattern, sometimes missed in estimates of child-headed households.

The grandmother had been a well-known herbalist in the area, and often took Matriq as an apprentice to gather herbs. Successful healing often resulted in gifts of groceries, which helped the healer to care for her grandchildren. Before her death, however, she had lost clients to a spiritual cleanser, a young boy who accused her of being a witch, an accusation that was apparently supported by the multiple deaths in her family and deaths of her patients by AIDS. Even her only remaining child, a son, shunned her.

Matriq wrote in her diary:

> It was a terrible time for us, my sisters and I had just lost our parents, but people turned us away, nobody wanted us to visit their houses or even help us with clothing or food. They said they were afraid that we would bewitch them and eat them. We almost starved to death while our relatives watched. What was surprising was that my father's brother was not afraid of utilising the land that belonged to witches. Even now, he refuses to let us use my late father's land. So this is my only way out... I have to be brave and work like the other girls. God will keep me safe.

Matriq's father's brother took over the property, cattle, and land his late brother had left, and should have taken over the care of the children; but they were left largely on their own in their grandmother's home. Matriq bitterly complained:

> I went to uncle's house to ask for money to pay my examination fees. He shouted at me, and complained that I pretend to be working with miners, yet only go there to look for men. He kept saying that I am lazy and wasteful, and that I should work as hard as he did when he worked on farms of White settlers. I would rather work more hours than go and hear that White farmer story again... I will work hard and get a good job... then I will buy a full chicken for each of my sisters with my first salary.

Matriq ensured that her siblings had food to eat at school, and invented recipes of her own from what she learnt from her grandmother:

> I often make '*mtukutu* buns' from sorghum flour that I combine with fruit from the *mtukutu* tree... My grandmother taught me how to make them, but I add honey to the recipe, to make them tastier, so I can sell them at interschool sports. When I cannot find vegetables, the new shoots of this tree can be gathered and boiled.

Table 7.1 Matriq's working day

Time	Task	Hours of work
5.00 a.m.–5.20 a.m.	Gather firewood	20 minutes
5.20 a.m.–5.40 a.m.	Prepare fire	20 minutes
5.40 a.m.–6.10 a.m.	Sweep yard	30 minutes
6.10 a.m.–6.40 a.m.	Wash plates and pots	30 minutes
6.40 a.m.–7.20 a.m.	Walk to school	
7.30 a.m.–1.00 p.m.	School	
1.00 p.m.–3.30 p.m.	Band activities	2 hours 30 minutes
3.30 p.m.–4.50 p.m.	Walk home	
4.50 p.m.–5.30 p.m.	Fetch water	40 minutes
4.50 p.m.–5.30 p.m.	Home garden	45 minutes
5.30 p.m.–6.30 p.m.	Cook supper	1 hour
6.30 p.m.–7.30 p.m.	Bathe child and siblings	1 hour
Total hours		**7 hours 35 minutes**

She stated that since she joined the gold diggers, there was always bus fare to take her sisters to the HIV/AIDS programme at Howard Mission hospital where they get free cotrimaxozole. She complained that since Howard was one of the few hospitals with such a programme, the hospital was always crowded. Children without connections were at a disadvantage in such crowds, and sometimes Matriq had to go home without any medication for her sisters.

Table 7.1 provides an approximation of Matriq's activities on a Monday, when she did not have band activities at night or clothes to wash. Band activities were interwoven into other activities, such as roasting and crushing stones at home, and collecting food on the way home. Matriq also worked at night whenever she could, usually two or three nights a week. The children pushed themselves for returns that were more immediate than in agricultural activities.

Dhevhi's story

Dhevhi was a sixteen-year-old boy who lived with his eight-year-old sister and their grandfather. After their father abandoned their mother for another woman, she remarried and moved away, leaving her children with their paternal relatives according to tradition. When Dhevhi's father died in 2007, the children lived with their grandparents and with their elder brother, who had two wives and five children of his own. Dhevhi felt that his brother's wives discriminated against him and his sister. Owing to family conflict and suspicions that multiple deaths in the family were due to his witchcraft, the grandfather was ostracized by other relatives: they were forcefully relocated and lost their land. Dhevhi decided that when he was hungry he would have to fend for himself with his friends outside: he had recurrent dreams about being surrounded by food and being stopped from eating it. He commented

Table 7.2 Dhevhi's activities

Time	Task	Hours of work
5.30 a.m.–6.00 a.m.	Gather and chop wood	30 minutes
6.00 a.m.–6.20 a.m.	Cook porridge	20 minutes
6.20 a.m.–6.50 a.m.	Sweep yard	30 minutes
6.50 a.m.–7.10 a.m.	Walk to school	
7.30 a.m.–1.00 p.m.	School	
2.00 p.m.–4.00 p.m.	Band activity	2 hours
4.00 p.m.–4.20 p.m.	Walk home	
5.30 p.m.–6.30 p.m.	Cook supper	1 hour
Total hours		**4 hours 20 minutes**

that he had to earn money in a variety of informal ways to look after his sister, because no one else in the village would do so. Subsequent to the research, the grandfather died and Dhevhi and his sister remained in the home alone.

Dhevhi was the leader of a foraging group partly on account of his skill in cooking. Since poor cooking methods may lead to food being unpalatable, or destroy nutrients, some skill is required. Dhevhi stated that he learnt to cook and be multi-skilled because even when his father was still alive, he rarely came home from South Africa. Dhevhi did nearly all the cooking and other housework in his grandfather's home. Table 7.2 presents Dhevhi's activities on a Monday. Without young siblings to care for, he had considerably less unpaid work in the home than did Matriq.

Child rights and child protection

Both Matriq and Dhevhi worked for the livelihood of themselves and their younger siblings, while they continued to attend school. Both were resource-ful in trying to improve their lives and to care for the younger children for whom they were responsible. Their responsibility was real: the younger children could and did depend on it. They were productive and contributing members of their society, although they complained that they were not treated as *vanhu* ('people of worth').

Apart from earning income, the children learned productive and social skills through their work. They learned the value of mutual support. They learned to operate within the kind of informal economy on which their future lives were likely to depend. They learned to assess and deal with risk: even without appropriate adult support (cf. Boyden and Mann, 2005), the children in the bands had the support of their peers and learning to deal with risk could still be ultimately protective. Through their work, they developed their own lives and the lives of those around them in a way that enabled them to utilize the resources around their homes in Chiweshe.

The children generally challenged restrictions on their work based on age and gender. While most adults seemed more concerned about the maintenance of traditional gendered, generational, and spatially differentiated roles, children were more concerned with surviving in the context of deprivation and inequality. Their criterion of acceptable work was its outcome on their lives. Their attempts to become more independent of adults reflected their concern for having a voice to ensure fair treatment and fair exchange.

Although much of their work (such as gathering food of various kinds) was relatively benign, some (particularly underground mining) was physically hazardous and took place at night. It was sometimes so extensive that schoolwork was compromised. Some of their work was illegal, and some (such as pimping) went against local community values and so could be considered harmful to moral development. Nevertheless, there is little likelihood that their lives would be improved by preventing them from undertaking such work. On the other hand, recognition of their initiatives may help and may make them less dependent on adults who exploit them. They did not need to be stopped from helping themselves, but they needed support that might reduce time and energy taken away from schooling.

The question arises over the obligation of society to protect children from exploitation: is there a tension between children's rights to provision and protection and their right to have some control over their own lives? Perhaps the problem lies rather in how 'protection' is perceived. Much child protection, inspired over the last two decades by the CRC and the African Charter, focuses on particular deviations from ideals of childhood set in high-income countries and communities (Punch and Tisdall, 2012: 256–9), protecting children from particular forms of risk or abuse following the model of traditional social work. There are three severe limitations to viewing child protection in this way (see Myers and Bourdillon, 2012).

First, it conceives protection too negatively: it considers only what protection is *against* and fails to attend to what protection is *for*. Ultimately, the responsibility of society is to protect the development of the child, and protection of opportunities is at least as important as protection from risk and abuse. In high-income societies, opportunities and resources are widely available, and protection from particular forms of harm that have occurred may seem more important than consequent restriction of opportunities. In low-income societies and communities, opportunities for children to improve their lives are scarce, and the removal of such opportunities must be weighed carefully against benefits offered to children in any truly protective policy. It seems likely that the situation of the children in Chiweshe would be even worse were they prevented from undertaking economic activities in accordance with international standards (see also Okyere, 2013, on children in artisanal mining in Ghana; see also Okyere, this volume).

Second, and deriving from the first, the social work model often fails to consider the context in which children are threatened.[9] When whole communities are under threat, protection of children must first deal with this threat. Poverty has been shown to subject the development of children to multiple risks (see, for example, Pells, 2012), so that dealing with specific risks is unlikely to provide significant protection unless the context of poverty is first dealt with. Dealing with poverty may require attention to political issues. Neil Howard (2012) argues that since many child labour migrants are trying to escape poverty at home, stopping migration is unlikely to help: we should rather attend to policies of international trade that damage the possibilities of income for the farming communities that the children are fleeing. Apart from poverty, Hart and Lo Forte (2010) show how futile it was when international child-protection agencies claimed to support Palestinian children without attending to the political violence that was disrupting their lives. In Chiweshe, it is not meaningful to speak of protecting children without attending to the macro-economic and political situation that was disrupting their wellbeing and impeding their development. Genuine protection should provide hope for their future.

Indicators of improved attention to child rights in Zimbabwe, although commendable, have little to say to the lives of the children of Chiweshe described here. In their case, multiple inequalities need to be addressed: the bulk of income from the gold in the area goes to international capital and people in power rather than to the local communities; adults control the trade to their own advantage and the disadvantage of children; adults control other family resources; and children already affected by multiple deaths in the family are further estranged from local resources. Child protection demands attention to local, national, and international structures. If the situation of these children were significantly improved, they would be in a position to avoid extensive and hazardous work.

A third limitation of the traditional social work model of child protection is that it easily considers children as victims to be rescued, paying insufficient attention to the children's ability to improve their situation. It appears that most of the children of Chiweshe are able to live through the traumas of their lives without evident psychopathology, as appears in studies of children amid violence (e.g. Seymour, 2012: 375). The survival bands we have described speak to the agency of the children as much as to the limiting social and economic structures, both local and wider. This agency, while enabling the children to survive, sometimes results in activities that conflict with the norms of the adult community, and so might be depicted 'ambiguous agency' (Bordonaro and Payne, 2012). The children, however, assess their activities in terms of outcomes for survival, both immediate and by developing entrepreneurial skills for the future: the ambiguity seems to fall away.

If, instead of focusing on avoidance of harm and risk, protection is perceived in terms of wellbeing and development, the right to participation becomes integral to the right to protection. While difficulties in deciding precisely what is in the best interests of the child remain, especially when values differ and conflict, the tension between protection and participation largely falls away.

The situation we have described questions the nature and meaning of children's rights. There is a problem with the idea of a bundle of rights, conceived as indivisible, based on ideals of childhood that are unrealistic for the children concerned. In practice, the children we have described exercise considerable agency, while their rights to provision and protection are poorly realized. There is also a problem with perceiving rights as determined and imposed by outsiders. Children have, in various contexts, claimed the right to work (Bourdillon *et al.*, 2010: 16), a claim that is more in line with the right to work of Article 23 of the UN Universal Declaration of Human Rights (1948) than with the ILO's Convention 138 on a Minimum Age for Employment and the corresponding clauses in the CRC (Article 32.2.a) and the African Charter (Article 15.2.a). Manfred Leibel (2012) argues that children's rights should be conceived as coming from the children themselves and their demands for justice. Further, rights must be adapted to local situations and needs to be effective. When children of Chiweshe claim a right to economic autonomy from exploiting adults, this should be taken seriously.

Besides asking about the extent to which CRC and the African Charter have been effective in African countries, we need also to ask how appropriate are the various clauses – or their interpretations – to the contexts of the children we meet. We need to ensure that protecting their rights is a form of empowerment to improve their lives. The current National Action Plan for Orphans and Vulnerable Children (Government of Zimbabwe, 2010) indicates that the government and cooperating agencies are aware of the need for broad-based protection of rights, and in particular for dealing with the poverty of children and their families: it remains to be seen how effective this plan will be in reaching children at the margins of society.

Acknowledgements

We wish to thank the children and their families for their time and cooperation. Also Patience Matambo and Godwin Kudzotsa of Save the Children, Zimbabwe, and Tara Miller and Marshall Kaseke of Childline, for their time and advice. Responsibility for what is in this chapter remains with the authors.

Notes

1 It was a component of doctoral studies sponsored by the University of Pretoria, South Africa.
2 This information comes from interviews with staff of the two organizations. Childline is a Zimbabwean NGO, founded in 1998 as a telephone helpline for children. It has expanded to be a leader in child-protection services in the country, cooperating well with government since 2009.
3 Reliable up-to-date figures are not available for Zimbabwe. The latest poverty figure given by the World Bank (2013) is 72% of the population in poverty in 2003, up from 35% in 1993. A UNICEF report in 2010 estimated 78% of the population in absolute poverty (VOA, 2013).
4 Human Rights Watch (2012) reports that the Zimbabwean authorities continue to harass and intimidate advocates for human rights in an attempt to prevent disclosure of abuses.

5 Accurate figures on migration are not available, but it is frequently suggested that over three million Zimbabweans (nearly 20% of all Zimbabweans) now live outside the country.
6 While we do not have accurate figures, approximately a quarter of the population of Zimbabwe are of primary school age (see population distribution for 2010 – Nationmaster, 2013). Even allowing for the fact that some of the children enrolled in primary schools are old for their grade, it appears that over 90% of children of primary school age were currently enrolled.
7 All names are pseudonyms.
8 A derogatory term dating from the time of the collapse of the Zambian kwacha, long before the much more dramatic collapse of the Zimbabwean dollar.
9 Lonne *et al.* (2009), spurred by the failure of the current social work model of child protection to help children in Aboriginal communities in Australia, point to the need for reform of child protection more broadly.

References

Bordonaro, L.I. and Payne, R. (2012) 'Ambiguous agency: critical perspectives on social interventions with children and youth in Africa', *Children's Geographies*, 10: 365–72.

Bourdillon, M. (ed.) (2000) *Earning a Life: Working Children in Zimbabwe*, Harare: Weaver Press.

Bourdillon, M., Levison, D., Myers, W., and White, B. (2010) *Rights and Wrongs of Children's Work*, New Brunswick, NJ: Rutgers University Press.

Boyden, J. and Mann, G. (2005) 'Children's risk, resilience, and coping in extreme situations', in M. Ungar (ed.) *Handbook for Working with Children and Youth: Pathways to Resilience across Cultures and Contexts*, Thousand Oaks, CA: Sage.

Chinyangara, I., Chokuwenga, I., Dete, R.G., Dube, L., Kembo, J., Moyo, P., and Nkomo, R.S. (1997) *Indicators for Children's Rights: Zimbabwe Country Case Study. Childwatch International* (available online at http://www.child-abuse.com/childhouse/childwatch/cwi/projects/indicators/Zimbabwe/ind_index.html) (accessed on 17 December 2012).

Chiweshe, M.K. (2011) *Farm Level Institutions in Emergent Communities in Post Fast Track Zimbabwe: Case of Mazowe District*, Grahamstown: Rhodes University, Department of Sociology.

Ennew, J. (2000) 'Why the Convention is not about street children', in D. Fottrell (ed.) *Revisiting Children's Rights: 10 Years of the UN Convention on the Rights of the Child*, The Hague: Kluwer Law International.

Government of Zimbabwe (1999) *Zimbabwe National Orphan Care Policy*, Harare: Department of Labour and Social Welfare.

Government of Zimbabwe (2006) *Child Labour Report, 2004*, Harare: Central Statistics Office.

Government of Zimbabwe (2010) *National Action Plan for Orphans and Vulnerable Children Phase II, 2011–2015*, Harare: Ministry of Labour and Social Services.

Harold-Barry, D. (ed.) (2004) *Zimbabwe: The Past is the Future. Rethinking Land, State, and Nation in the Context of Crisis*, Harare: Weaver Press.

Hart, J. and Lo Forte, C. (2010) *Protecting Palestinian Children from Political Violence: The Role of the International Community. Refugee Studies Centre Policy Briefing*, Oxford: Refugee Studies Centre.

Holleman, J.F. (1952) *Shona Customary Law: With reference to Kinship, Marriage, the Family and the Estate*, Manchester: Manchester University Press.

Howard, N. (2012) 'Protecting children from trafficking in Benin: in need of politics and participation', *Development in Practice*, 22: 460–72.

Human Rights Watch (2012) *World Report 2012: Zimbabwe* (available online at http://www.hrw.org/world-report-2012/world-report-2012-zimbabwe-0) (accessed on 20 February 2013).

IRIN (2012) *ZIMBABWE: Child Labour on the Rise* (available online at http://www.irinnews.org/report/94939/ZIMBABWE-Child-labour-on-the-rise) (accessed on 18 December 2012).

Liebel, M. (ed.) (2012) *Children's Rights from Below: Cross-Cultural Perspectives*, Basingstoke: Palgrave Macmillan.

Lonne, B., Parton, N., Thomson, J., and Harries, M. (2009) *Reforming Child Protection*, London and New York, NY: Routledge.

Mail and Guardian (2009) 'Zim unemployment skyrockets' (available online at http://www.mg.co.za/article/2009-01-29-zim-unemployment-skyrockets) (accessed on 10 October 2012).

Maphosa, F., Kujinga, K., and Chingarande, S.D. (eds) (2007) *Zimbabwe's Development Experiences Since 1980: Challenges and Prospects for the Future*, Harare: Organization for Social Science Research in Eastern and Southern Africa.

Myers, W. and Bourdillon, M. (2012) 'Concluding reflections: how might we really protect children?' *Development in Practice*, 22: 613–20.

Nationmaster (2013) *Age Distribution* (available online at www.nationmaster.com/country/zi-zimbabwe/Age-distribution) (accessed on 20 December 2012).

Okyere, S. (2013) 'Are working children's rights and child labour abolition complementary or opposing realms?' *International Social Work*, 56: 167–79.

Pare, M. (2003) 'Why have all the street children disappeared? The role of international human rights law in protecting vulnerable groups', *International Journal of Children's Rights*, 11: 1–32.

Pells, K. (2012) '"Risky lives": risk and protection for children growing-up in poverty', *Development in Practice*, 22: 562–73.

Punch, S. and Tisdall, E.K.M. (2012) 'Not so "new"? Looking critically at childhood studies', *Children's Geographies*, 10: 249–62.

Seymour, C. (2012) 'Ambiguous agencies: coping and survival in eastern Democratic Republic of Congo', *Children's Geographies*, 10: 373–84.

Turnbull, C.M. (1972) *The Mountain People*, New York, NY: Simon & Schuster.

UNAIDS (2010) *Global Report: UNAIDS Report on the Global AIDS Epidemic 2010*, Geneva: Joint United Nations Programme on HIV/AIDS.

UNAIDS (2012) 'UNAIDS highlights Zimbabwe's progress in responding to AIDS' (available online at http://www.unaids.org/en/resources/presscentre/featurestories/2012/may/20120528fszimbabwe/) (accessed on 19 February 2013).

VOA (2013) 'Unicef says 6.6 million Zimbabweans living below food poverty line' (available online at http://www.voazimbabwe.com/content/unicef-says-66-million-zimbabweans-living-below-food-poverty-90257362/1457690.html) (accessed on 19 February 2013).

World Bank (2013) *Data: Zimbabwe* (available online at <http://data.worldbank.org/country/zimbabwe) (accessed on 19 February 2013).

8 In the best interests of the child

The case of child domestic workers in Ghana and Nigeria

Evelyn Omoike

Introduction

In recent times, attention has been drawn to the situation of children who undertake domestic activities in homes other than their own. This practice is widespread with an estimate of over 15.5 million children aged 5–17 years engaged in domestic work worldwide (ILO, 2013). For the most part, domestic work is considered safe and suitable for children to undertake. But reports of exploitation and abuse have made it a subject of international concern. The protection of children as championed by the United Nations Convention on the Rights of the Child (CRC) potentially guarantees children everywhere regardless of race or gender, basic rights and protection against exploitation and abuse. Like other forms of child exploitation, the CRC's principle of 'best interests' acts as a guide for interventions targeted at protecting children. But the realities of many children are far removed from the ideals proposed by the CRC. In this chapter, I argue that the principle of 'best interests' is of no effect for child domestic workers if it does not consider children's own perceptions of best interests. There is a growing recognition that children are competent social beings (Valentine, 1996, cited in Panelli *et al.*, 2007) with the capacity to act upon their environments and the ability to articulate their needs. The CRC also provides that children's voices be heard in matters concerning them. However, there is no provision that recognizes that child workers' views might be different. And what happens if the children's voices or ideas are different from the notion of best interests as interpreted and implemented by state parties?

With this understanding, this chapter draws on the testimonies of child domestic workers in Ghana and Nigeria to explore the notion of best interests as it applies to child domestic workers. The children's experience of domestic work and the priorities they set for themselves will be used to examine the notion of best interests and how this corresponds, or conflicts, with the child domestic workers' perceptions of their best interests.

The first section discusses the CRC's principle of 'best interests'. The next section goes on to address child domestic work and the forms in which it exists. Their experience as live-in domestic workers and the positives and negatives of child domestic work are examined. The chapter concludes by examining the children's perception of what is in their best interests in relation to the international conception of the notion of best interests.

Children who work as domestics either 'live in' (live with as well as work for their employers) or live away from their employers. This chapter focuses on child domestics who 'live in'. Child domestic workers can be male or female but the children involved in this research were predominantly girls. The term employer is used to refer to people the children lived with and provided domestic services for.

Methodology

Data for this chapter were obtained through fieldwork undertaken for an on-going doctoral thesis. Sixty-nine child domestic workers were interviewed in Ghana and Nigeria between September 2009 and May 2010. There were 19 boys and 50 girls between the ages of 9 and 18 years. The children were accessed through non-governmental organizations (NGOs) and three state-owned primary and secondary schools with high concentrations of domestic workers in Ghana, the Nigerian National Agency for the Prohibition and Trafficking of Persons and Other Related Matters (NAPTIP) and an evening school in Nigeria, and personal contacts in both countries. Individual interviews and group sessions were held with current and previous child domestic workers within and outside formal educational systems.

The principle of best interests

Article 3 of the CRC provides that the best interests of the child shall be a primary consideration in all actions concerning children. Conceptually this means that states parties must consider the principle as the basis of all policies and interventions regarding children. There is no single meaning provided for the term 'best interests' but it can be broadly defined as whatever constitutes the well-being of a child. The United Nations Committee on the Rights of the Child (2005) emphasized the interrelationships between the articles of the CRC. And the interpretation of best interests must be consistent with the spirit of the entire Convention. The principle of best interests is included in a number of other CRC articles relating to individual children in particular situations. It often applies to situations of child custody and has to be interpreted in the specific case of the child concerned. The CRC provides a yardstick that offers parameters on child protection. Guidelines are provided relating to situations of child custody but there is an absence of a precise definition for situations covering areas such as child work which leaves room for subjective interpretation by various state parties. Van Bueren (2007, cited in Zermatten, 2010) highlights the uncertainty and indeterminacy inherent in the best interests' principle. It can be argued that the flexibility of the principle is what allows it to be adapted to the variety of social and cultural contexts of various state parties. However, this flexibility could conceivably produce outcomes that are counterproductive for child workers.

On a regional level, the best interests principle was enshrined in the African Charter on the Rights and Welfare of the Child adopted by the Organization of African Unity (OAU) in 1990. It was domesticated into Nigerian national law with the passage of the Child Rights Act 2003 and into the Ghanaian legislative framework by the Children's Act 1998. The African Charter on the Rights and Welfare of the Child further provides that the best interests of the child should not just be 'a' but 'the' primary consideration in all actions concerning children: 'In all actions concerning the child undertaken by any person or authority the best interests of the child shall be the primary consideration' (art. 4 (1) African Charter).

The Charter also provides for the protection of children from all forms of economic exploitation and from performing any work that is likely to be hazardous or to interfere with the child's physical, mental, spiritual, moral, or social development (UNHCR, 2008).

The case of child domestic workers

Child domestic workers are people under the age of 18 who work in households of people other than their closest family doing domestic chores, caring for children, running errands, and sometimes helping the employer run a small business from home. This includes children who are paid for their work, as well as those who are not paid or who receive 'in-kind' benefits, such as food and shelter (Flores-Oebanda, 2006; Blagbrough, 2008). The International Labour Organization (ILO) (2013) refers to child domestic work as children's work in the domestic sector in the home of a third-party employer. Child domestic labour refers to domestic work undertaken by children under the legal minimum working age (as prescribed by national governments) as well as by children above the legal minimum age but under the age of 18 under slavery-like, hazardous, or other exploitative conditions (ILO, 2004). This form of exploitation would include working for long hours with little or no wages. Where such exploitation is extreme and includes trafficking, slavery, or practices similar to slavery, or work which by its nature or the circumstances in which it is carried out is hazardous and likely to harm the health, safety, or morals of children, then this constitutes a worst form of child domestic labour which needs to be tackled as a matter of urgency (ILO, 2004). Child domestic work generally encapsulates both permissible and non-permissible situations. Child domestic labour is regarded as harmful and exploitative work requiring urgent elimination. A child undertaking domestic activities within their home is common place and acceptable in many parts of the world. But such work is open to exploitation and abuse when undertaken in third-party homes. Such children are often invisible and difficult to protect as they work within the confines of their employers' homes and their work is often seen as part of the expected roles of children in the household. There are an estimated 15.5 million children involved in paid or unpaid domestic work in the home of a third party or employer (ILO, 2013), but it is difficult to obtain accurate numbers as situations of child domestic work are hidden and often difficult to identify.

Child domestic work occurs in different forms and Jacquemin (2009) highlights that a number of child domestics switch between the different forms of child domestic work during their time as domestic workers. Some child domestic workers receive monetary compensation for their services and there are others who receive compensation in form of 'in-kind' benefits, such as food and shelter (Flores-Oebanda, 2006). There are child domestic workers with formal employment contracts most of which are employed though placement agencies and those without formal contracts. Some child domestic workers work full time and do not attend school or any form of training or apprenticeship, while some other child domestics work part time and attend school or an apprenticeship. The categories the child domestic workers belong to are not always precise but they are often determined by their age, the way the children came to be child domestics, and their relationship with their employers.

The children's accounts of their lives as domestic workers indicated both positive and negative aspects. The children who participated in this research highlighted the benefits of life as domestic workers and for most of the children, life as domestic workers encompassed advantages and disadvantages. There was no archetype of the life of a typical child domestic worker; however, the children shared similar experiences although in varying degrees.

Negatives of child domestic work

The basis of the children's negative experience of domestic work can often be traced to the exploitation and abuse they receive from their employers. This exploitation takes different forms such as sexual and physical abuse, mistreatment, exposure to hazardous products and tools or unsafe kitchens, being confined to the house for extended periods of time, long working hours, with little or no wages, limited educational opportunities, discrimination, or simply children working below the minimum working age. Child domestic workers are highly isolated due to their invisibility behind closed doors and, because they are hidden, it is almost impossible to tell how many children work in domestic service. Child domestic labour is one of the most common and traditional forms of child labour (ILO, 2004) and this category of child labourers are particularly difficult to protect as their labour is not considered work, but rather a mere extension of their obligations to the household. Child domestics are often expected to perform skilled tasks such as childcare with minimum training and are severely punished for their mistakes. They can be on call 24 hours a day and may be awakened during the middle of the night to tend to the needs of their employers. It is estimated that around 70% of child workers carry out unpaid work for their families with girls being particularly in demand for domestic work (Anti-Slavery International, 2013). Some children work full time and others combine schooling with economic activities. Some children are sent to live with relatives in the urban areas to serve as domestics in exchange for education or training. Often it is the female children that are sent and in situations where the children are sent to strangers, the wages of those children can be sent home for the upkeep of the rest of the family. Child domestic workers are predominantly girls due to the gendered nature of domestic work.

The children in this study undertook a variety of tasks such as sweeping, cleaning and dusting, washing dishes and linen, caring for babies and children, making beds, scrubbing the bath house (bathroom), cleaning the urinal (toilet); cooking for members of the household; ironing; washing cars; cleaning gutters; clearing pig droppings; and fetching water. These tasks were often undertaken under harsh conditions. The children were expected to undertake tasks that were difficult for them and for which no training had been provided. For instance, 15-year-old Nigerian girl, Halima, explained that:

> because some work that I used to do here I've never do it one day for my parents. But this one self some work that you cannot do they will force you to do it so you can't have the chance to tell them that you can't do this thing.

Some of the children had to walk long distances to get water for the household. They cooked for the household but could not eat until the employer and their families had eaten.

In addition to the domestic tasks undertaken, a number of the children were contributing to their employer's domestic economy by engaging in various commercial activities. Thorsen's (2012) research on West and Central Africa indicates that in addition to domestic tasks, children in low-income households are often required to engage in income-generating activities. Oloko's (1991) work with street children in Nigeria draws attention to the number of children who undertook commercial activities such as hawking various items on the streets for their employers. Many children seen on the streets of Ibadan (a metropolitan city in south-western Nigeria) were actually domestic workers involved in their employer's commercial enterprises. The child domestic workers cooked and sold food in chop bars (restaurants) in smoke-filled kitchens, under intense heat. A few of the children cooked food such as *akara* (bean cakes) which was sold in front of the house. Other food items included fried fish and the sale of provisions (groceries) in the market and in front of their employers' houses. Some employers had cold rooms in the house where the children sold frozen items such as fish and chicken. The children complained about having to constantly pound *fufu* (a local dish), fetch water, and hew and carry heavy firewood for cooking. Most of the children hawked items such as packaged water and sold phone/call cards on the streets and in the market place. The children spoke of the dangers encountered while hawking on the streets and working in bars and restaurants. Such dangers included working under extreme heat on major motorways; the danger of being knocked down by cars; rape of both boys and girls; theft of their goods and sales money; sexual harassment while working on the streets and bars; and punishment by their employers when insufficient sales were made.

Domestic work is associated with chores within the family which means that hours of work for domestic workers are rarely defined (Bourdillon *et al.*, 2009). Jacquemin (2004) reported that no 'little maid' in Abidjan works fewer than 11 hours a day. The child domestic workers involved in this research lacked definite working hours and were on call 24 hours a day as living with their employers blurred the lines of their working hours. Living with their employers heightened their exploitative situation as there is no division between the place of work and the place of rest. They often had inadequate time to sleep as some of the children took care of employers' babies during the night and some others attended to their employer's needs day and night. These often included the needs of other members of the household such as the employer's children and relatives. For instance, 13-year-old Ghanaian girl, Agatha, lived with a woman whom she referred to as grandma. Grandma had a problem with her leg and Agatha was required to pull (massage) grandma's leg with *koto* (a local ointment) anytime she was in pain. Agatha complained that sometimes she was up late at night pulling Grandma's leg. These children were often the first in the household to wake up with their activities commencing once they woke up in the morning. Wake-up time varied on average between 4 a.m. and 6 a.m. in the morning. However, in some instances the children woke up earlier to undertake additional tasks as prescribed by their employer. For children who found it difficult to wake up in the morning, shouting of their names, slaps from their employer, or in one case a splash of cold water on the face from the employer were some of the methods employed to wake them up. Some employers issued threats to children who woke up late. For instance, 15-year-old Ghanaian girl, Tabitha, explained that her employer threatened to sack her each time she woke up late for her morning tasks.

Bedtime was not as clear cut as wake-up times as this was dependent on the employer, completion of household tasks, and sleeping arrangements. Only a minority of the children had designated sleeping places, and the children slept in locations ranging from bedrooms, to front rooms, living rooms, corridors, hallways, bars, and stores. For instance, 16-year-old Ghanaian boy, Kweku, slept on a mattress in the bar he managed for his employer. Most of the children had to wait till their employer went to bed but it was harder for the children who slept in communal areas as they had to wait until the area was clear before they could go to bed. For instance, 15-year-old Nigerian girl, Halima's bedtime was dependent on the time her employer went to bed: 'well they sleep anytime, we used to sleep like 10.30 to 11.

Almost sometimes to 12 because if them [employer and family] no sleep I won't sleep.'

The children's accounts of their day indicated a cyclical nature which involved the daily repetition of tasks, leaving them with hardly any respite as each day rolled into each other in an unending cycle of work. Rita, a 12-year-old Ghanaian girl, provides an account of her day:

> In the morning, when I wake up, sometimes when I am in the afternoon [school shift], I will wash the clothes and I will sweep the compound. After sweeping the compound, I will eat my breakfast. Then I will go and sell water at the market. When I sell the water and the time is 11.30, I'll come home and bathe, and go to school. Then I come to school. After the school, when we close, when I come home, when I go home, my mother [non-biological] is selling porridge at the roadside. So I will help her doing the porridge, and I will sell something, some chairs at the roadside. After I finish that thing, I will go to the market and sell water again. After selling the water, I'll come and sit at the roadside. After the porridge will finish, then we come home. Sometimes it finish at 11.00, sometimes at 12 o'clock, sometimes 10 o'clock, when I will come home. When we come home, early, I will put the bowls down and I will went to sleep. After the morning come, then I will sweep again.

The children complained that their employer always had tasks for the children to undertake. It would seem that they needed to ensure that the children were constantly engaged in an activity. Fourteen-year-old Ghanaian girl, Faustina, believed her employer could not stand to see her idle or resting:

> When I was helping the woman and the woman come, if I am thinking, she will come and tell me that I should go and sweep. If the job has finished in the house, she will come and tell me that the bowl she and her husband have eaten, I should go and wash it. I will go and wash it, after that if I am sitting down, I will go and take a book and she will come and slap me that I should go and do this.

The children's endless cycle of work is reinforced by Faustina's comment that she wasn't allowed time to think. This was reiterated by most of the children and some complained that they had to work even when they were ill. Sixteen-year-old Ghanaian girl, Kate, for instance, said:

> What I don't like is if maybe I am sick and I told her that today I will not go and sell then she said I am lying because I don't want to go and sell... then she will allow [make/force] me to go and sell.

Detecting the number of children working in domestic service is beyond human capabilities. But, according to the International Labour Organization

(ILO), more girls under 16 worldwide are engaged in domestic service than any other kind of employment (Plan UK, 2009). The domestic realm is traditionally regarded as the domain of women and children (Plan UK, 2009). Hence, in many countries girls are required to undertake these roles in preparation to become better wives and mothers in the future. Domestic work is so common place that it is hardly regarded as employment but the nature of work and its performance within the household creates an ambiguous relationship that is reflected in the way the children are treated. They work and live with the family but are not treated as part of the family thereby making them vulnerable to exploitation and abuse. This notwithstanding, despite the challenges the children face, many child domestic workers see benefits in the work that they do. For most of the children, domestic work was a means to an end as it offered opportunities that they would not otherwise have had access to.

Benefits of child domestic work

Child domestic work offers a number of benefits to children who undertake such work. The idea that domestic work is safe often makes it a vocation of choice for girls, with parents expressing a preference to send girls into domestic service (Black, 2002). Sixty-three of the child domestic workers involved in this research left their homes in the rural areas to go to the cosmopolitan cities of Accra and Lagos. The children often spoke of a rural crisis in which access to education, jobs, social amenities, and facilities such as electricity and pipe-borne water was difficult. Seventeen-year-old Ghanaian boy, Musa, showed the contrast of his life in the northern region of Ghana to life in the city of Accra:

> I like everything here because this is a city. We have water and I don't go far away for water. Electricity is also a good thing because I have never seen light before in my life until I came to the city. I have the chance to watch television set... I can tell you that before Allah and man I really love Accra.

Most of the child domestic workers spoke of their excitement at the prospect of moving to the city. For them, it was an opportunity to improve their lives and those of their families. Jacquemin (2004) highlighted the significance of the city to the child domestic workers in Abidjan. Going to Abidjan was seen as 'promotion', as 'bettering oneself'. For instance, 15-year-old Ghanaian girl, Miriam, expressed her excitement at being told she was moving to Accra. She saw it as an opportunity to better herself and make her family proud. Related to this, was the desire for better prospects and particularly the desire to obtain quality education which was lacking in their villages of origin. The majority of the children left home with the view to obtaining formal education or some form of vocational training. In one instance, 14-year-old

Ghanaian girl, Ama, linked her excitement of moving to the city to the opportunity to access an education:

Evelyn: What do you like about living in Accra?
Ama: Because I want to finish my school and I want to be educate so that I will become someone in the future.

Over half the child domestic workers involved in this research attended schools in their homes of origin but they regarded education in the city to be of better quality. For most of the children, the schools in their villages were far from their homes, the quality was low as it was difficult to recruit teachers to areas where there was no water or electricity, and the nearest hospital was miles away. The schools were often not equipped with facilities such as chairs, tables, and books. The idea that education in the city was of better quality than what was offered in the villages is highlighted in the case of 10-year-old Ghanaian girl, Afua:

> I was going to school at my place but they don't hear English so he [her father] brought me here to hear English so that if am going to my home town I can speak it then people will know that am coming from Accra.

For Afua's father, a key indicator of an education was the ability to speak English, the achievement of which represented a marked difference from the education offered in Afua's home town. In several instances, parents and children actively sought opportunities for the children to better them- selves by moving to the cities. Flores-Oebanda (2006) argues that the pri- mary motivation of many children entering into domestic service is the desire for a quality education. For the children, the lure or the appeal of the city was often the chance to be educated as a number of the children were promised an education in exchange for the provision of domestic services. Ondimu's (2007) work in Nairobi and Hashim's (2005) work in Ghana high- light this trend where migration offers the children the opportunity to access school or training in exchange for their labour. Hashim (2003) and Ondimu (2007) highlight the propensity of rural children migrating to work as domestic workers in the urban centres with the idea that domestic labour can be a pathway to education. Ondimu (2007) further highlights that some of the children are lured to move to urban areas with a promise to further their education. Some of the child domestic workers earn money to go to school while others exchange their labour for the opportunity to attend school. Other benefits highlighted in the literature (Bourdillon, 2009) include the fact that income from domestic work improves the lives of the children and their families. Despite the benefits that domestic work offers to many children, millions of children find themselves in exploitative and abu- sive situations.

The children's perception of best interests

Discussions with the children on the subject of best interests often revealed the children's pragmatism and their demonstration of agency. Child workers' demonstration of agency is often presented through their decision to work and the pride they take in their work (Liebel, 2004; Bourdillon, 2009). The strategies they employ to survive as child labourers further demonstrate their agency (Hashim, 2007; Ondimu, 2007; Mizen and Ofosu-Kusi, 2013). However, their expression of agency through their ability to endure their negative circumstances by projecting themselves into the future has scarcely been addressed. In the group sessions undertaken with this group of child domestic workers, there was a general consensus that it was better for a child to be with their biological parents. In one instance Afua believed a child should be with his/her biological mother:

Evelyn: So do you think that a child should stay with the father and the mother or should stay with other people?
Afua: They should stay with their mother.
Evelyn: Why?
Afua: Because what their mother is treating them is not like here that they are treating them.

Nevertheless the children placed a caveat that this was only possible when the parents were alive and were able to take care of the children. However, over half the child domestic workers who participated in the study felt it was in their best interests to live with their employers. The children's determination of their best interests was often based on the benefits they obtained from living with their employers as opposed to living with their parents. Fifteen-year-old Ghanaian girl, Esther, explained the basis of her preference for living with her employer: 'Because maybe when I finish school my mother will not get money to send me to school.'

The children's focus on their future and their lives as domestic workers was a means to an end. The believed it was in their best interests to stay with their employers in order to secure a better future. They aspired to be educated as they believed this would secure their future. This emerged in the interview with 16-year-old Ghanaian girl, Naadua:

Evelyn: If you had the opportunity to go back home, would you go back home?
Naadua: I want to finish schooling here then get a nice future. I don't want to go back there so that my schooling will stop. I want to continue everything.

Like so many working children, education was a key consideration for child domestic workers. In another instance, 12-year-old Ghanaian girl, Adjoa, created a link between schooling and wealth: 'I want to attend school and become a big and a wealthy woman.'

The children placed a high premium on education and linked it to obtaining respect in the society and becoming a 'somebody'. For instance, 17-year-old Ghanaian girl, Agnes, explained that:

> In Ghana, this world if you haven't go to school before or if you don't have your own job, nobody will respect you or even *po* [expression of distaste] you won't get any money to buy food.

In another instance, 16-year-old Ghanaian girl, Mabel, pointed out that: 'In Ghana now, the situation is changing and without education, you are nobody.'

Despite the challenges the children faced, the children believed it was in their best interests to endure life as child domestics in order to secure their future. This belief in education as the means to obtaining a nice future keeps some children in domestic labour. For instance, 15-year-old Nigerian girl, Halima, was taken from the northern part of Nigeria under false pretences. Her parents agreed for her to be taken to Jos (also in northern Nigeria) to live with a family friend, but without the knowledge of her parents, she was taken to Lagos (in the south west of the country) to provide domestic services. She was not allowed to use the home phone to call her parents and she had no money to do so herself. She was not happy with the treatment she received but despite her situation, she was particularly interested in the fact that she was being sent to school:

Evelyn: Why would you stay in Lagos?
Halima: Because I like the person and if you put me for school. But if the person treat me well and no school, I didn't think I can live with that person.
Evelyn: But if you are in school and the person is not treating you well, will you still stay?
Halima: Yes I will stay because I came to look for something and I have see it so I have to wait. I'm a human, one day I will leave, one day you will be surprised.

In another instance, 15-year-old Ghanaian girl, Miriam, although not happy with the treatment she received, did not want to go back home if given the opportunity:

Evelyn: If you had an opportunity to go back, will you go back?
Miriam: No.
Evelyn: Why?
Miriam: Because I want to study. I want to become what I want.

Bourdillon (2009) draws attention to how the possible benefits of work for children might override the hazards. He argues that working children often value the opportunities work offers for the future, a factor that weighs more heavily for them than any hazards work may involve (Bourdillon *et al.*, 2009). His work with child domestic workers in Zimbabwe indicates that despite the complaints the children had about their work, fewer than half of them wanted to stop working (Bourdillon, 2007). The child domestic workers involved in this study had complaints about their employers and did not think children should have to work but they responded to their situations by taking decisions they felt were in their best interests. Like so many child domestic workers, the children were unhappy with their lives as domestic workers but they made pragmatic decisions based on the benefits they obtained from living with their employer rather than on their situation as child domestics. Their decisions reflected what they believed to be in their best interests, but these were not always compatible with international perception of best interests.

In the best interests of the child domestic worker

Weston (2005) defines child labour as work done by children that is harmful to them or otherwise contrary to their best interests. Myers and Boyden (1998) interpret activities that are detrimental to children's educational, health, physical, and psychological development to be inconsistent with the children's best interests. The situation of many child domestics has been likened to intolerable child labour, a modern form of slavery (Black, 2002; Blagbrough, 2008), and one of the worst forms of labour requiring urgent eradication (ILO, 2007). The CRC recognizes the right of children to be protected from economic exploitation and from work which is likely to be hazardous, which interferes with their education, or is harmful to their health or physical, mental, spiritual, moral, or social development (Article 32). In addition, the African Charter on the Rights and Welfare of the Child also states that 'every child should be protected from all forms of economic exploitation and from performing any work that is likely to be hazardous or to interfere with the child's physical, mental, spiritual, moral or social development'.

In line with international conventions and the principle of best interests, child domestic workers should perceive domestic work as inconsistent with their best interests. However, the actual realities of these children and the views they present conflict with international perceptions of their rights and best interests. Reynolds *et al.* (2006) refer to this tension as a refraction of children's rights, where the practice of the language of rights, enshrined in international policies, clashes with the actual realities of children's lives and the priorities children set for themselves. International standards regard these children as requiring protection from harm and exploitation – i.e.

removal from their employer's homes and sending back to their families in the villages. However, children make conscious decisions in response to dire circumstances. Such interventions seemingly undertaken in the best interests of the children would clash with the priorities the children set for themselves and infringe on what the children regard as their best interests. Thus tension is created between the state's obligation to protect children on the one hand and the agency children exercise on the other hand, and there is a need to strike a balance when addressing these tensions. Are we to ignore international standards and allow children to be harmed and exploited by the work that they do or do we intervene in their lives and deny them the opportunity for better prospects? In the situation of these children, what they consider to be in their best interests goes beyond their conditions of work and their experience of life as child domestics. Their notion of best interests is closely linked to their perception of their future and how they negotiate what is best for them. Mizen and Ofosu-Kusi (2013) argue that principle of best interests enshrined in international conventions must confront the detours established by the priorities and aspirations that children knowingly set for themselves. Without this consideration, there is a real risk of obscuring 'alternatives that may be more sensible, more realistic and more attractive to the children concerned' (Reynolds *et al.*, 2006: 292). The principle of best interests is of no effect if it does not consider children's perceptions of their best interests particularly when these are markedly different from international conceptions of best interests.

Conclusion

The notion of best interests is relative and complex particularly in the case of child domestic workers. In determining the best interests of child domestic workers, it is imperative to recognize that they are individuals with the capacity to negotiate their lives within the confines of their situation, and to consider the strategies employed by this group of children to secure their future. Children set priorities for themselves and the intention of the best interests principle is lost if interventions targeted at child domestic workers produce contradictory effects or outcomes conflicting with the children's definition of their best interests. The children's account of their lives as domestic workers indicates the need for protection. But in trying to determine what is best for child domestic workers, it is imperative that their definition of best interests be taken into consideration, particularly when they define their best interests in ways which are markedly different. It is not feasible to solely use the views of children to determine their best interests, but it is possible to consider what they define as their best interests in relation to interventions targeted at them. In the case of these child domestic workers, education is the driving force. Therefore, the focus should be on providing the means to achieve quality education both in the rural and urban centres which will, to a large extent, reduce the need for children to become child domestic workers.

Children are social actors who to some extent are able to negotiate and impact upon their lives. As argued by Cunningham (2005, in Bourdillon, 2006), failure to consider the agency of children has resulted in an unrealistic view of children that has become dominant in developed societies. Until the views of working children are considered, what child domestic workers define as their best interests will be at odds with the ideals of the CRC's principle of best interests.

References

Anti-Slavery International (2013) 'What is child labour?' (available online at <http://www.antislavery.org/english/slavery_today/child_labour.aspx>) (accessed on 16 July 2013).

Apt, N.A. (2005) *A Study of Child Domestic Work and Fosterage in Northern and Upper East Regions of Ghana*, Accra: Centre for Social Policy Studies, University of Ghana Legon, UNICEF.

Black, M. (2002) *A Handbook on Advocacy. Child Domestic Workers: Finding a Voice*, London: Anti-Slavery International.

Blagbrough, J. (2008) *They Respect their Animals more: Voices of Child Domestic Workers*, London: Anti-Slavery International.

Blagbrough, J. and Glynn, E. (1999) 'Child domestic workers: characteristics of the modern slave and approaches to ending such exploitation', *Childhood*, 6: 51–6.

Bourdillon, M.F.C. (2006) 'Children and work: a review of current literature and debates', *Development and Change*, 37 (6): 1201–26.

Bourdillon, M.F.C. (2007) 'Child domestic workers in Zimbabwe: children's perspectives', in B. Hungerland et al. (eds) *Working to be Someone: Child Focused Research and Practice with Working Children*, London and Philadelphia, PA: Jessica Kingsley.

Bourdillon, M.F.C. (2009) 'Children as domestic employees: problems and promises', *Journal of Child Poverty*, 15 (1): 1–8.

Bourdillon, M.F.C., Levinson, D., White, B., and Myers, W.E. (2009) A Place for Work in Children's Lives? Plan Canada (available online at <http://plancanada.ca/downloads/A%20place%20for%20work%20in%20children's%20lives.pdf>) (accessed on 16 July 2013).

Cunningham, H. and Stromquist, S. (2005) 'Child labour and the rights of children: historical patterns of decline and persistence', in B. Weston (ed.) *Child Labor and Human Rights: Making Children Matter*, Boulder, CO and London: Lynne Rienner.

Flores-Oebanda, C. (2006) 'Addressing vulnerability and exploitation of child domestic workers: an open challenge to end a hidden shame.' United Nations Division for the Advancement of Women (DAW) in collaboration with UNICEF Expert Group Meeting 'Elimination of all forms of discrimination and violence against the girl child', Florence: UNICEF Innocenti Research Centre.

Hashim, I. (2003) 'Child migration: pathological or positive?' Paper presented to the Conference on Child Abuse and Exploitation: Social, Legal and Political Dilemmas, Onati, Spain, 29–30 May.

Hashim, I. (2005) *Exploring the Linkages between Children's Independent Migration and Education: Evidence from Ghana*, Brighton: Development Research Centre on Migration, Globalization and Poverty, University of Sussex.

Hashim, I. (2007) 'Independent child migration and education in Ghana', *Development and Change*, 38 (5): 911–31.

ILO (2004) *Helping Hands or Shackled Lives? Understanding Child Domestic Labour and Responses to it*, Geneva: ILO/IPEC.

ILO (2007) *Hazardous Child Domestic Work: A Briefing Sheet*, Geneva: ILO.

ILO (2013) 'Ending child labour in domestic work and protecting young workers from abusive conditions' (World Day against Child Labour report), Geneva: ILO.

Jacquemin, M. (2004) 'Children's domestic work in Abidjan, Cote D'Ivoire, the petites bonnes have the floor', *Childhood*, 11 (3): 383–97.

Jacquemin, M. (2006) 'Can the language of rights get hold of the complex realities of child domestic work: the case of young domestic workers in Abidjan, Ivory Coast', *Childhood*, 13: 389–406.

Jacquemin, M. (2009) 'Invisible young female migrant workers: "little domestics" in West Africa. Comparative perspectives on girls and young women's work', in *Child and Youth Migration in West Africa: Knowledge Gaps and Implications for Policy*, Paris: African Studies Centre EHESS/IRD.

Kielland, A and Tovo, M. (2006) Children at Work: Child Labour Practices in Africa, Boulder, CO: Lynne Reinner.

Klocker, N., Robson, E., and Bell, S. (2007) 'Conceptualising agency in the lives and actions of rural young people', in R. Panelli *et al.* (eds) *Global Perspectives on Rural Childhood and Youth: Young Rural Lives*, London: Routledge.

Liebel, M. (2004) *A Will of their Own? Cross Cultural Perspectives on Working Children*, London: Zed books.

Mizen, P. and Ofosu-Kusi, Y. (2013) 'A talent for living: exploring Ghana's "new" urban childhood', *Children and Society*, 27: 13–23.

Myers, W. and Boyden, J. (1998) *Child Labour: Promoting the Best Interest of Working Children*, London: Save the Children.

Oloko, B.A. (1991) 'Children's work in urban Nigeria: a case study of young Lagos street traders', in W.E. Myer (ed.) *Protecting Working Children*, London: Zed Books.

Ondimu, K.N. (2007) 'Workplace violence among domestic workers in urban households in Kenya: a case of Nairobi city', *Eastern Africa Social Science Review*, 23 (1): 37–61.

Panelli, R., Punch, S., and Robson, E. (eds) (2007) *Global Perspectives on Rural Childhood and Youth: Young Rural Lives*, London: Routledge.

Plan UK (2009) *The State of the World's Girls. Because I am a Girl: Girls in the Global Economy: Adding it all up*, London: *Plan UK* (available online at <http://plan-international. org/files/global/publications/campaigns/BIAAG%20Summary%20ENGLISH%20 lo_resolution.pdf>) (accessed on 30 May 2013).

Reynolds, P., Nieuwenhuys, O., and Hanson, K. (2006) 'Refractions of children's rights in development practice: a view from anthropology', *Childhood*, 13: 291–302.

Thorsen, D. (2012) *Child Domestic Workers: Evidence from West and Central Africa*, Dakar-Yoff, Senegal: UNICEF.

UNHCR (2008) *Guidelines on Determining the Best Interest of the Child* (available online at <http://www.essex.ac.uk/armedcon/story_id/000821.pdf>) (accessed on 12 March 2013).

United Nations (2005) General Comment No. 7 by the Committee on the Rights of the Child, Fortieth Session, Geneva, 12–30 September, 'Implementing child rights

in early childhood' (available online at http://www2.ohchr.org/english/bodies/
crc/docs/AdvanceVersions/GeneralComment7Rev1.pdf) (accessed on 21 August
2013).

Weston, B. (ed.) (2005) *Child Labor and Human Rights: Making Children Matter*, Boulder,
CO and London: Lynne Rienner.

Zermatten, J. (2010) *The Best Interest of the Child: Literal Analysis, Function and Implementation* (working report of the Institut International Des troit De Lenfants) (available
online at www.childrights.org) (accessed on 13 March 2013).

Why are aspirations for children in Tanzania not translating into substantive change?

Kate McAlpine

Introduction

The purpose of this chapter is, first, to remind readers of the centrality of children if development outcomes are to be achieved in a country where over 50% of the population is under the age of eighteen and, secondly, to provide evidence that differences in progress in realizing child rights in the domains of survival, education, and health can be attributed to the comfort of policy-makers and public planners with the technical aspects of development over human development. I argue that there is a virtuous cycle between realizing children's rights and fostering human development and this requires that space be created for a multiplicity of perspectives. A rights discourse by itself does not do this because it does not offer strategies or approaches that support behavioural change or the development of more compassionate forms of relationships, which are ultimately fundamental to ensuring that children's rights are advanced.

This chapter starts with me locating my own interest, history, and bias as a scholar-activist. I do this because there is never a perspective-free universe and we enact our reality from our own developmental gravity.

After introducing the backdrop of Tanzania's extraordinary demographics, the rapid pace of social and economic transition, generalized insecurity, and the diverse lifestyle, cultural, and social worldviews of its people, I suggest that national development plans and priorities have focused on monolithic responses that require technical and financial inputs controlled from the centre of government. This is instead of supporting families and communities to use their own local knowledge, what is known in Swahili as *maarifa*, to nurture the best interests of their children.

I back up this assertion by conducting a child rights audit of progress in the domains of child survival, education, and protection, exploring whether the commitments made by the government when it ratified the United Nations Convention on the Rights of the Child (CRC) and the African Charter on the Rights and Welfare of the Child (ACRWC) have translated into real change for children. I chose these domains because in spite of similarities in the scope and impacts of the problems facing Tanzanian children each domain has seen substantively different levels of investment and attention, has been subject to varying approaches, and thus has achieved vastly different outcomes for children. I attribute this to a comfort with technical interventions over the more complex business of engaging with humans and their diverse worldviews, the effects of chronic stress on people's functioning, and the partiality of a child rights discourse, in spite of its claims to universalism.

What do I bring to the table?

I start this chapter with a brief introduction of myself. Openness about how I identify and understand myself is important because in the absence of a perspective-free universe we all understand reality in a certain way. We also all create reality depending on our histories, and on our cognitive and ego development that determines our meaning-making and perspective-taking capacities (Wilber, 2003; Fuhs, n.d.). My perspective is informed by how I identify myself, by my own developmental level of gravity, by my emotional and physical state in the moment, and by the disciplinary 'baggage' that I bring to my analysis.

I identify myself as a scholar-activist who works across disciplinary and geographic boundaries and on the inter-section between scholarship, practice, and activism. My worldview is underpinned by a commitment to social justice and a belief in universal human rights. But, in my work in child protection and in facilitating large-scale social change I increasingly see a tension between universalist and particularistic approaches to facilitating individual and collective development, and it is this tension that I try to explore in this chapter.

My own developmental level shifts depending on my state (Wilber, 2006). Am I tired? Am I emotionally balanced? When I am out of sorts I become limited and show concern for members of my own group, understanding phenomena through the comfort zone of my own education and socialization. But, when I am at my best I am better able to take up a world-centric concern that honours all humans regardless of group distinctions, that recognizes the inter-connectedness between phenomena, and that integrates understanding of people's emotions and behaviours within their contextual system and culture.

My personal experience informs this chapter because I believe that a similar tension occurs in the realization of child rights. While the text of the Convention honours all individuals and makes explicit reference to ending discrimination, the Convention is also a set of injunctions that guide how we should behave towards children. The underlying paradox is that the Convention offers no strategies to equip individuals or states to take up new practices towards children. The aspirations of the Convention become undermined by our own human frailties. It is thus the argument of this chapter that emphasis now needs to be placed on supporting the moral and emotional development of individuals and groups so that they are better able to demonstrate consistent compassion and empathy for children, particularly those children who lie outside their immediate familial circle of care.

In this chapter I draw on the work of Ken Wilber (1996, 1997, 1998) who emphasizes that it is impossible to fully understand the experience of being human without exploring the domains of the individual's subjective and objective experience and the group's inter-subjective and inter-objective worlds. My framing of human development draws on the work of Kegan (1982) who studied the process of identity development, Beck and Cowan (1996) who look at values development, Piaget (1975) who pioneered study into children's cognitive development, and Kohlberg and Mayer (1972) who explored moral development. All adopted a structuralist approach to studying humans' interior realities. Their goal, no matter which line of development they were studying, was to reveal the internality codes or agency that awareness follows. While many academics are 'sceptical of the principles of hierarchy... and therefore seek to deconstruct any concepts and structures that presuppose order, rationality, and the need for control' (Fuhs, n.d.: 17), the hierarchical nature of human development cannot be judged as either good, or bad. It is purely that as human awareness becomes increasingly complex it is able to encompass, transcend, and include the awareness that came before.

My interest in writing this chapter lies in scrutinizing why and where progress in realizing child rights has stalled. In my own research I have found that adults only rarely refer to children's rights as a motivator for the protective actions that they take towards children (McAlpine, 2013b). And yet the Tanzanian Government, non-governmental organizations (NGOs), and international donor partners pay homage to the discourse of rights, if not to their practice. I hope that this chapter will provoke the reader to at least question whether real change for children can be achieved only through reliance on a child rights discourse. I hope that the reader will bring different perspectives and that together, albeit at a distance from each other, we can co-create new questions and new insights into the state of child rights in Tanzania.

The backdrop to child rights in Tanzania

I describe here the backdrop of Tanzania's extraordinary demographics, the rapid pace of social and economic transition, and the diverse lifestyle, cultural, and social choices of its people. I do so to provide context for my subsequent argument that despite this diversity, national development plans and priorities have focused on monolithic responses that require technical and financial inputs controlled from the centre of government, rather than supporting families and communities to use their local knowledge to nurture the best interests of their children.

Demographics

Tanzania can be characterized as a youth bulge state (National Intelligence Council, 2008). In its 2002 census, children constituted more than 50% of Tanzania's population. With an annual population growth rate of 2.9%, Tanzanian children now significantly outnumber the country's adults (National Bureau of Statistics, 2011). However, their rights and needs continue to be considered non-essential to development efforts (UNICEF Tanzania, 2012).

Neither birth rates nor death rates have changed substantively over the past ten years, but Tanzania has a massively young population whereby 52.4% of people are between the ages of 16 and 24 years (National Bureau of Statistics, 2011). This means that Tanzania faces a demographic tipping point as its working-age population grows and its dependency ratio falls. Scenario planners such as Evans (2011) project that countries with such demographics could face social revolutions characterized by out-migration, unemployment, political violence, and civil conflict. But, an alternative and more optimistic view is that the young population could catalyse a developmental shift within the entire country. This would occur as people take up a socio-centric perspective that places emphasis on interpersonal communication, majority rule, community harmony, and equality, and as they explore with others the caring dimension of community (Beck and Cowan, 1996). This would result in social transformation, but it will not occur without an investment in progressive social initiatives that invest in children's survival, education, protection, and participation. Should the investment and transformation take place, Tanzania would witness a virtuous cycle that results in the better fulfilment of children's rights.

Economic transition and generalized insecurity

Tanzania is facing a period of rapid transition as its economy shifts from a moral economy to a market economy (Manjolo *et al.*, 2008). Socioeconomic development, urbanization, and technological change caused Tanzania to leapfrog the Industrial Age and the country has almost no manufacturing economic base. Rather, the country is characterized by a diverse combination of subsistence and cash-crop farming, pastoralism, and a small number of urban service industries.

Generalized insecurity is prevalent. The incidence of poverty is high and social protection is low, leaving only a few pockets of robust socioeconomic security among those who are at the very top of the country's income distribution (Wuyts, 2006). Macro-economic growth has not translated into reductions in household poverty levels for most Tanzanians. In fact, 34% of Tanzanians fell below the basic-needs poverty line in 2007 (Government of the United Republic of Tanzania, 2007a).

Diverse worldviews

Worldviews are the deep structures and surface features that determine the meaning that individuals give to their behaviour (McAlpine, 2013b) and Tanzania's varying socioeconomic bases are mirrored by diverse cultures and social norms, all of which have value, legitimacy, and relevance to their context. Many of these particularistic ways of seeing the world do not concur with the notion of universal rights and the reader should not assume that child rights is an uncontested notion in many communities.

Human development has been understood as a hierarchical process whereby each stage is not better than that which comes before, but is certainly better able to deal with complexity. Thus the development of cognition, values, and morals is a staged approach (Kohlberg and Mayer, 1972; Piaget, 1975; Beck and Cowan, 1996). Wilber (2002) argues that 'politically correct coercive movements' consider it politically incorrect and lacking in reflexivity to characterize one group of people as less developed than another; or to consider modernism or postmodernism 'more developed' than what came before. I concur with him that the point is not that one stage of development is better than another, but that developmental stages mirror and adapt to the socioeconomic base of a population.

Thus in Tanzania the diverse socioeconomic base and the rapidly changing context of urbanization are creating an imperative for people to develop capacities for new cognitive, moral, and interpersonal competencies that will enable them to better thrive in this new environment. For example, over millennia the hunter gatherers such as the WaHadzabe, who are the last full-time hunter-gatherers in Africa, thrived in their ethnocentric tribal configuration where the world was perceived as being orderly, predictable, and controllable and where morality was dictated by the desire to be considered good by their peers. This is no longer viable for them because the boundaries of their social world have become porous, they are exposed to others who want their land, and are forced to engage with the operations of the state in a way that they have never known. Consequently, there is a pressure on them to build their capacities to deal with a complex and rapidly changing world.

Similar dynamics are at play with the small, nascent middle class, which represents pockets of robust socioeconomic security in Tanzania. Many of these individuals grew up in villages with families who were peasants or pastoralists. Since universal primary education became a reality for people in 2001, with the abolition of school fees, many urban dwellers have been educated through the formal school system that values rationality and reasoning, morality that is premised on ethical principles rather than on relationships, and beliefs that people are entitled to a certain set of rights, individual dignity, and self-respect. The complexity of these worldviews is neither better nor worse than those of the WaHadzabe. Function is following form – the form of the urban, modern world demands a worldview that is different from that needed in a traditional society.

Tanzania is grappling with this transition. The discourse and practice of international development are at its heart – a question of how individuals and nations build ability to deal with increasing complexity, while holding on to the historical, spiritual, and practical values that were inherent to their ancestral worldviews. The tension as I see it, in the domain of children's rights in Tanzania, is that a rush to rationality creates reverberations and instabilities between the perspectives that individuals carry over from their childhoods in the village and the behaviours that are considered acceptable by the modern world.

Thus, Tanzanians now live in a country where development is the over-riding imperative in political discourse, but development is primarily positioned as a set of economic interventions. Even education, which is the government's primary site of long-term stimulus, is positioned as an economic intervention to build a society of employable citizens (Revolutionary Government of Zanzibar, 2006; Government of United Republic of Tanzania, 2007c). The national strategies for poverty reduction are monolithic development plans that rely on foreign investment and macro-economic growth and position humans as cogs in the wheel. While homage is paid to children's rights and community empowerment, there has been little discussion of such matters in the mainstream of political life since the days of Nyerere (1967, 1968; see also Chachage and Cassam, 2010).

In the child rights audit that I now conduct I provide evidence that despite Tanzania's cultural and social diversity, national development plans and priorities have focused on technical and financial inputs that are controlled from the centre of government, rather than supporting families and communities to use their local solutions or *maarifa* to nurture the best interests of their children. The result of this has been progress, particularly in the domains of children's access to education and health services, but as this progress slows there is a real need to start engaging with human development rather than relying on technical quick fixes.

A child rights audit in the domains of survival, education, and protection

This child rights audit of progress in the domains of survival, education, and protection has been conducted using three approaches. I draw on data and thinking in UNICEF's comprehensive situational analysis of women and children, of which I was a lead researcher (McAlpine *et al.*, 2009). I also review recent secondary demographic data, media commentary, and local research findings and finally I draw on the thinking and research of the Caucus for Children's Rights, a Tanzanian local development network, about the impacts of violence against children. I chose to focus on the three sectors of survival, education, and protection because although the negative impacts of the problems in the health, education, and protection sectors are similar in scope, each has received substantively different levels of investment, attention, and approach from the Tanzanian government and their international donor partners and they thus have achieved quite different outcomes for children.

The extent of the problem and the impact on children and society

Child survival is a key site of intervention for the Tanzanian Government in line with its commitment to advance Millennium Development Goal (MDG) 4 to reduce child mortality. Each year 50,000 children die in their first month of life (Government of the United Republic of Tanzania, 2008a). One in twelve children do not live to see their fifth birthday (Government of the United Republic of Tanzania and Macro International, 2005).

In Tanzania the wealthiest children are 22% more likely to survive beyond their fifth birthday than their poorest peers. This can be attributed partly to the underlying social determinants of health and partly due to the inequitable distribution of government health resources across districts whereby the most prosperous receive relatively and absolutely more income than those districts that are larger, but poorer (National Bureau of Statistics, 2010).

A consultation with children about their experience in clinics conducted by Save the Children (2007) revealed that falling ill is a real problem for them, particularly when their parents are unable to pay for health services. Often their carers borrow money for treatment, visit a local witch doctor, or keep the child at home and hope they will get better. In the same consultation children complained of routinely waiting for long periods to receive treatment at clinics, rarely seeing the same doctor or nurse when they come for an appointment, and only infrequently receiving age-appropriate information about what is happening or being encouraged to ask questions.

Children's access to primary and secondary education has improved considerably since 2001, when primary school fees were abolished. The focus is now on achieving improvements in the quality of education and in addressing the inequity of teacher distribution and school resourcing which means that poorer regions have fewer teachers than wealthier regions and schools in remote areas have fewer teachers than those in urban centres.

It is in the domain of child protection that I have the most engagement through my work with the Caucus for Children's Rights (CCR). Here I draw on their thinking that violence against children is Tanzania's greatest developmental challenge (McAlpine, 2013a). Nearly three in 10 females and approximately one in seven males have experienced sexual violence prior to the age of 18. Almost three-quarters of both females and males experienced physical violence as a child by an adult or intimate partner. One-quarter of respondents have experienced emotional violence by an adult during childhood (UNICEF Tanzania *et al.*, 2011).

The domestic magnitude of the challenge lies not just in the humanitarian consequences of such endemic violence towards children, but in the developmental impacts as children's potential to become the human capital of the nation is being compromised. The CCR (McAlpine, 2013a) argues that as violence becomes normalized in the social norms of the country, individuals who are victims, perpetrators, and bystanders are damaged and their subjective understanding of themselves is negatively affected. They may feel fear, not believe that they have value or that they can influence their life. This affects behaviour in self-sabotaging ways. They may be unable to focus and fail to consider the consequences of their actions or take risks.

This contention was supported by a recent study that sought the voices of Tanzanians about the impact of violence on their own lives (Habdedank, 2013b). Findings revealed that pervasive child maltreatment affects both survivors and those who bear witness in ways that permeate many domains of their lives. These include making communities less safe and desirable, taking an emotional toll – it 'hurts' and causes 'pain' – and sometimes putting witnesses at personal risk because it may trigger a willingness to speak or intervene on behalf of an affected child, which can result in confrontations or conflicts (Habedank, 2013b).

Violence against children is a global problem (United Nations, 2006, 2012), but the scale of violence in Tanzania is particularly significant because both the global community and Tanzanian citizens are making such significant financial investments in education, health, agriculture, and manufacturing to promote macro-economic growth. Endemic violence against children undercuts these investments because people's experience of violence prevents them from achieving their potential. Rather than becoming productive members of society they become dependants (Habedank, 2012, 2013a). The costs of anti-social behaviour have to be borne by the state. The immediate costs associated with an increase in crime will have to be borne by the state which employs police, prison, and enforcement officers, but there is also a longer-term risk of that a critical number of disenfranchised, unemployed youth who have experienced personal and structural violence will feed political instability.

Child rights commitments made by the CRC and by the Government of Tanzania

The Convention on the Rights of the Child considers those under the age of 18 to be children who need protection because of their physical, mental, and emotional immaturity (United Nations, 1989). The Tanzanian government ratified the Convention in 1991 and the African Charter on the Rights and Welfare of the Child (ACRWC) in 2003, but the government did not follow this up with legislation until 18 years later when it domesticated the CRC into the Law of the Child Act 2009.

While during the interim period various policies, services, resources, and administrative reforms have been put in place in the health and education sectors, the Law of the Child Act was the first piece of legislation that enshrined children's fundamental rights and set out a comprehensive framework for child protection, child justice, and child labour (Government of the United Republic of Tanzania, 2009). One reason why progress in the domains of education and survival seems to be more extensive than that of protection is that only since the publication of the United Nations Study on Violence against Children (2006) has international attention of any scale been brought to bear on child protection and this is only now slowly rippling through the domestic instruments of state in Tanzania.

The Convention recognizes that every child has the inherent right to life (Article 6). It also asserts that states parties shall endeavour to ensure the survival and development of the child and to ensure that children access health care. The Law of the Child Act mirrors these commitments, emphasizing that a person shall not deprive a child of access to immunization, health, and medical care.

To advance the achievement of the Millennium Development Goals, Tanzania has a raft of health-related strategies. Key among these are the health objectives in the country's National Strategy for Growth and the Reduction of Poverty (2010–15), the Health Sector Strategic Plan, and the Primary Health Services Development Strategy, all of which focus on universal access to basic health services, albeit constrained by a limited resource base. They place the greatest emphasis on expanding health infrastructure to provide one dispensary per village and one health centre per neighbourhood or ward.

The Convention recognizes the rights of all children to education and encourages states to take measures such as the introduction of free education and offering financial assistance in case of need. Additionally, the ACRWC requires that the state take 'special measures… to ensure equal access to education for all sections of the community' (Organization of African Unity, 1990). In Tanzania, the Education Act of 1978 was amended in 2001 to make primary education free for all and the Law of the Child emphasizes that no person shall deprive a child of access to education. In Tanzania's strategy for poverty reduction education has been given priority status because of its importance in improving human capabilities in addressing poverty.

The Convention protects children from all forms of physical or mental violence, injury, abuse, neglect or negligent treatment, maltreatment or exploitation (Article 19), and from sexual abuse (Article 34). The Convention and the ACRWC also protect children from both school discipline and parental discipline that undermines their dignity.

Tanzania acceded to the Optional Protocol on the Sale of Children, Child Prostitution, and Child Pornography in April 2003 (Government of United Republic of Tanzania, 2007b). The trafficking of people, child prostitution, and pornography are also prohibited under domestic law. For the first time in Tanzanian law, the Law of the Child Act 2009 defined child abuse as a 'contravention of the rights of the child which causes physical, moral or emotional harm including beatings, insults, discrimination, neglect, sexual abuse, and exploitative labour.'

Although the Law of the Child Act was adopted in 2009 and was ratified by the President in 2010, it has remained largely unimplemented, as there are no regulations providing guidance about compliance and adherence to front-line workers. Regulations for children's homes, foster care, adoption, child employment, apprenticeships, juvenile detention and care homes, approved schools, day-care centres, and the child protection system are still in development and are not yet informing practice (UNICEF Tanzania, 2012).

Investment made and approaches used to turn commitments into practice

The key strategy towards improving children's rights to survival has been to improve their access to medical assistance through the construction of neighbourhood clinics and to develop primary health-care services. The financial investment has been huge with 4.5% of GDP being spent on health provision (equating to USD $57 per person per year) (WHO figures for 2008). But the health system emphasizes clinical services over health promotion.

The Integrated Management of Child Illnesses (IMCI) programme to combat disease and malnutrition is showing positive results with an international evaluation of IMCI finding that a 14% reduction in under-five deaths was attributable to its implementation. However, scaling up the strategy has proved to be a major challenge because of the sheer number of front-line health workers that need to be trained and the substantial gap between treatment protocols and actual practice.

There has been a massive investment in building locally accessible clinics in every neighbourhood across the country. But, there is evidence that the construction of new facilities is outpacing the government's ability to staff, equip, and supply them. The Tanzanian Ministry of Health and Social Welfare describes the human resources situation in its health sector as a 'crisis'. The Human Resources Strategic Plan (2008) envisages a tripling of the health workforce over a decade, but this vastly exceeds current production capacity as well as budgetary resources and leads to the conclusion that the strategy may be more aspirational than realistic (McAlpine *et al.*, 2009). Employment of new health sector employees by local government authorities between 2002 and 2008 averaged 1,600 per year and this is barely enough to compensate for attrition. There is also a chronic problem of mal-distribution of workers across the different regions of the country. The 'better-off' regions continue to hire staff while the poorer regions and districts do without.

The Tanzanian Government conceives of education as its primary long-term development intervention and the investment in the sector has been large with the focus on increasing children's access to primary and secondary education and reversing the decline that took place in the 1980s and the 1990s as a result of the consequences of the structural adjustment programme which hit government spending on education and brought in unaffordable user fees for students.

The government increased funding for the education sector by 112% between 2004 and 2009. However, as a share of the total government budget, the allocation to education has remained more or less constant. Further investment is still required. Over 90% of the primary education budget is spent on recurrent operational costs, and this is reflected in the under-resourcing of teacher education, which only gets 0.3% of the development budget. This has serious implications for the quality of education that children receive.

The Convention speaks of the need for protective measures for children who have been deprived of their family environment (Article 20). These include mechanisms for the prevention, identification, reporting, referral, investigation, treatment, and follow-up of instances of child maltreatment. The Law of the Child's innovation was to be explicit about the envisaged judicial and social welfare response to children who need care and protection. Under the new Law, courts can make a range of orders to remove a child from a situation where s/he is suffering or likely to suffer significant harm.

However, the law is largely hypothetical because in practice the rules and regulations pertaining to child protection are yet to be published. Only a handful of magistrates have been sensitized to ensure that their decisions advance the protective safeguards outlined in the Act. There is no central government budget for child protection and insufficient social workers exist to intervene when a child faces a situation of violence or abuse.

Efforts are underway with a number of NGOs and the Department of Social Welfare trying to build models for a child protection system. Eight districts are currently piloting multi-sectorial child protection teams. There is increasing recognition of the value of sectors working together and coordinating referrals for children. The objective is to scale up these models nationally (UNICEF Tanzania, 2012), but in the absence of a budget line for child protection it is unclear who is expected to finance these new child protection services.

The achievement of outcomes

Significant progress has been made in realizing children's rights to survival in Tanzania. There has been a reduction in under-five mortality equivalent to saving nearly 100,000 children every year. Nonetheless, the toll of under-five deaths still amounts to roughly 155,000 deaths per year. Neonatal mortality has improved, but it still accounts for approximately 30% of all under-five deaths (Government of the United Republic of Tanzania, 2008a).

The focus on investment in infrastructure and clinical care requires technical interventions. These have been prioritized over interventions that require hiring, training, managing, and nurturing community-based health professionals. The result is that survival outcomes for children have improved, but a programme of community-based integrated management of childhood illness (IMCI) has only recently begun. The effects of this can be seen in children's health status. Children are surviving, but many are unable to reach their potential because their health is so compromised. Out of every 100 children under the age of five years, 38 are stunted, 72 are anaemic, one-third were sick during the previous two weeks, and two-thirds lack access to an improved latrine. There has been a decline in the proportion of under-fives suffering fever and acute respiratory infections, stemming from the reduction in the burden of malaria. But, there has been no discernible change in the incidence of diarrhoea (National Bureau of Statistics, 2010).

Uncontestably there have been increases in the financial investments in child survival, but only a small proportion of these investments is directly reaching children. Expenditure often remains in the hands of the central government. For example, in 2007–8 the total expenditure on HIV/AIDS prevention, care, treatment, and support services was Tsh 595.7 billion (approximately GBP 2,367,520). While this was more than a 100% increase from 2005–6, only 5% was directly channelled to the districts and regions (Government of the United Republic of Tanzania, 2008a).

There has been a massive school-building programme in Tanzania, to which communities contributed at considerable cost. Between 2004 and 2009, the number of secondary schools increased by 218% (Government of United Republic of Tanzania, 2008a). Along with the abolition of primary school fees in 2001 enrolment in both primary and secondary education has risen exponentially. Numbers of secondary students rose from 345,441 in 2003 to 1,466,402 in 2009 (Government of United Republic of Tanzania, 2008b).

The key challenge now is to ensure that educational attainment mirrors the investments that have been made. This is of major concern to parents, students, practitioners, and policy-makers because more than 30% of children fail to complete primary school (Government of United Republic of Tanzania, 2008a). Furthermore, many graduates from primary school can barely read or write (Mrutu *et al.*, 2005). Students who sat for the National Form IV secondary examination in secondary schools in 2012 performed awfully. In fact, 240,903 of the 397,136 candidates scored division zero (Mwakyusa, 2013). Moreover, full capitation grants are not reaching schools, teachers are only instructing students for an average of two hours and four minutes each day, and the majority of students in all levels of primary school are unable to pass a Standard 2 test (Sumra, 2011).

There has been an outcry following the recent poor performance in the Form IV secondary exam results and politics has started to prevail in the education sector. Professor Herme Mosha explains that the crisis in educational outcomes is the result of the intersecting factors of:

- teacher quality – knowledge gaps, lack of training to implement the new curricular changes, poor pay, and demotivation;
- inadequate textbooks, a growing culture of not using books, and the short supply of laboratory facilities and equipment;

- lack of clear synchronization of lines of authority and powers to make binding decisions and oversee their effective implementation;
- changing of the curriculum from a content-based approach to a competency-based approach in 2006 before making adequate preparations; and
- student and teacher indiscipline.

Needless to say a number of politicians have focused on the issue of student indiscipline, loudly calling for more corporal punishment in schools (Mosha, 2013). There is considerable government denial about the structural and underlying causes of dysfunction within the school system. Rakesh Rajani, a member of the government commission that was convened to investigate the causes of the poor exam results explained in his letter of resignation to the Prime Minister 'the Commission quickly realized that the core problems were not the nature of the examinations but the utter collapse of the education system' (Rajani, 2013).

Tanzania still has a long way to go before its children receive a quality basic education. In order to do so the government needs to acknowledge the primacy of teachers – their training, their motivation, and their numbers – as a force for educational improvement. Tanzania has an absolute shortage of teachers with the Pupil Teacher Ratio (PTR) of 1:54 that is well above the recommended PTR of 1:45 (Government of the United Republic of Tanzania, 2010) and relationships between the government and the teachers' union is at an all-time low with the unending threat of teacher strikes.

The World Bank and International Monetary Fund caution the government against mass recruitment of teachers, health professionals, and social workers fearing the impact on the government purse and the inflationary pressures of a large public-sector workforce. But, the reality is that without investing in the right people to run progressive social programmes in health, education, and protection the investments that have been already made in infrastructure will only accrue a limited return.

In the domain of protection little progress has been made to protect children's right to live in safety. At the moment there are no regulations, insufficient staff, no procedures, only one juvenile court in the country, and little chance of redress or justice for victims of violence. While a quick win could be achieved by finalizing the child protection regulations that would bring the Law of the Child to life, this is yet to be completed almost four years after the law was passed.

There exists a National Multi-Sectorial Task Force to respond to violence against children and a National Costed Plan of Action for vulnerable children (2012–16), but there is not yet a national child protection strategy, or a central government budget line for child protection services, nor minimum standards for agencies that come into contact with children.

Child protection, as it is conceived of in the Law of the Child, is primarily the responsibility of social workers. But there is a massive shortfall of social workers across the country with only 437 currently employed by the government (Ministry of Health and Social Welfare, 2012). This feasibility of implementing the Law given this shortfall and the absence of a substantive social workforce recruitment strategy suggests that caution is required before one can make claims about Tanzania's commitment to protecting children's rights to live in safety.

The underlying determinants of these differential outcomes

To conclude this chapter I suggest that there are three underlying factors that influence what progress is made and where it stalls in terms of realizing children's rights in Tanzania. These are around the comfort zones of policy-makers, public planners, and international donor partners; the effects of generalized insecurity and persistent stress on the behaviour of individuals towards children; and the partiality and limited traction of the child rights approach itself.

The system that underpins development in Tanzania militates against progressive social programmes

In Tanzania development technocrats are keen to act and politicians are keen to equate acting with solving the problems of a country. Thus manipulating financial flows, building infrastructure, and dispersing commodities are seen by them as 'development interventions'.

It is not an attractive political position for either domestic politicians or aid bureaucrats to engage with the more complex business of supporting humans to move along their own developmental trajectories at their own pace. And to be fair a strong case could be made that doing so is not the business of planners, politicians, and policy-makers.

This leaves them doing what they do best, which is to 'throw things' at problems. Essentially, the neoliberal Western paradigm of development, which has been adopted almost whole-heartedly by the Tanzanian government, puts the cart before the horse. It frames economic growth as the driver, equating prosperity with development. It does not see development as something that happens in people's interiors and that subsequently generates economic growth.

This equation of development with the economy means that investing in progressive social policies that support people's interior growth is unpopular with donors, with politicians, and with government planners. There is also little space within their discourse of economics to appreciate the significance that context plays and the importance of designing interventions with nuance in mind. And thus in Tanzania we get one generic form of state schooling, irrespective of the lifestyles, culture, language, or preferences of children growing up in pastoralist, fishing, and urban situations.

An underestimation of the effects of generalized insecurity and persistent stress on the behaviour of individuals towards children

There is extensive empirical evidence in the domains of interpersonal neurobiology about the negative effects of chronic stress on people's relational functioning (Siegel, 1999, 2010). A recent review of the literature on the impacts of childhood maltreatment reminds us that the violence is borne over individuals' life-courses and has negative impacts on their emotional, cognitive, behavioural, and interpersonal functioning (Habedank, 2012). Given the prevalence of generalized insecurity and violence against children in Tanzania, I think it would be fair to assert that few individuals are reaching their potential and performing at their peak.

As I discussed at the beginning of this chapter, when I am off balance and stressed I revert back to an ethnocentric perspective where the needs of me and mine take precedence. I may be committed to putting the interests of those outside my family first, but my claimed values and those I practise start to diverge in the face of frustration, exhaustion, and stress (Argyris, 1996, 1999).

This is not a phenomenon that is unique to me and given the chronic stress under which many Tanzanians live, it becomes clearer why few people take positive actions to protect children's best interests at cost to themselves. An on-going study about the worldviews of Tanzanian adults who protect children (McAlpine, 2013a) reveals that one of the greatest challenges they face lies in the perception of their fellow community members that they are foolhardy in taking action to intervene when children are at risk. Participants have described being teased, humiliated, stigmatized, and threatened all because they have stepped outside their familial circle of care and taken action to educate, house, or save a child's life. This is an on-going study and final conclusions are yet to come in, but these findings do indicate that altruistic behaviour towards children is increasingly not accepted as a social norm.

The partiality of the child rights approach

Finally, it is naïve to think that the concept of children having rights is uncontested in Tanzania. I have heard too many times individuals arguing that children's rights are a Western imposition or a luxury that Tanzania cannot afford. For adults who conceive of childhood as a period of life to be got through as quickly as possible before children enter the adult social world, the idea that children are social actors who can claim entitlements is an anathema. Arguing that the government has made a commitment to children's rights has little traction with people who hold this position.

While the Convention is universal in the sense that almost all nations bar three have signed up to it, I believe that the child rights discourse is partial. The Convention is essentially a set of behavioural injunctions that set out expected practices towards children. The Convention tells us what should be done, but not how to go about enacting these practices.

Behaviour is informed by the interior worlds of individuals, by the political and economic system in which the collective lives, and by the cultural and interpersonal norms of the group. The Convention is quiescent about these dimensions of social experience, but if real change is to occur for children in Tanzania we need to adopt a more inclusive understanding of our context and to design interventions that tap into people's emotional and relational experience and into the political and economic system of governance.

References

Argyris, C. (1996). 'Unrecognised defenses of scholars: impact on theory and research', *Organisation Science*, 7(1): 79–87.

Argyris, C. (1999) *On Organisational Learning*, Oxford: Blackwell.

Beck, D.E. and Cowan, C.C. (1996) *Spiral Dynamics: Mastering Values, Leadership and Change*, Oxford: Blackwell (Kindle edn).

Chachage, C. and Cassam, A. (2010) *Africa's Liberation: The Legacy of Nyerere*, Pambazuko Publishers (available online at http://www.pambazuka.org/en/) (accessed on 9 August 2011).

Evans, A. (2011) *2020 Development Futures*, ActionAid (available online at http://www.globaldashboard.org/2011/01/28/2020-development-futures/) (accessed on 11 April 2012).

Fuhs, C. (n.d.) *Toward an Integral Approach to Organisation Theory: An Integral Investigation of Three Historical Perspectives on the Nature of Organisations* (available online at http://www.clintfuhs.com/files/pdf/Fuhs_Toward%20An%20Integral%20Approach%20to%20Org%20Theory.pdf) (accessed on 25 June 2012).

Government of the United Republic of Tanzania (2007a) *Household Budget Survey 2007*, Dar es Salaam: National Bureau of Statistics.

Government of the United Republic of Tanzania (2007b) *Initial Report to the Committee on the Rights of the Child on the Optional Protocol on the Convention of the Rights of the Child on the Sale of Children, Child Prostitution and Child Pornography*, Dar es Salaam: Government of the United Republic of Tanzania.

Government of the United Republic of Tanzania (2007c) *National Higher Education Policy*, Dar es Salaam: Ministry of Higher Education, Science, and Technology.

Government of the United Republic of Tanzania (2008a) *MKUKUTA Annual Implementation Report 2007/08*, Dar es Salaam: Ministry of Finance and Economic Affairs.

Government of the United Republic of Tanzania (2008b) *Basic Education Statistics in Tanzania (BEST) 2004–2008*, Dar es Salaam: Ministry of Education and Vocational Training.

Government of the United Republic of Tanzania (2009) *The Law of the Child Act, 2009*, Dar es Salaam: Government of the United Republic of Tanzania.

Government of the United Republic of Tanzania (2010) *Basic Education Statistics in Tanzania (BEST) 2006–2010*, Dar es Salaam: Ministry of Education and Vocational Training.

Government of the United Republic of Tanzania and Macro International (2005) *Tanzania Demographic and Health Survey 2004/5*, Dar es Salaam: National Bureau of Statistics.

Habedank, M. (2012) *How Chronic Stress from Childhood Maltreatment Affects Brain Development, Emotional Regulation and Cognitive Functioning*, Arusha: Caucus for Children's Rights.

Habedank, M. (2013a) *The Social Return on Investments in Child Protection Infrastructure: A Summary of Accrued Value and a Tool for Advocacy*, Arusha: Caucus for Children's Rights.

Habedank, M. (2013b) *Voices of the People: A Qualitative Research Study Exploring the Impact of Child Maltreatment on Survivors and Witnesses in Tanzania*, Arusha: Caucus for Children's Rights.

Kegan, R. (1982) *The Evolving Self: Problem and Process in Human Development*, Cambridge, MA: Harvard University Press.

Kohlberg, L. and R. Mayer (1972) 'Development as the aim of education', *Harvard Educational Review*, 42: 449–96.

Manjolo, I., Likwelie, S.B., Kamagenge, A.M., Mesik, J., and Owen, D. (2008) *Community Foundations – The Relevance of Social Funds in Urban Areas: The Tanzania Social Action Fund Experience. Social Funds Innovation Notes* 5(1) (available online at http://openknowledge.worldbank.org/handle/10986/11154) (accessed on 9 August 2011).

McAlpine, K. (2013a) *CCR's Social Impact Strategy (2013–2017): An Application of Integral Activism to Programming for Social Change in Tanzania*, Arusha: Caucus for Children's Rights.

McAlpine, K. (2013b) 'The world-views of Tanzanian adults who take micro-actions to protect children: towards the development of a theory of altruistic social action.' Unpublished thesis in progress, Fielding Graduate University.

McAlpine, K., Smithson, P., Taylor, B., Sumra, S., Shariif, H., and Mtandu, R. (2009) *Children in Tanzania: A Situation and Trends Analysis*, Dar es Salaam: UNICEF.

Ministry of Health and Social Welfare (2012) *Assessment of the Social Welfare Workforce in Tanzania*, Dar es Salaam: Department of Social Welfare.

Mosha, H. (2013) 'CSSE results: where did we lose our way?' *The Citizen* (available online at http://africa.widmi.com/index.php/tanzania/the-citizen/magazine/5582-csse-results-where-did-we-lose-our-way) (accessed on 23 June 2013).

Mrutu, A., Ponera, G., and Mkumbi, E. (2005) *The SACMEQ II Project in Tanzania: A Study of the Conditions of Schooling and the Quality of Education*, Dar es Salaam: Ministry of Education and Culture.

Mwakyusa, A. (2013) 'Tanzania: form four results out', All Africa.Com (available online at http://allafrica.com/stories/201302190430.html) (accessed on 11 March 2013).

National Bureau of Statistics (2010) *2010 Tanzania Demographic and Health Survey*, Dar es Salaam: National Bureau of Statistics.

National Bureau of Statistics (2011) *Tanzania in Figures 2010*, Dar es Salaam: National Bureau of Statistics.

National Intelligence Council (2008) *Global Trends 2025: A Transformed World* (available online at http://www.acus.org/publication/global-trends-2025-transformed-world) (accessed on 10 March 2012).

Nyerere, J. (1967) *The Arusha Declaration: Socialism and Self-Reliance*, Arusha: Tanganiyka Africa National Union.

Nyerere, J. (1968) *Freedom and Socialism/Uhuru na Ujamaa*, Dar es Salaam: Oxford University Press.

Organization of African Unity (1990) *The African Charter on the Rights and Welfare of the Child*, Addis Ababa: Organization of African Unity (available online at http://www.refworld.org/docid/3ae6b38c18.html) (accessed on 25 June 2013).

Piaget, J. (1975) *The Child's Conception of the World*, London: Rowman & Littlefield.

Rajani, R. (2013) *Letter of Resignation to Hon Mizengo Pinda, Prime Minister of Tanzania. Dar es Salaam* (available online at http://twaweza.org/go/form-iv-statement) (accessed on 20 June 2013).

Revolutionary Government of Zanzibar (2006) *Education Policy*, Zanzibar: Revolutionary Government of Zanzibar.

Save the Children (2007) *Child Rights Situation Analysis – Health in Tanzania*, Dar es Salaam: Save the Children.

Siegel, D.J. (1999) *The Developing Mind: How Relationships and the Brain Interact to Shape Who We Are*, New York, NY and London: Guilford Press.

Siegel, D.J. (2010) *Mindsight: The New Science of Personal Transformation*, New York, NY: Bantam Books.

Sumra, S. (2011) *Are Our Children Learning? Annual Learning Assessment Report*, Dar es Salaam: Uwezo.

UNICEF Tanzania (2012) *Thematic Child Protection Report*, Dar es Salaam: UNICEF.

UNICEF Tanzania, National Center for Injury Prevention and Control, Centers for Disease Control and Prevention, and Muhimbili University of Health and Allied Sciences (2011) *Violence against Children in Tanzania: Findings from a National Survey, 2009 Summary Report on the Prevalence of Sexual, Physical and Emotional Violence, Context of Sexual Violence, and Health and Behavioural Consequences of Violence Experienced in Childhood*, Dar es Salaam: UNICEF.

United Nations (1989) *The United Nations Convention on the Rights of the Child*, Geneva: United Nations.

United Nations (2006) *Report of the Independent Expert Committee for the United Nations Study on Violence against Children*, New York, NY: United Nations.

United Nations (2012) *Annual Report of the Special Representative of the Secretary-General on Violence against Children*, Geneva: United Nations.

Wilber, K. (1996) *A Brief History of Everything*, Dublin: Gill & Macmillan.

Wilber, K. (1997) 'The integral vision: the good, the true, and the beautiful,' in K. Wilber (ed.) *The Eye of the Spirit: An Integral Vision for a World Gone Slightly Mad*, Boston, MA: Shambhala.

Wilber, K. (1998) *The Essential Ken Wilber: An Introductory Reader*, Boston, MA: Shambhala.

Wilber, K. (2002) *Excerpt A: An Integral Age at the Leading Edge* (available online at http://www.kenwilber.com) (accessed on 2 February 2013).

Wilber, K. (2003) *Excerpt D: The Look of a Feeling: The Importance of Post/Structuralism* (available online at http://www.kenwilber.com) (accessed on 2 February 2013).

Wilber, K. (2006) *Excerpt G: Towards a Comprehensive Theory of Subtle Energies* (available online at http://www.kenwilber.com) (accessed on 2 February 2013).

Wuyts, M. (2006) *Developing Social Protection in Tanzania within a Context of Generalised Insecurity. REPOA Briefs*, Dar es Salaam: REPOA.

10 Accessing and participating in education in Lesotho

Children in the early years with special needs

Jacqui O'Riordan, James Urwick, Matemoho Khatleli, Stella Long, Grace Ntaote, Florence Nyakudya, and Nthabeleng Maketela

Introduction

This chapter examines a range of issues facing children with special needs, their families, and educational professionals in relation to access to, and participation in, education in Lesotho. In the first instance, an overview of issues arising for children living with disabilities in Lesotho is offered, particularly those of educational access, with a focus on IECCD (Integrated Early Childhood Care and Development). The discussion includes an examination of policy at national level, aimed at increasing access to, and participation in, IECCD for children with special educational needs (SEN). Attention is drawn to an emphasis of including children with SEN, as well as the importance attached to early intervention. Research findings highlight a range of gaps between policy and practice that impact on access to, and participation in, education for children with SEN, with particular reference to Articles 23, 28, and 29 of the Convention on the Rights of the Child (CRC) and Articles 11 and 13 of the African Charter on the Rights and Welfare of the Child (ACRCW).

The research on which the analysis presented is drawn includes two inter-related research exercises. The methodology informing both exercises views educational opportunities of children with special needs as influenced by a range of organizational and social units which intersect with their local-specific contexts. The first research exercise was coordinated by the Centre for Global Development through Education (CGDE), supported by an African-Irish institutional partnership, and led to a detailed report (CGDE, 2011). Briefly, it attempted to map the capacity of relevant organizations in Lesotho to contribute to a national system of identification, assessment, and support for children with special educational needs in Lesotho. A total of 75 interviews in urban and rural areas, in four districts of Berea, Leribe, Maseru, and Quting, were undertaken for this research. It included interviews with managerial and professional bodies at national and district levels, representatives of international agencies, national non-governmental organizations (NGO), representatives of schools of different kinds and levels as well as interviews at household and local community levels. The overriding objective of this study was to assess key capacities in each of the areas to contribute to quality inclusion of children with special educational needs in education.

The later research was undertaken in 2012 and was developed in collaboration with the Catholic Relief Services, Maseru and supported by the Good Shepherd Sisters, based in the highland area of Auray. It was a more limited and localized research exercise, the aim of which was the beginning of a process of identification of young children with SEN, and their access to IECCD in a specific community: Auray, near Mantsonyane, Thaba-Tseka District, where the Catholic Relief Services and the Good Shepherd Sisters are developing their support of IECCD centres and of young children with disabilities more generally. Inquiry focused on eliciting local perspectives on disability in general, and on issues arising within the community in accessing education for children with SEN. It included a focused group discussion with members of the Auray community, visits to IECCD centres in the locality, and in-depth interviews with teachers and parents of children with disabilities.

Children with disabilities in Lesotho

We have discussed the context of people living with disabilities elsewhere (CGDE, 2011; O'Riordan *et al.*, 2013) and summarize key issues arising here. National data on disability in Lesotho are available through the *Population and Housing Census 2006*.[1] Figures resulting from this census estimate that 3.7% of the population of Lesotho are living with disabilities of some sort (Bureau of Statistics, 2009). However, criticisms on the nature of the questions that were asked in the census draw attention to its narrow interpretation of disability, and suggest that this has led to the omission of disabilities such as autism, Attention Deficit Hyperactive Disorder (ADHD), Development Coordination Disorder (DCD) and mild forms of disability in general (LCE, 2007). The reported rate is below what would be expected, given international averages, and so in some ways tends to add strength to those criticisms. Importantly, however, *The Population and Housing Census 2006* gives a recorded rate of disability of 1.5 for the 5–9 age group (2,233 children) and 0.7 (899 children) for the 0–4 age group. This difference suggests that many young children acquire disabilities through disease or accidents and that some disabilities are not identified until children reach primary school. Kamaleri and Eide (2010) also suggest that over one-third of people acquired their disabilities as a result of an illness or disease, while just under one-third of disabilities were related to birth or were congenital conditions. They present figures on the distribution of people living with disabilities under six main domains: vision, hearing, mobility, remembering, self-care, and communicating. According to these figures, those who reported living with a disability were likely to report severe disability in one core domain (62.3%) or across two or three core domains (23.9%). The most common types of disability identified in their study related to mobility (34.7%) and remembering (27.2%).

As elsewhere, there are cultural traditions in Lesotho that attach stigma to disability. Often the result is social and economic isolation of people with disabilities and of their families (Kamaleri and Eide, 2010). Beliefs that connect disability to either a curse on the person/household/family, and/or suppose that it has roots in some type of supernatural realm, combine to stigmatize people with disabilities. It is suggested that stigma is the outcome of a complex web of inter-related factors. Khatleli *et al.* (1995: 6) suggest that the supposed causes of disability include 'contact with other disabled people when pregnant, eating protein, transgression in a previous life, unfaithfulness during pregnancy, witchcraft, incest, evil spirits, lack of proper attention to ancestral sprits and heredity'. Resulting attitudes and service provision can impact on the daily activities of people, the access they have to services, and general attitudes of others towards them. Negative assumptions may be made about their capabilities. These factors combine to act as barriers to people's full participation in society, as well as the normalization of exclusion (Khatleli *et al.*, 1995; Mokoena, 2007; Kamaleri and Eide, 2010).

Regarding the reproduction of stigmatized attitudes and processes of exclusion, in Lesotho it has been found that children without disabilities are often afraid of people with disabilities (Mokoena, 2007). Furthermore, Kotze (2012) found that regionally, and specifically in Lesotho, people with disabilities often do not know about services or campaigns that might be useful to them. She found (2012) that this was particularly so with regard to awareness of health services in Lesotho and reflected on the resourcing and development of these services. She reports (2012: 29) that people with disabilities in Lesotho often:

> Do not know about various services that are available for them to address their health needs. [They] do not have access to appropriate health treatment and care. Health centres do not have suitable infrastructure, necessary expertise, and equipment to cater for the health needs of various disabilities.

While, as stated, this criticism refers to health-related services, poor awareness of them can have a significant associated impact on education provision and participation. Access to appropriate health services and interventions might well be necessary in order for meaningful participation in education to become a reality.

As part of an attempt to counter and challenge barriers presented to people with disabilities in Lesotho, the Ministry of Education and Training

(MoET) has, since 1989, maintained a programme, though with very limited resources, to facilitate primary school attendance by children with disabilities (see LCE, 2007). The Bureau of Statistics (2009) reports that such children are likely to attend primary education, but that only 12.2% of people with disabilities have attended secondary education. This compares unfavourably with more general participation rates in secondary education for girls of 42%, and 33% for boys.

We are reminded again, however, about criticisms of the narrow definition of disability employed by the Bureau and questions also arise regarding the quality of such education. Mokoena (2007) is very critical of the quality of education that is deemed acceptable for children with disabilities in Lesotho. She also alerts us to the vulnerability of children with mental and speech impairments to sexual abuse. She considers that education for children with disabilities is often inappropriate, making it difficult for them to progress through to higher levels; that poorly trained teachers contribute to the marginalization of such children; and that teachers often do not understand children's needs, in particular those of children with speech and hearing difficulties. Astonishingly, she contends that teachers contribute to children's marginalization by calling them degrading names like *seqouala* or *sekooa*.[2] Furthermore, children with SEN commonly repeat classes at primary-school level and in some cases do not access education at all (CGDE, 2011). Identification of children's SEN is often not evident or is informal. Furthermore, the development of individual educational programmes (IEPs), to plan their development and progress through the grade levels, is unlikely. There is also a lack of appropriate resources to aid in the identification and assessment of children (LCE, 2007; CGDE, 2011).

Recent initiatives of NGOs

This relative neglect of children with special needs in Lesotho has been challenged, in recent years, by national organizations consisting of, and representing, people with disabilities, who have come together to lobby the government and oppose discrimination. The Lesotho National Federation of Organizations for the Disabled (LNFOD) is the umbrella organization under which four other national-specific issue-based organizations operate. As a result of their intense campaigning, the Government of Lesotho ratified and signed the UN Convention on the Rights of Persons with Disabilities (CRPD) on 2 December 2008. The following extract from Kotze (2012: 43) is one example of the extent of this lobbying as well as the cooperation of NGOs:

> One such strategy [pressure on the government to ratify the Convention] was the 'Joint Open Letter on the Convention on the Rights of Persons with Disabilities' which, together with stakeholders from non-governmental organizations, service providers, international agencies, religious groups

and trade unions, wrote to the Prime Minister. This letter outlined the benefits that PWD [Persons With Disabilities] would gain if the Convention was ratified. For instance, the stakeholders maintained that the Convention would offer guidance to the government on protecting the rights of the PWD.

Article 24 of the CRPD requires that 'states recognize the right of persons with disabilities to education', with a view to realizing this right 'without discrimination and on the basis of equal opportunity', and that inclusive educational systems be developed at all levels. It also makes the connection between meaningful education participation and participation in society.

As a sequel to the signing of the CRPD, a *National Disability and Rehabilitation Policy* was developed, in 2011, by the Ministry of Health and Social Welfare (MoHSW). The stated aim of this policy is to 'to create an environment where PWDs living and working in Lesotho would be able to realize their full potential' (MoHSW, 2011: viii). It identifies the removal of cultural and social barriers, including negative attitudes that inhibit employment opportunities; and the promotion of equal opportunities and the encouragement of good practice in private and civil society sectors as key factors in the pursuit of this aim. Importantly, 'prevention, early identification, and intervention', are emphasized in this policy. The potential of IECCD in prevention and early identification of disability among young children is recognized. So is the role of appropriate education, starting from early childhood, in promoting and supporting the empowerment of people with disabilities, through to adulthood.

Lesotho's obligations on education of children with disabilities under CRC and ACRWC

Lesotho is also a signatory to the United Nations Convention on the Rights of the Child (CRC), having signed the Convention on 21 August 1990 and ratified it, with no reservations, on 10 March 1992 (UN Treaties Collection, n.d.). Furthermore, as a member of the African Union, Lesotho ratified the African Charter on the Rights and Welfare of the Child (ACRWC) on 27 September 1999. Together, these international conventions provide a strong international framework focused on ensuring that the rights of children are promoted and their provisions are wide-ranging. They can be viewed as symbolizing an increasing global recognition that children will not necessarily be included in more general instruments developed to promote and protect people's rights. Their development indicates agreement, globally and among African Union member states that, because of the particular circumstances of children, including their need for care and positions within families and institutions, the promotion and development of children's rights need specific international agreements. As signatories to these conventions, countries recognize their obligations to promote children as rights holders. As our concern in this chapter is with examining children's access to education within a rights framework, it is worth examining in more detail both the relevant provisions within these conventions regarding children's access to education and those provisions regarding children with disabilities in particular.

Article 23 (1) of the CRC is concerned with children with disabilities. It states that signatories will 'recognize that a mentally or physically disabled child should enjoy a full and decent life, in conditions which ensure dignity, promote self-reliance, and facilitate the child's active participation in the community'. Section 2 of Article 23 recognizes a disabled child's right to special care and states that such will be encouraged and provided to the child and to her/his carers, subject to a state's resources and with regard to the particular circumstances of the child. Importantly, Article 23 (3) goes on to state that assistance, where possible, will be provided free of charge to children with disabilities in order to ensure that the child has effective access to education, health, and other appropriate services. The final subsection of this article commits to information sharing across a range of disciplines, aimed at improving services and, in particular, recognition of the needs of countries with lower incomes.[3]

Article 28 recognizes children's right to education in the context of equal opportunities. It states that primary education should be made available to all children (28 (1) (a)) and places the onus on states to encourage attendance at school (28 (1) (e)). It addresses the issue of school discipline, which should be 'administered in a manner consistent with the child's human dignity and in conformity with the present Convention' (28 (2)). Finally, international cooperation is encouraged in the third section of Article 28 (3) for its role in furthering the 'elimination of ignorance and illiteracy throughout the world and facilitating access to scientific and technical knowledge and modern teaching methods', again with regard to the needs of low-income countries.

The focus of Article 29 is on education, which it proposes should be directed to the holistic development of children's mental and physical capacities, have respect for the communities in which they live and their cultural orientations, and encourage respect for other cultures and civilizations. Section 1 (d) perhaps sums up the orientation of this article in stating that the direction of education should be 'the preparation of the child for responsible life in a free society, in the spirit of understanding, peace, tolerance, equality of sexes, and friendship among all peoples, ethnic, national and religious groups and persons of indigenous origin'.

Article 3 of the ACRWC, which is concerned specifically with promoting and protecting the rights and welfare of African children, states that 'every child shall be entitled to the enjoyment of the rights and freedoms recognized and guaranteed in this Charter'. It specifically states that every child will have a right to education (11 (1)) and that such education will be concerned with the promotion of the child's personality and fulfilment of her/his capacities (11 (2) (a)). Section 11 (2) (b) states that respect for human rights nationally and internationally, with particular reference to provisions incorporated into African instruments, be fostered. This article also states that education should be directed at strengthening positive African morals, values, and culture and preparing the child 'for responsible life in a free society, in the spirit of understanding tolerance, dialogue, mutual respect and friendship among all peoples, ethnic, tribal and religious groups' (11 (2) (d)). Article 11 (3) goes on to place an onus on states to ensure that such rights are realized by ensuring access to education for children, by providing free and compulsory primary education, and encouraging progression to higher levels of education. It specifically states that states shall 'take special measures in respect of female, gifted and disadvantaged children, to ensure equal access to education for all sections of the community' (11 (3) (e)). Directing its attention to handicapped[4] children, Article 13 (1) states that:

> [e]very child who is mentally or physically disabled shall have the right
> to special measures of protection in keeping with his physical and moral
> needs and under conditions which ensure his dignity, promote his self-
> reliance and active participation in the community.

This article goes on to ensure that the child will be provided with, within state resource limitations, 'effective access to training, preparation for employment and recreation opportunities in a manner conducive to the child achieving the fullest possible social integration, individual development and his cultural and moral development' (13 (2)).

Together, these articles provide a strong rights framework with much potential for the development of services for children with disabilities. Furthermore, their orientation towards a positive and inclusive perspective on disabilities is noteworthy, as is their recognition of the role of education in fostering inclusive values and in holistically developing and promoting mental, physical, and emotional capacities of children within their particular cultural milieus. These instruments provide a robust starting point towards achieving greater inclusion for children with disabilities, based on a rights framework. However, their potential is constrained by their frequent reference to limitations of state resources.

The IECCD sector in Lesotho

It could be argued that the development of Lesotho's IECCD sector has benefited from its international obligations in combination with internal pressure. It is a relatively vibrant sector, which has been growing since the early 1970s. While its development is uneven, the presence of IECCD centres is now evident, at some level, throughout the country. In terms of access to IECCD, gross enrolment estimates for children aged 3–5 in 2006 varied from 18% (UNESCO, 2008: Table 3b) to 33% (UNESCO-IICBA, 2010). Participation in IECCD is thought to be less likely for children who (i) live in rural and highland areas and (ii) come from poorer families (UNESCO-IICBA, 2010). Our research also indicates that children with disabilities face difficulties in accessing and continuing their participation in IECCD centres (CGDE, 2011; O'Riordan and Maketele, 2012).

The sector has its origins in a number of advocacy groups concerned with issues pertaining to the intersecting interests of women, children, and childcare. The sector came together under the umbrella of the Lesotho Preschool and Day Care Centre in the mid-1980s, focusing on the development and service provision of early years care and education through crèches, preschools, and kindergartens. Later on, the IECCD unit was established at the Ministry for Education and Training, which assumed responsibility for monitoring and inspecting all early years centres in Lesotho and is involved in training and support. Furthermore, the IECCD National Council oversees the sector at a national level, supported by District IECCD Councils and committees at community levels. This structure is consistent with Lesotho's commitments as a signatory to the UN Convention on the Rights of the Child (1989) and the Dakar Agreement on Education for All (UNESCO, 2000), in which early childhood education and inclusion of children with disabilities are identified as important goals.

IECCD provision includes a range of structures. There are IECCD community-centres, centres attached to primary schools, privately-run centres, and home-based resource persons. Reception classes have also been developed in some primary schools specifically to offer one year of preschool to 5–6-year-olds and increase their school-readiness. The diverse provision is thought to facilitate the inclusion of as many children as possible and especially to ensure IECCD centres are developed in highland areas, which can be quite inaccessible. The inclusion of home-based provision has been noted as an example of good practice in a study of early childhood care and education in selected sub-Saharan African countries. Its strengths are said to include (i) its targeting of 'children from poor families and other disadvantaged backgrounds' and (ii) its working 'according to parents' expectations in terms of its impact on the children, their parents and the community' (UNESCO-ICCBA, 2010: 28–9). Furthermore, the location and contextualization of home-based centres within the community, with parents taking active roles as educators/carers have been particularly noted as having very positive potential. These home-based centres are the only type of early years provision available in Lesotho to which, in principle, fees do not apply, as they comprise groups of parents who co-operate in providing preschool care and education for their children.

The *Final Draft of the National Policy Document: Early Childhood Care and Development* is effectively the guiding policy on IECCD in Lesotho. According to this policy, dated November 2000, the IECCD Unit's stated goal is that all children aged 0–6 who are not yet in primary school have access to IECCD provision. Such provision should 'facilitate [a] child's survival, growth, development, and learning'. It states that priorities are to be given to those populations identified as being 'at risk' (MoET, 2000: 10). Within its definition of care it includes 'the early detection of disabilities and early intervention' (p. 9). It also specifically recognizes the importance of integration of children with special educational needs at an early stage and its connection with on-going integration throughout educational levels and sectors, as is clear from the following statement:

> In accordance with the Ministry of Education and Training (MoET) – Special Education policy on integration, the integration exercise should start from early childhood education through primary, secondary, right up to tertiary and vocational level (MoET, 2000: 1–2).

However, the document goes on to highlight a lack resources and expertise pertaining to SEN within the IECCD sector: it views these limitations on resources as serious impediments to achieving the potential of early identification of disabilities and setting interventions in place – a potential that, it states, is not achieved in practice. It seems that these limitations continue to be a feature within the sector. UNESCO-ICCBA (2010: 20), in its assessment of IECCD in Lesotho in the late 2000s, suggested that the sector *should* continue to develop in line with '[i]ts constitutional duty to protect the rights of young children and to provide them with security, nutrition, health and education as a matter of right'. They and others (Sebatane and Lefoka, 2011) point out that IECCD trainers and teachers often have very low levels of qualifications, although they might have been working in the sector for some time. They also tend to have very little SEN training and there are problems associated with low levels and delayed payments for teachers and carers in the sector. Obstacles to progress also arise in limited public funding for the sector, and in that priority is thought to be given to primary schools and the development of Reception Centres for 5–6-year-olds, within primary school facilities. Urwick and Griffin (2012: 76–7) point out that MoET has focused on developing such Reception Classes in a number of primary schools rather than supporting the existing network of IECCD centres. They argue that MoET has provided no subsidies to IECCD centres and that in-service training at this level has depended upon workshops funded by UNICEF as well as the on a network of volunteer resource teachers at the district and community levels.

Lesotho's IECCD policy is currently under review and is expected to be finalized in 2013. In commenting on the development of the sector, particular reference to its role in supporting children with SEN has recently been emphasized (Makhele, 2011). The IECCD Unit's information officer indicated a continuing commitment to 'ensure vulnerable children receive early childhood intervention services... especially for children in difficult circumstances' (Makhele, 2011: 4). Furthermore, as part of the review, a consultation process was undertaken. This consultation process reiterated evidence from earlier studies that many children with SEN are currently not accessing services and that their parents are often unsure where to go for information and assistance. It should also be noted that, across neighbouring countries in sub-Saharan Africa, difficulties in accessing information and services for people with disabilities are also reported to be commonplace (Kotze, 2012). This was an issue to which the Centre for Global Development though Education's final report (to which most of the authors of this chapter contributed) also drew attention. One of its recommendations was that, in addressing this issue, a network of school-based SEN coordinators should be developed to link with IECCD centres as well as schools in their areas (CGDE, 2011).

One of the more positive developments in this context was the development, in 2007, of a Certificate in Early Childhood Education (CECE) programme at the Lesotho College of Education (LCE). This is a two-year in-service programme, where practitioners are taught and supervised by personnel of LCE and MoET. The programme is 'designed for the education and training of teachers and caregivers who are or will be responsible for children aged three to six' (LCE, 2007: 2) and is thought to signal the beginning of professional development of IECCD teachers in Lesotho (UNESCO-IICBA, 2010: 17). It recognizes the importance of early identification and intervention and includes a short module on Child and Parent Counselling and one on Special Educational Needs. There is also a compulsory module on SEN within the initial teacher-training diploma programmes for primary and secondary education, indicating the importance that SEN is afforded by the key teacher-training institution in Lesotho. Additionally, it offers an Advanced Diploma in Special Education (ADSE) which is a one-year, full-time programme, aimed at qualified teachers who have responsibility for SEN in primary, secondary, and special schools.

Those working within the IECCD sector currently, because of their low levels of qualification, do not qualify for the Advanced Diploma and relatively few qualify for admission to the undergraduate teaching diploma. However, these programmes do offer the possibility of progression in the future. They also indicate the pro-activeness of the educational establishment in reaching out to meet the needs of the sector, and an understanding of the importance of including SEN components in more generalized programmes as well as offering SEN as a specialism.

Children with disabilities in early childhood education in Lesotho

Within this context we now specifically turn our attention to findings arising from research that we have undertaken in Lesotho since 2009 as detailed above. We draw particular attention to those issues arising with regard to the inclusion of children in IECCD, as well as more general perspectives on disability encountered during the course of the research. Given the structure of the IECCD sector as outlined above, with national, district, and local structures and networks, and its stated recognition of education of children with disabilities, it might be expected that children with disabilities would be participating in IECCD and that identification of their SEN would be recognized. However, in both research exercises it was found that there were few children with disabilities attending early years centres and that, in practice, their inclusion was, at best, rudimentary. There was some evidence of negative views on disability, formal identification and assessment of their SEN was lacking, and an understanding of the importance of early identification was not well developed. Having said this, however, a potential for early identification was also demonstrated.

In the 2009 study, initial answers to questions posed on whether there were children with SEN attending IECCD centres, suggested that there were none (CGDE, 2011). This was similar in the 2012 study where we found that there were few children with SEN attending IECCD centres. However, on further questioning it was often revealed that principals and teachers might have had concerns about children who didn't seem to act in ways that would be expected of children of their age. Thereafter, accounts of informal identification of disabilities were revealed. For instance, IECCD teachers reported that they had noticed young children had problems with their sight, and they mentioned children attending IECCD classes whom they thought had difficulties in hearing.

The teachers might then convey their concern to the children's parents (CGDE, 2011) or they might not take any action (O'Riordan and Maketele, 2012). This seemed to depend on their views about their role as an IECCD teacher/carer, on disability, and on their relationship with the parents. Responses of teachers ranged from assuming that the child was 'undisciplined' and that this was likely to be as a consequence of poor parenting, often by mothers about whom the teachers held low opinions. Alternatively, the teacher might consider that nothing could be done to accommodate children's needs. We observed children with hearing problems being left at the back of a class and obviously unable to understand what was going on, as well as children who had sight problems being given no particular attention (O'Riordan and Maketele, 2012). In these instances their teachers were aware of the children's hearing and sight difficulties, but having acknowledged it, did nothing more to identify, assess, or accommodate them. More worryingly again, centres involved in the latter instances had personnel who were enlisted in the Certificate in Early Childhood Education in LCE and/or were well integrated into the local IECCD resource network, through which we were informed there were regular workshops in SEN. On a more positive note we also encountered occasions when an observed difficulty was brought to the attention of the parents in an attempt to further investigate a child's needs. In one particular case this resulted in a child being treated by a specialist in South Africa and their potentially sight-losing condition being addressed successfully (CGDE, 2011).

In discussing their children's experiences of, and participation in, IECCD, parents highlighted a number of issues. At times they found that their children were not accepted in the centres by the other parents, children, and teachers. This also usually meant that the children remained, largely, in or near the vicinity of their homes and had limited interaction with anyone outside the family. For instance, issues arising for one boy, who is now ten years old and currently attending IECCD offer a poignant example of the challenges faced in accessing, and participating in, meaningful education (O'Riordan and Maketele, 2012). He was enrolled in primary school when aged six, but very shortly problems began to occur. Complaints were made to his parents that he was not 'behaving normally', and that he was fighting with other children. The message that was conveyed to his mother was that he was the cause of trouble in the school, and that teachers and other parents were unhappy with this. As time progressed he became isolated and his parents withdrew him from school. They felt that the conflicts at the school were part of their son's reaction to being singled out as different and ridiculed because of these differences. They also felt that, had there been a greater understanding by teachers and parents within their community of his needs, the outcome could have been different. Later on, when the boy was nine years old, his parents enrolled him in a home-based preschool. Again problems began to arise. Complaints were made to his parents that the other children, who were now much younger and smaller than him, were afraid of him and that the other parents were unhappy. However, at this time, following discussion with the other parents, teacher/carers, everybody arrived at a greater understanding of the boy and he continued to attend preschool, make friends, and enjoy the experience. However, while this meant that there was some level of inclusion in education for him, it was now within a sector not appropriate to his age, and there was no formal recognition of his special educational needs.

While we found no systematic approaches to identifying children with disabilities and there were no official mechanisms for assessment internal to any of the preschools, the role of IECCD in furthering an understanding of disability was evidenced. While their level of qualifications was often low, some teachers in this sector displayed an amount of creativity, using a range of materials for demonstration and learning purposes and showed good levels of interest in the progress that children were making. For instance, they reused packaging, made their own demonstration symbols, and/or copied illustrations from workbooks to use in their teaching. They might also, for instance, ask children whom they suspected could not see very well to stand at a distance from illustrations, to gauge the extent of their vision. If they then approached the child's parents the tendency was to discuss their observations with parents and encourage them to seek medical assessments. In such cases, the hope was that medical intervention would contribute to identifying any problem that child might have and lead to the development of interventions for them. However, even if the teacher followed up on their observations, this hope might also not be realized, as is discussed below.

One issue that arose starkly in the 2012 research exercise was that even where children had been attending health centres or hospital clinics from very early on this might have little impact on recognition or interventions. In one instance a boy, again who was 10 years old and attending IECCD, had been attending health clinics since he was just a few months old. Yet, he had never been diagnosed with any specific condition and he had never been educationally assessed in any way, although a referral to a SEN specialist was promised some years ago. In another instance, the parents of a boy who was attending medical appointments because of severe fits he was experiencing had been given no idea that his speech and language delays could be addressed. And in another case we found that a grandmother was now spending all her time sitting with her granddaughter who had severe physical disabilities, with no contact with, or advice on, any occupational or physical therapy that would help to increase the child's level of mobility. In yet another instance that arose in the 2009 research, as a result of an accident while attending crèche, a three year old was now cared for in her home. Following this accident the child was unable to sit up. Despite her mother's attempts to access support for her, she was having little or no success, informally or formally. When she was working at one of the local factories, she asked that the child be taken out with the other children, but this did not happen. She was also unable to access any formal educational support for the child.

Conclusion

Both research exercises indicate that some children with disabilities, at least, become isolated from their communities at an early stage and face challenges in accessing education, because of their disabilities. Such isolation affects the children themselves and their families. Stigma, it seems, continues to be a barrier they and their families face; a barrier presented by other parents, teachers, and other children. However, there is reason to believe that isolation might be alleviated through medical consultations, identification of their needs through teachers, followed by interventions, as well as through discussions about disability and greater awareness within communities. On the other hand, such cannot be assumed and even where SEN is included in, for instance, IECCD community workshops, poor understanding can continue. Poor communication by medical personnel and inaction on referrals across education and medical sectors are also of concern. The latter also indicates little progress on another aim of Article 23 of the CRC which seeks to foster interdisciplinary cooperation. This chapter has focused on inclusion and early intervention at IECCD level. The potential that this has for meaningful inclusion of children with SEN in education is evident. However, this potential is hampered by a lack of training, poor communication, and low levels of aware-ness and understanding of challenges faced by children with disabilities and their families within communities.

Together, these findings indicate that, in practice, much remains to be achieved in the realization of appropriate education for children with SEN. The rights of children with disabilities, as stated in UNCRC Article 23, to live in conditions that ensure their dignity are upheld, to conditions that promote their active participation in the community and access to appro-priate education, are not being fulfilled. Nor is there evidence that the pro-visions of ACRWC's Article 11, which is concerned with ensuring a child's capacities are fulfilled, that their dignity is upheld and that they are offered education appropriate to their needs, are being achieved. However, the positive developments, as in the development of the Certificate in Early Childhood Education and some evidence of good communications between teachers and parents at IECCD level offer signs of hope for the future.

Notes

1 The 2001 Lesotho Demographic Survey was the first official survey in Lesotho to collect data on disability and the 2006 Housing and Population Census drew on the questions asked in 2001 in incorporating questions on disability into its questionnaire.
2 *Sekooa*: the correct term is *seqhoala*. The prefix *se-* is used to refer to objects with disability. The preferred term of people with disabilities is *motho ea nang le bokooa*, which translates as 'people with disabilities'. *Seqouala* refers to physical disability and is also a degrading term.
3 The terminology used in the UNCRC is 'developing countries'. However, there is much controversy regarding the use of developed/developing countries, particularly with reference to their assumption regarding progress and assumed 'stages of development'. Of the terms in current usage, our preference is to use Global North/Global South or to make reference to low/high/medium-income countries, where no such assumptions on progress follows.
4 This is the term used in the Charter, although our preference is to focus on a child's abilities vis-à-vis her/his context/society, or on any particular needs applicable to the child. The former has a tendency to place the onus of change on the wider community and society rather than locating a problem within the child.

References

Bureau of Statistics (2009) *2006 Lesotho Population and Housing and Census: Analytical Report. Volume IIIB: Socio Economics Characteristics*, Maseru: Ministry of Finance and Development.
Centre for Global Development through Education (CGDE) (2011) *Identification, Assessment and Inclusion for Learners with Special Educational Needs: Towards a National System for Lesotho: Final Report of the Research Team*, Limerick: CGDE, Mary Immaculate College.

Kamaleri, Y. and Eide, A.H. (eds) (2010) *Living Conditions among People with Disabilities in Lesotho*, Oslo: SINTEF Technology and Society and Global Health and Welfare.

Khatleli, P., Mariga, L., Phachaka, L., and Stubbs, S. (1995) 'Schools for all: national planning in Lesotho', in B. O'Toole and R. McConkey (eds) *Innovations in Developing Countries for People with Disabilities*, UK: Lisieux Hall, Italy: AIFO (available online at www.eenet.org.uk/resources/docs/inno_dev_coun.php) (accessed on 8 March 2012).

Kotze, H. (2012) *Status of Disability Rights in Southern Africa*, Open Society Foundation for South Africa, the Open Society Initiative for Southern Africa, and the Open Society Foundations Disability Rights Initiative.

Lesotho College of Education (2007) *Education Policies, Programmes and Legislation Relating to Disadvantaged Children and Children with Disabilities: Final Report*, Maseru: Ministry of Education and Training, Special Education Unit.

Makhele, M. (2011) 'IECCD policy reviewed', *Informative*, 10 October.

Ministry of Education and Training (MoET) (2000) *Final Draft of the National Policy Document: Early Childhood Care and Development*. Prepared by ECCD Task Force and Dr Martha Llanos, Maseru: MoET.

Ministry of Health and Social Welfare (MoHSW) (2006) *National Policy on Orphans and Vulnerable Children*, Maseru: MoSHW.

Ministry of Health and Social Welfare (MoHSW) (2011) *The National Disability and Rehabilitation Policy: Mainstreaming Persons with Disabilities into Society*, Maseru: MoSHW.

Mokoena, N. (2007) *International Report for Foundation. Report on the Lesotho Disability Project, October to December 2007,* Maseru: Skillshare International.

O'Riordan, J. and Maketele, N. (2012) 'Understanding the needs of children, households, and communities in rural villages for improving services to children with disabilities.' Report prepared for Catholic Relief Services, Maseru and Good Shepard Sisters, Auray, Mantasanyane, Thaba Tseka.

O'Riordan, J., Urwick, J., Khatleli, M., Long, S., Ntaote, G., and Maletela, N. (2013) 'Accessing and participating in education in Lesotho: children in the early years with special needs', in J. O'Riordan *et al.* (eds) *Early Childhoods in the Global South: Local and International Contexts*, Oxford: Peter Lang Publications.

Sebatane, E.M. and Lefoka, P.J. (2011) *Knowledge, Attitudes and Practices of Parents and Caregivers of Children aged 0 to 8 Years Regarding Early Childhood Care and Development (ECCD)*. A report submitted to the Ministry of Education and Training, Institute of Education, Roma: National University of Lesotho.

UN Enable (n.d.) *Factsheet on Persons with Disabilities*, New York, NY: UN Enable.

UNDP (2009) *Human Development Report*, New York, NY: UNDP.

UNESCO (2000) *The Dakar Framework for Action, Education for All: Meeting our Collective Commitments,* Paris: UNESCO.

UNESCO (2008) *EFA Global Monitoring Report 2009. Statistical Tables 2009: Final Longer Version*, Paris: UNESCO.

UNESCO (2009) *The Inclusion of Children with Disabilities: The Early Childhood Imperative. UNESCO Policy Brief on Early Childhood* 46 (April–June).

UNESCO-IICBA (2010) *Country Case Studies on Early Childhood Care and Education (ECCE) in Selected sub-Saharan African Countries 2007/2008: Some Key Teacher Issues and Policy Recommendations. A Summary Report*, Addis-Abba: UNESCO-IICBA.

UN Treaties Collection (n.d.) Chapter IV: 'Human rights.' Convention on the Rights of the Child (available online at http://treaties.un.org/Pages/ViewDetails. aspx?src=TREATY&mtdsg_no=IV-11&chapter=4&lang=en) (accessed on 17 December 2012).

Urwick, J. and Griffin, R., with Opendi, V. and Khatleli, M. (2012) 'What hope for the Dakar goals? The lower levels of education in Lesotho and Uganda since 2000', in R. Griffin (ed) *Teacher Education in Sub-Saharan Africa: Closer Perspectives*, Oxford: Symposium Books.

11 Barriers to the effective implementation of the UN Convention on the Rights of the Child in the Niger Delta of Nigeria

Emilie Secker

Introduction

Nigeria ratified the UN Convention on the Rights of the Child (CRC) in 1991, and domesticated this through the national Child Rights Act in 2003 (CRA). Nigeria is also a party to the African Charter on the Rights and Welfare of Child (ACRWC), which it ratified in 2000. However, there remain significant barriers to the effective implementation of the CRC and the consequent enjoyment by children of their rights within Nigeria. This analysis focuses on violations of children's rights in the Niger Delta region of Nigeria, and uses data from the Niger Delta Child Rights Watch project (NDCRW), run by the UK-based non-governmental organization (NGO) Stepping Stones Nigeria in partnership with local Nigerian NGOs and the Bar Human Rights Committee of England and Wales, to identify specific problem areas and practical recommendations for improvement.

The NDCRW project was implemented in a context of social inequality, low levels of education, and significant violence and corruption. Although the transition from military to civilian rule in 1999 has improved democracy, governance, and human rights protection in Nigeria, and the country recently celebrated its first civilian-to-civilian transition of power following elections in 2011, Nigeria continues to face considerable challenges. Levels of inequality are high, with the United Nations Development Programme (2009: 11) identifying that 'despite its vast resources, Nigeria ranks among the most unequal countries in the world'. The incidence of relative poverty in Nigeria was 69% in 2010 (National Bureau of Statistics, 2010: 11).[1] These problems are compounded by high levels of corruption within Nigerian institutions. Transparency International's Global Corruption Barometer 2010/2011 showed that 73% of Nigerians believe levels of corruption in the country are increasing, and that political parties, police, and judiciary were seen as particularly corrupt. This has a clear impact on the enjoyment of children's rights. Save the Children (2009: 2–3) estimate that 15 million children are engaged in some form of child labour and 11 million children are out of school across Nigeria. Poor access to safe drinking water and to improved sanitation facilities[2] – with only 58% and 32% of the population having these respectively in 2008 – dramatically affect children's mortality as diarrhoea primarily attributed to these causes is the cause of 17% of child deaths in Nigeria (UNICEF, 2010: 1–2).

The effect of inequality and corruption is particularly evident in the Niger Delta region. Despite the region being the source of Nigeria's vast oil wealth, poverty levels remain high. The United Nations Development Programme summarized the Niger Delta in 2006 as 'suffering from administrative neglect, crumbling social infrastructure and services, high unemployment, social deprivation, abject poverty, filth and squalor, and endemic conflict' (2006: 9). In addition, few international human or children's rights organizations currently operate in the Niger Delta. Amnesty International has a long history of campaigning against human rights abuses related to oil extraction, and UNICEF also run a range of programmes across Nigeria including in the Delta region, but few other major organizations choose to operate in the region, reportedly due to the risk of violence, the high levels of corruption, and the logistical challenges. There are, however, a large number of local Nigerian human and children's rights organizations working in the region, many extremely small in scale. Although growing in influence and capacity, most of these organizations have a limited impact on the child rights violations discussed below, due primarily to having restricted access to funds and training, in addition to the identified constraints of inequality, poverty, low levels of education and literacy, violence, and corruption.

The Niger Delta child rights watch project

The NDCRW project was piloted between June 2010 and May 2011, and the first full phase of the project took place between October 2011 and September 2012. The pilot phase involved Stepping Stones Nigeria and a Nigerian NGO, the Centre for Environment, Human Rights, and Development, based in Port Harcourt, the capital of Rivers State in the Niger Delta. The first phase expanded the project to include other Nigerian NGOs (Basic Rights Counsel Initiative, based in Calabar, the capital of Cross River State, and Stepping Stones Nigeria Child Empowerment Foundation, based in Eket in Akwa Ibom State) and also placed an intern from the UK Bar Human Rights Committee (BHRC) in the Niger Delta for the duration of the project. The NDCRW project covered the following states in the Niger Delta: Bayelsa, Cross River, Akwa Ibom, and Rivers.

The aims of the project were to investigate, document, and monitor abuses of children's rights as protected under the CRC in the Niger Delta and to promote awareness of children's rights within this region. The first phase of the project expanded its remit beyond documentation of abuses and awareness-raising, to also include the provision of direct emergency support including counselling, family tracing and reunification, medical care, and educational support to victims of abuse, and the provision of free legal support to children who had suffered rights violations. The first phase also included a specific capacity-building element for Nigerian project partner organizations via a legal intern from the BHRC being placed in the Niger Delta for a year in order to train, mentor, and support the local Nigerian partners on case management and child rights litigation.

Between June 2010 and September 2012 the NDCRW project documented 177 cases of child rights abuse in four Niger Delta states, including accusations of witchcraft, sexual assault, child labour, trafficking, abandonment, physical violence, and neglect. Three cases involved the murder of a child and others were cases of attempted murder. The cases were documented first via written case reports gained through interviews with the children and later through the use of case logbooks which had been specifically designed for the project and which also documented interactions with police, government, parents, and teachers among others. Case summaries and monthly statistical analyses of case data were also produced. During the first phase of the NDCRW project, when emergency and legal support to children were included in project activities, 150 children received some form of support via the project, including legal advice, counselling, medical care, relocation, and family tracing. Various advocacy activities were undertaken as part of the project, which were designed to promote awareness of the legal protections for children's rights and sources of support if a child's rights were abused. These included market outreach sessions, live TV debates between schools, children's rights-themed radio jingles, children's rights school clubs, the production and distribution of materials including posters, leaflets and newsletters, and meetings with key stakeholders including community leaders, pastors, government officials, teachers, and police. The advocacy activities were estimated to have reached over 500,000 people.

There currently exists a lack of reliable data on violations of the CRC in the Niger Delta region, as identified by the UN Committee on the Rights of the Child in their most recent Concluding Observations on Nigeria, which noted 'the lack of information about the extent and forms of child abuse and about the legislative and administrative framework in place to prevent and protect children from all forms of violence, abuse and neglect' (2010: para. 54). Local NGOs do not have the capacity to collect and collate extensive data, and there is little relevant information on child rights violations in the region publically available from either the state or federal governments. The NDCRW project results therefore provide extremely useful information both on the range of violations of the CRC occurring in the Niger Delta and on the various factors which cause these violations. It is also a key source of information on the potential for NGO-led interventions to positively affect children's enjoyment of their rights.

The following discussion will use the NDCRW project data to analyse some of the main barriers to the effective implementation of the CRC in the Niger Delta region. First, it will examine the high incidences of violence against children reflected in the NDCRW case data, and will analyse the main forms that these take and their key causes. Secondly, it addresses how lack of access to justice exacerbates violations of children's right to freedom from violence, and considers the degree to which low levels of awareness of children's rights affect children's enjoyment of their right of access to justice and consequently their right to freedom from violence. Finally, the discussion addresses the extent to which NGO-led interventions can have a positive impact on overcoming violations of the CRC, and concludes with several key recommendations for future action.

Violence against children

The project recorded significant numbers of cases of violations of children's right to freedom from violence as protected by Article 19 of the CRC: 'States Parties shall take all appropriate legislative, administrative, social, and educational measures to protect the child from all forms of physical or mental violence, injury or abuse, neglect or negligent treatment, maltreatment or exploitation, including sexual abuse.' Using this wide-ranging definition of violence against children, reiterated in the ACRWC Article 16, the 2006 World Report on Violence Against Children (Pinheiro, 2006: 4), and in Section 11 (a) of the Child Rights Act, nearly all the NDCRW cases involved clear violations of children's right to freedom from violence. However, the NDCRW case data are particularly useful as they both reflect previously identified types of violence against children, and demonstrate forms of violence against children which have received relatively little attention.

First, the NDCRW project data reflected several well-recognized forms of violence against children. Some 43 cases involved a child being physically abused in some way, including a 12-year-old girl who was severely beaten by the woman for whom she worked as a maid; a 7-year-old girl who was beaten with wire and a cane for failing to return with money after being sent out to sell water on the street; a 12-year-old girl who was burnt with a hot knife because she had stolen a biscuit; a 14-year-old girl who was flogged after being accused of stealing; and a 10-year-old boy who was beaten with wire and had pepper put in his eyes after being accused of stealing money. Eighteen cases involved child labour, here defined as participation in work activities that negatively affected the children's safety, personal wellbeing, and/or ability to access education, and/or child trafficking. Some 73 cases involved the neglect and/or abandonment of a child, including a case where two siblings aged 6 and 11 were beaten and neglected by their step-mother, leading to them leaving home. Although in some cases poverty was a clear factor leading to the neglect of children and/or involvement in child labour, in others neglect was used as a form of punishment, for example, if the child had misbehaved or was considered to be a 'witch' (see further discussion below).

The project also recorded a large number of cases of sexual abuse of children, with 20% of documented cases being of this nature. The majority of these cases took place in Rivers State. The victims of this form of abuse were all girls. In the vast majority of cases the perpetrator was known to the victim, being either a family member or a neighbour. In several cases the initial abuse had further serious consequences. For example, in one case a 13-year-old girl was raped by a group of local youths, who then made death threats against both the girl and the project officer who investigated the case. This resulted in the girl having to be relocated by the project team. In another case, a 12-year-old girl was kidnapped and raped by several members of a local gang, resulting in significant and long-term health problems. She and her family were then subjected to further violence and death threats, again requiring their relocation by the project team.

Sexual abuse, including rape, is clearly prohibited by the CRA in Sections 31 and 32. Although sexual abuse and rape of children are reported by local project staff to be generally socially unacceptable in the region, project data also indicate that there is considerable reluctance to formally report this form of abuse in particular to either the statutory authorities, such as the police or relevant government agencies, or to local NGOs. In general, these cases came to the attention of the project team due to their links with the local community and their personal relationships with community members. Project reports indicate that the primary reason for this unwillingness to formally report sexual violence against children is that rape is generally considered to be a private matter, and while there may be forms of community justice, such as violence against the perpetrator or payment of compensation to the parents of the child, in very few cases were formal charges brought against the perpetrator. This is supported by the Committee on the Rights of the Child (2010: para. 88), which is 'seriously concerned at reports on the high number of children who have experienced some form of sexual abuse, including in schools, and that such abuse is not documented and reported to the police'.

Data from the NDCRW project also identify a particular cause of violence against children which has received relatively little attention. Over the two-year period, 32 documented cases concerned accusations of witchcraft against children. These involved both boys and girls and occurred primarily in Akwa Ibom and Cross River States. In the documented cases, children suffered significant abuses of their rights including violence, abandonment, and neglect as a result of the witchcraft accusation. Several of the children ended up living on the street as a result. In some cases, the consequences for the children were extremely severe. For example, in one case a 12-year-old girl was beaten, cut with razor blades, and dumped naked by the side of a road due to the belief that she was a witch. In another case, an 8-year-old boy was beheaded because he was believed to be a witch.

The nature and scale of rights abuses resulting from accusations of witchcraft against children identified in the NDCRW project data reflect those identified in other analyses. The UN Special Rapporteur on Extra-Judicial, Summary, or Arbitrary Executions has described accusations of witchcraft as being 'tantamount to a death sentence' (Alston, 2009: para. 43), and the NDCRW case data clearly support this analysis. Abandonment resulting from witchcraft accusations has also been identified as a contributing factor to the numbers of street children (Alston, 2009: para. 49 (i)) which is further demonstrated by the NDCRW project data which document several cases where children ended up living on the streets following accusations of witchcraft, either because they were forced out of their homes by family members or because they chose to leave in order to avoid further abuse.

In addition, the NDCRW data further demonstrate other identified aspects of witchcraft accusations against children. For example, it is widely believed that the witchcraft spirit can be transferred to, and between, children using food (Foxcroft, 2009). This was reflected in a case in which a teacher sent a boy home from school as he was eating meat that he had picked up off the floor and she was concerned it might 'spiritually infect' other children. Pastors, often from revivalist Pentecostal churches, are often involved in accusations of witchcraft against children (Cahn, 2006: 422), either through making the initial accusation or by confirming the belief of the child's family that the child is a witch, and Molina (2005: 24) considers that 'the boom in revivalist churches is undoubtedly closely related to the accusations of witchcraft against children'. This is also reflected in several of the NDCRW project cases, where children believed to be witches were taken to a local church or prayer house in order to confirm the accusation. One of the root causes of witchcraft accusations against children is the attribution of misfortune to spiritual causes (Falola, 2001; Smith, 2001; Molina, 2005). This is again reflected in the NDCRW case data, with one boy stating that whenever he makes a mistake he is accused of being a witch, due to the belief that misbehaviour or 'problems' in children are evidence of witchcraft.

The belief that children can be witches therefore clearly results in wideranging and significant violations of their rights and thus constitutes a major barrier to the effective implementation of the CRC in the region. Following a Shadow Report from Stepping Stones Nigeria on this issue (Battarbee *et al.*, 2009), the UN Committee on the Rights of the Child concluded (2010: para. 67) that it remained:

> extremely concerned at the reportedly widespread practice of the witchcraft stigmatization of children in the State party and reports that these children are tortured, abused, abandoned and even killed as a result of such stigma and persecution. The Committee is particularly concerned at the reported roles of certain churches and the film industry in promoting the belief in child witchcraft and that already vulnerable children, including children from poor families and children with disabilities, are at greater risk of witchcraft stigmatization. In this respect, the Committee express utmost concern at reports of arbitrary killings of children during the course of activities designed to extract a confession of witchcraft or resulting from exorcism ceremonies.

The committee further recommended that Nigeria take specific action to address this barrier to the effective implementation of the CRC, through criminalizing accusations of witchcraft against children, ensuring law enforcement and other relevant agencies received specific training on the issue, undertaking public sensitization campaigns, regulating religious institutions engaged in such practices, and undertaking further research and data collection on the issue (2010: para. 68). The NDCRW project data therefore underline the concerns recognized by the Committee on the Rights of the Child and demonstrate that witchcraft accusations against children remain a significant concern in the Niger Delta region.

Although the African Committee on the Rights and Welfare of the Child has, to date, made no explicit comments in relation to accusations of witchcraft against children in Nigeria, the ACRWC specifically identifies 'harmful social and cultural practices affecting the welfare, dignity, normal growth and development of the child' (Article 21) as an area of concern and requires states to take action to eliminate these, as well as requiring that 'Any custom, tradition, cultural or religious practice that is inconsistent with the rights, duties and obligations contained in the present Charter shall to the extent of such inconsistency be discouraged' (Article 1 (3)). It is clear that the rights violations resulting from accusations of witchcraft against children would fall within this remit.

There is a lack of clarity at the national level concerning the legal prohibition of witchcraft accusations against children. Although the Child Rights Act clearly prohibits the types of abuse of children's rights which result from accusations of witchcraft, it does not specifically criminalize accusations of witchcraft against children, nor does it contain a general provision on harmful social or cultural practices as is found in the ACRWC, although it does prohibit other specific harmful cultural practices including child marriage/betrothal and tattooing (Sections 21–24). However, witchcraft accusations against both adults and children are specifically criminalized under the Nigerian Criminal Code 2004 (Section 210) and, at the state level, the Akwa Ibom State Child Rights Law 2008 prohibits both accusations of witchcraft against children and any abusive action taken to 'cure', 'purge', or 'exorcise' a child of witchcraft (Sections 274–275).

To date Akwa Ibom State is the only state in Nigeria to have criminalized accusations of witchcraft against children, meaning that legal prohibition of this form of abuse remains geographically variable. The failure to include any specific provision on this in the CRA further indicates either a lack of awareness of this issue or an unwillingness to consider it as a form of child rights abuse by the Federal government. There are, however, indications that the problem of witchcraft accusations against children is being accorded higher political priority. The Federal government convened a three-day technical meeting on witchcraft accusations against children in June 2011 and issued a public statement on the need to address the issue (Amusan, 2011). This indicates that the issue of witchcraft accusations against children has now been placed on the policy agenda, although these initiatives are yet to result in concrete policy development.

The NDCRW case clearly demonstrates that witchcraft accusations against children should be recognized as a form of violence against children. Although some studies are beginning to take account of this (see, for example, International NGO Council on Violence Against Children, 2012: 39), the issue of witchcraft accusations remains absent from some of the major discussions and reviews of violence against children, even when these address other forms of violence resulting from traditional beliefs and practices. For example, Female Genital Mutilation (FGM) receives considerable attention in the UN World Report on Violence Against Children (see Pinheiro, 2006: 60–1); yet there is no mention of witchcraft accusations. Witchcraft accusations against children, therefore, need to be addressed in a far more consistent manner when analysing and responding to violence against children.

Violence against children in Nigerian society

It can also be seen that the NDCRW case data support other analyses of the ways in which both the status of children and the normalization of violence in society affect the acceptability of violence towards children. First, the abuse of children's rights resulting from violence against children may be considered as both reflective of, and as a contributing factor to, the way the 'child' is understood within Nigeria. The traditional Nigerian perception of the child places them at the bottom of the social hierarchy, with obedience and respect for adults being paramount. The traditional Yoruba family structure privileges seniority, with junior members of society expected to provide services in a submissive and deferential manner (Falola, 2001). Traditional social stratification within southern Nigeria – the area covered by the NDCRW project – accords children the lowest social status (Akhilomen, 2006). This social status of children has been identified as a contributing factor to levels of violence against children. As Pinheiro (2006: 71–2) claims:

> where parent–child relationships are excessively controlling and afford a low status to children, this is likely to increase violence, particularly when coupled with the belief that corporal punishment or other humiliating forms of punishment are a necessary means of discipline.

This analysis is clearly supported by the NDCRW case data.

Secondly, certain forms of violence against children are plainly normalized and are therefore widely socially acceptable within Nigeria. Akhilomen (2006: 240) comments that 'in Nigeria, like most parts of Africa, children are daily harassed, assaulted, beaten, bruised or maimed for the least trivial [sic] of reasons'. Jones agrees that 'Child domestic abuse is often regarded as part of the socialisation process in Nigeria, and children cannot speak out, given their subordinate position in the home' (2011: 2). Reports from project workers on justifications for violence against children further underline the acceptability of violence against children, and demonstrate social perceptions that violence against children is in some situations necessary to support the effective functioning of social norms and relationships. For example, one project worker reported that the successful prosecution of a woman who had burnt a child with an iron sent 'shockwaves' through the local community, as they had not realized that the physical punishment of children, which often takes very serious forms as demonstrated by the NDCRW case data, and is broadly regarded as common and acceptable, could result in legal action being taken and a potential custodial sentence. Other project workers report adages such as 'spare the rod and spoil the child' being used as justifications for violence against children. The problem of the normalization of violence against children is also recognized by the UN Committee on the Rights of the Child, which considered in 2010 that little or no action had been taken by Nigeria to address the issue of the corporal punishment of children, and recommended that:

> the State party... ensure the prohibition of corporal punishment in all settings, including in the home [and] conduct awareness-raising campaigns to ensure that alternative forms of discipline are used, in a manner consistent with the human dignity of the child. (2010: paras 40–41)

This normalization of violence means that violence towards children is more acceptable and therefore more frequent, and that violence as a form of punishment for even very minor misbehaviour is considered justifiable, or is in some cases not considered as 'violence' but as 'discipline'. However, Nigeria is far from unique concerning such distinctions. As Pinheiro (2006: 10) identifies:

> Persistent social acceptance of some types of violence against children is a major factor in its perpetuation in almost every State. Children, the perpetrators of violence against them and the public at large may accept physical, sexual and psychological violence as an inevitable part of childhood. Laws in a majority of States still condone 'reasonable' or 'lawful' corporal punishment and reflect societal approval of violence when it is described or disguised as 'discipline'. Corporal punishment and other forms of cruel or degrading punishment, bullying and sexual harassment, and a range of violent traditional practices may be perceived as normal, particularly when no lasting visible physical injury results.

The NDCRW case data therefore highlight both well and less recognized forms of violence against children, all of which constitute violations of children's rights under the CRC. It is also evident that there is an urgent need to improve interventions directed to reducing violence against children in the Niger Delta to take account of social and cultural attitudes and perceptions of the 'child' and of acceptable ways to treat children. A simple reliance on legal prohibitions will not suffice.

Access to justice

A further key challenge to the effective implementation of the CRC in the Niger Delta identified through the NDCRW project data was the lack of access to justice for children who have suffered violations of their rights. Although this is more pronounced regarding certain violations than others, for example in relation to sexual abuse as discussed above, in all cases children struggled to receive justice. One of the key findings of the pilot phase of the project was the need to include free legal support to children in subsequent phases. Although project staff were able to report cases to the police during the pilot phase, in very few cases was further action taken as the children and families concerned could not afford legal representation. While every child has the right to legal aid under Section 155 of the Child Rights Act, in practice this is almost completely unavailable to children without NGO assistance, as the Nigerian Legal Aid Council has struggled to make an impact due to capacity and funding constraints (Ehighalua, 2012). The first full phase of the project therefore included significant provision to provide children and families with free legal advice and, if necessary, legal representation.

However, this element of the project continued to face significant challenges during the first full phase in 2011–12. The final project statistics show that just under 50% of cases were reported to the police. Two primary reasons were identified for this. First, in several cases legal action was not considered to be in the best interests of the child, usually because the perpetrator was the primary care-giver for the child, and pursuing legal action against them would result in the abandonment of the child. This is due to the almost total lack of alternative care provision for child victims of abuse, from either the public or private sector, despite the rights of children to this under the Child Rights Act (Sections 16, 42–44, 53–55), which was identified as a major area of concern by the Committee on the Rights of the Child (2010: paras 48–51; see also Akhilomen, 2006: 242). In these cases family counselling, often including a commitment from the perpetrator not to commit further abuse of the child, and on-going monitoring of the child by the project team, was considered a more appropriate course of action.

Secondly, in several cases the project team did not feel enough information was available to support pursuing legal action. This further highlights a failure by the statutory authorities in relation to guaranteeing children's right of access to justice. Although the police have a duty to investigate cases of child rights abuse, the NDCRW project demonstrates that in practice the burden of investigation, including gathering evidence and taking witness statements, primarily falls upon local NGOs. A number of reasons for this may be identified. First, the police and other statutory bodies do not have the capacity to effectively investigate cases of child rights abuse, due to a lack of training on the provisions of the law and suitable ways to interact with children. Project staff reported that some police officers were not aware of the existence of the Child Rights Act and that few had any detailed knowledge of its content. In addition, police knowledge and practice of appropriate ways to treat both child victims of abuse and child witnesses were considered in need of significant improvement. This has also been identified by the Committee on the Rights of the Child (2010: para. 20), which noted:

> the lack of sustained and comprehensive training programmes for key professional groups, including law enforcement officials, members of the judiciary, prison staff, health professionals, social workers, local government administrators and traditional and religious leaders on the Convention and the Child Rights Act.

Project data also report claims by the police that they lack the financial resources to investigate cases, with police officers requesting funds for fuel and other expenses from the project team. However, these claims must be assessed in relation to the endemic corruption in the Nigerian legal system. Amnesty International (2009) found that high levels of unlawful killings occur, with the majority of cases going un-investigated and most police officers not being punished. This evidence supports the reports from the NDCRW project team that the police do not lack resources, but that internal corruption results in the unavailability of resources to properly investigate cases.

Corruption also continues to constitute a barrier to children's enjoyment of their right of access to justice for those cases which were reported to the police. Less than 10% of cases resulted in legal charges being brought; in most cases the suspect was released on bail and no further action was taken. The perception of the project team was that 'bail' is being used by the police as a means to extort money and that there is little police interest in ensuring that children receive justice. Project statistics indicate that in at least 25% of cases the reason for a reported case not proceeding to prosecution was bribery or extortion. Furthermore, corruption in the judiciary constitutes a further barrier to children's right of access to justice; Arewa (2012: 239–40) argues that there is a 'dire need' for the Nigerian public to regain confidence in the sanctity and impartiality of its judiciary, and that such confidence has been lost due to corruption, lack of technical skills, and lack of independence. As a result, people are reluctant to institute legal proceedings as there is a significant lack of faith that the case will be heard in an impartial and independent manner.

It should be noted that there is no specific right of access to justice contained in either the CRC or the ACRWC, although the international legal protection for this is found via reference to the International Covenant on Civil and Political Rights, Article 2 (3), which Nigeria ratified in 1993 and which states:

3. Each State Party to the present Covenant undertakes:
(a) To ensure that any person whose rights or freedoms as herein recognized are violated shall have an effective remedy, notwithstanding that the violation has been committed by persons acting in an official capacity;
(b) To ensure that any person claiming such a remedy shall have his right thereto determined by competent judicial, administrative or legislative authorities, or by any other competent authority provided for by the legal system of the State, and to develop the possibilities of judicial remedy;
(c) To ensure that the competent authorities shall enforce such remedies when granted.

The Child Rights Act, although not providing an explicit right of access to justice for children, contains a number of provisions which provide for this in practice. Primary among these is the obligation of all states to establish Family Courts 'for the purposes of hearing and determining matters relating to children' (Section 149) and which have unlimited jurisdiction to hear both civil and criminal cases concerning offences committed by or against children (Section 151 (a) and (b)).

The establishment of family courts illustrates further barriers to the enjoyment of the right of access to justice for children in the Niger Delta. To date, a family court has been instituted in only one of the nine Niger Delta states, having been established in Cross River State in late 2011 following a concerted campaign by local civil society organizations. The first application to the Cross River State family court for child rights abuse was made by the local project partner, the Basic Rights Counsel Initiative, as part of the NDCRW project, and they also recorded the first successful judgement in a child rights case by the family court in a case where a girl was deliberately burnt with a hot iron. However, in the remaining Niger Delta states, child rights abuse cases must currently be taken to the criminal courts, meaning that children do not have access to a dedicated and child-friendly judicial system, and that cases are often subject to long delays. For example, one case, concerning three girls who were burnt with hot water following an accusation of witchcraft, has been in the criminal justice system for over three years with no resolution.

The lack of access to justice for children who have suffered violations of their rights therefore constitutes a significant barrier to the effective implementation of the CRC in the Niger Delta. Lack of access to justice affects the enjoyment of other rights as it undermines the potential to secure other rights; rights will continue to be denied if right-holders have no effective means to claim them. Furthermore, the children supported by the NDCRW project reported feeling 'helpless' and 'hopeless' because they thought no one would assist them to gain justice or would take seriously what had happened to them, indicating significant negative psychological consequences resulting from a lack of access to justice. Finally, it is also clear from reports of community reactions to successful prosecutions that these could have a considerable deterrent effect on future violations and play an important role in disseminating the legal provisions for the protection of children's rights. Access to justice therefore has a broader and important impact on children's rights protection beyond securing the rights of the individual concerned.

In order to be able to realize a right of access to justice, there must first exist a legal system under which rights claims can be made. There must also exist awareness of and support for this legal system and for the principle of access to justice for violations of human rights. As identified, Nigeria is a party to relevant international legislation for the protection of child rights, and has developed national legislation on child rights via the Child Rights Act which provides fairly comprehensive legal protections for children, including the rights to survival and development (Section 4), the right to freedom from discrimination (Section 10), the right to freedom from physical, mental, or emotional injury, abuse, neglect, or maltreatment, and to freedom from torture, inhuman, or degrading treatment (Section 11), and the rights to health (Section 13), and education (Section 15). These broadly reflect the rights of protection and provision found in the CRC and the ACRWC.

One area of divergence is the right to participation, which is not as strongly emphasized in the Child Rights Act as in the CRC. Under the Act, reference is made to court proceedings being conducive to 'allowing the child to express himself and participate in proceedings' (Section 158), whereas Article 12 of the CRC provides the much broader right of the child to 'express those views freely in all matters affecting the child' and for 'the views of the child being given due weight in accordance with the age and maturity of the child'. In this respect the Child Rights Act more closely follows the ACRWC which provides for an opportunity for children's views to be heard in judicial or administrative proceedings which affect them (Article 4). In addition, the Child Rights Act also follows the ACRWC in containing specific provisions which outline the responsibilities of the child, rather than the CRC which provides no explicit statement on the responsibilities of the child. These provisions, found in Section 19 of the Child Rights Act closely reflect those in Article 31 of the ACRWC. While it does diverge from the CRC in some areas, the Child Rights Act should be considered adequate domestic legislation to support the implementation of the CRC in Nigeria. As UNICEF (2007: 3) have identified, 'the CRA in its rights-responsibilities approach, is culturally sensitive, compatible, relevant and above all in the best interest of the Nigerian child'.

However, there are two significant problems with the implementation of the Child Rights Act within Nigeria, which in turn prevent the effective implementation of the CRC. First, it has not been universally enacted across the country, as each of the 36 states has to individually pass their own state Child Rights Law for it to come into force in that state. The Niger Delta has a comparatively good record in this regard, with only Bayelsa State of the nine Niger Delta states not having enacted a state Child Rights Law to date. However, as identified above, this does mean that the legal protection of children's rights remains geographically variable.

Secondly, and arguably of more significance, is that levels of awareness of the Child Rights Act are reported as being extremely low; very few of the children or families assisted by the NDCRW project knew that children's rights were protected under Nigerian law, nor what this implied for how children should be treated. Likely causes of this include difficulties in accessing both electronic and hard copies of state child rights laws, as consistently reported by local NGOs. Furthermore, the Child Rights Act, like most legal instruments, including the CRC, is written in legal terminology and is therefore largely inaccessible to non-specialists, and especially to those with poor literacy skills.

The CRC entails specific obligations on governments to disseminate its provisions: 'States Parties undertake to make the principles and provisions of the Convention widely known, by appropriate and active means, to adults and children alike' (Article 42), although the Convention provides little information about what specific obligations of provision this requires of government in practice. This has been clarified to some extent by the Committee on the Rights of the Child, which has identified the lack of dissemination of the provisions of the Convention in Nigeria as being a key area of concern, describing current initiatives as 'ad-hoc' and recommending that both the CRC and the Child Rights Act be translated into local languages and that particular efforts be made to publicize these instruments in rural areas (2010: paras 20–22). However, the NDCRW project data demonstrate that in practice little is being done by state authorities to ensure that both adults and children are not only aware of the provisions of child rights legislation but also understand how these principles can, and should be, practically realized. This indicates that children's rights, and especially dissemination of the legal protections for these, are not accorded high political priority, as reflected in Nigeria's Human Rights Action Plan (Federal Government of Nigeria, 2009: 94).

Although discussions with local NGO workers strongly indicate their belief that lack of awareness of the law is a key causal factor in violations of children's rights as protected under the CRC, the ACRWC, and the CRA, a further problematic factor may be that these laws do not adequately reflect the reality of people's lives and their fundamental beliefs. Especially in a context of poor access to justice and significant police corruption, resulting in little or no faith in the rule of law, the development and dissemination of laws concerning children's rights with which people essentially disagree will have little impact. As identified above, in relation to the use of violence as a means to correct wrongdoing and to punish children, there is a significant disconnect between the legal provisions of both the CRA and the CRC and socially acceptable ways to treat children. Similarly, action to criminalize accusations of witchcraft against children as a means to reduce abuse may well be unsuccessful if it conflicts with the genuinely held belief that it is acceptable or even obligatory to treat children considered to be witches in the negative ways identified above.

The NDCRW project data, therefore, highlights on-going tensions in human rights concerning the cultural acceptability of international human rights legislation and the ways that this is implemented at the local level.[3] In relation to violence against children and in particular concerning the prohibition of witchcraft accusations, there is clear conflict with local values and the simple dissemination of what may be perceived to be 'external' or 'alien' principles is unlikely to result in improved protection of children's rights. Although there is a significant relationship between lack of access to justice and the high levels of violence against children reflected in the NDCRW case data, it is also evident that solely focusing on implementation of the law would not fully address the violations of the CRC highlighted in this discussion, due to the disconnection between perceptions of children's rights and the legal provisions existing for their protection. More attention needs to be paid both to informing communities about the law – both the CRC and the Child Rights Act – and to ensuring that this law is meaningful and acceptable to those communities.

Efficacy of NGO activities

As part of the NDCRW project, local NGOs undertook a series of activities, as detailed above, to address the identified barriers to the effective implementation of the CRC. These had a number of positive results. First, the NDCRW generated considerable data on the nature, scale, and causal factors for a range of child rights violations in the region, through documenting cases in detail. Secondly, the project significantly improved access to justice for children and their families, through the provision of free legal services, the investigation of cases, and the securing of convictions. Thirdly, the project positively impacted children's rights to health, alternative care, education, and shelter, through intervening to support children who required these services.

However, analysis of the role of NGOs in the NDCRW project also highlights concerns. Most importantly, in relation to all the areas of success identified above, the NGOs involved in the NDCRW project were providing services for children which the government is legally obliged to provide. Although this has resulted in improved rights enjoyment for those children, this approach remains inevitably limited due to resource constraints. The NDCRW project was able to support a restricted number of children in a limited geographical area, and while those children enjoyed improved access to their rights as a result, these forms of support do not offer a long-term solution to the identified barriers to the implementation of the CRC. The problems identified above require widespread and coordinated action if the outcomes are to be other than partial and this action needs to be developed and implemented by government.

Conclusion

There clearly exist considerable barriers to the effective implementation of the CRC in the Niger Delta region of Nigeria concerning violence against children, access to justice, and awareness of legal protections for children's rights. It is also evident that tension exists between international and national legal provisions and local beliefs and practices concerning acceptable ways to treat children. While analysis of the data provided through the NDCRW project is of value in providing information on the nature of the problem, it is also essential to address potential means of addressing and overcoming these barriers. A number of recommendations, both practical and analytical, may therefore be identified.

First, there is a need to research and explore means of publicizing international and national legal provisions on children's rights in a manner that allows for community-level discussion. These laws must be meaningful to people if they are to be upheld and the corresponding increase in children's enjoyment of their rights is to be achieved. Any publicity campaigns on children's rights laws, whether government or NGO-led, should therefore be interactive rather than simply informative.

Secondly, specific policies should be developed to address harmful cultural and social practices and beliefs, including accusations of witchcraft against children, sexual abuse of children, and violence towards children. These must take account of local interpretations of acceptable ways to treat children, and should not simply force or encourage people to abandon their beliefs. Rather, policies should be developed in consultation with communities to develop alternative courses of action which fulfil the same social needs. This is particularly imperative in relation to appropriate forms of punishment for children.

Finally, local, national, and international actors must continue to emphasize the government's role and obligations in ensuring child rights protection. In particular, efforts to address police corruption must be improved and wider initiatives to promote access to justice, including training for key personnel and provision of legal aid must be developed. While NGOs will inevitably continue to have a role to play in children's rights protection in the Niger Delta, continued reliance on service provision by NGOs both risks a series of uncoordinated and partial interventions and does not result in the large-scale, systematic change required to ensure that the CRC is implemented effectively.

Notes

1 Relative poverty is here defined as per capita expenditure of N 66,802.20 (approximately £270.00 GBP).
2 Improved sanitation facilities is here defined as technologies which provide a barrier between the faeces and human, animal, and fly contact.
3 For further discussion of this see, for example, Cerna (1994), Brown (1997), Ibhawoh (2001), Donnelly (2003), Harris-Short (2003).

References

Akhilomen, D. (2006) 'Addressing child abuse in southern Nigeria', *Studies in World Christianity*, 12 (3): 235–48.

Alston, P. (2009) *Report of the Special Rapporteur on Extrajudicial, Summary or Arbitrary Executions* (available online at http://daccess-dds-ny.un.org/doc/UNDOC/GEN/G09/134/39/PDF/G0913439.pdf?OpenElement) (accessed on 26 March 2013).

Amnesty International (2009) *Nigeria: Police 'Kill at Will'– New Amnesty Report* (available online at http://www.amnesty.org.uk/news_details.asp?NewsID=18543) (accessed on 26 March 2013).

Amusan, B. (2011) *Stakeholders Meet to Save 'Child-Witches'* (available online at http://www.thenationonlineng.net/2011/index.php/newsextra/10736-stakeholders-meet-to-save-%E2%80%98child-witches%E2%80%99.html) (accessed on 26 March 2013).

Arewa, J.A. (2012) 'Judicial integrity in Nigeria: challenges and agenda for action', in E. Azinge and D. Dakas (eds) *Judicial Reform and Transformation in Nigeria*, Lagos: Nigerian Institute of Advanced Legal Studies (available online at http://www.nials-nigeria.org/journals/Arewa-Judicial%20Integrity.pdf) (accessed on 26 March 2013).

Battarbee, L., Foxcroft, G., and Secker, E. (2009) *Witchcraft Stigmatization and Children's Rights in Nigeria: Shadow Report to the UN Committee on the Rights of the Child* (available online at http://www.steppingstonesnigeria.org/images/pdf/Shadow_Report_Low_Res.pdf) (accessed on 26 March 2013).

Brown, C. (1997) 'Universal human rights: a critique', *International Journal of Human Rights*, 1 (2): 41–65.

Cahn, N. (2006) 'Poor children: child "witches" and child soldiers in sub-Saharan Africa', *Ohio State Journal of Criminal Law*, 3: 413–56.

Cerna, C. (1994) 'Universality of human rights and cultural diversity: implementation of human rights in different socio-cultural contexts', *Human Rights Quarterly*, 16: 740–52.

Donnelly, J. (2003) *Universal Human Rights in Theory and Practice* (2nd edn), London: Cornell University Press.

Ehighalua, D. (2012) *Is the 'Legal Aid Architecture' Failing Nigerians?* (available online at http://wrongfulconvictionsblog.org/2012/02/24/is-the-legal-aid-architecture-failing-nigerians/) (accessed on 26 March 2013).

Falola, T. (2001) *Culture and Customs of Nigeria*, Westport, CT: Greenwood Press.

Federal Government of Nigeria (2009) *National Action Plan for the Promotion and Protection of Human Rights in Nigeria 2009–2013*, Abuja: Federal Government of Nigeria.

Foxcroft, G. (2009) *Witchcraft Accusations: A Protection Concern for UNHCR and the Wider Humanitarian Community* (available online at http://www.steppingstonesnigeria.org/images/pdf/witchcraft_accusations.pdf) (accessed on 26 March 2013).

Harris-Short, S. (2003) 'International human rights law: imperialist, inept and ineffective? Cultural relativism and the UN Convention on the Rights of the Child', *Human Rights Quarterly*, 25 (1): 130–81.

Ibhawoh, B. (2001) 'Cultural relativism and human rights: reconsidering the Africanist discourse', *Netherlands Quarterly of Human Rights*, 19 (1): 43–62.

International NGO Council on Violence Against Children (2012) *Violating Children's Rights: Harmful Practices Based on Tradition, Culture, Religion or Superstition* (available online at http://www.crin.org/docs/InCo_Report_15Oct.pdf) (accessed on 27 March 2013).

Jones, N. (2011) *Strengthening Linkages between Child Protection and Social Protection Systems in Nigeria*, London: Overseas Development Institute (available online at http://www.unicef.org/nigeria/62_Strengthening_linkages_between_child_protection_and_social_protection_system.pdf) (accessed on 27 March 2013).

Molina, J. (2005) *The Invention of Child Witches in the Democratic Republic of Congo* (available online at http://www.crin.org/docs/The_Invention_of_Child_Witches.pdf) (accessed on 26 March 2013).

National Bureau of Statistics (2010) *Nigeria Poverty Profile* (available online at http://www.tucrivers.org/tucpublications/Nigeria%20Poverty%20Profile%202010.pdf) (accessed on 26 March 2013).

Pinheiro, P.S. (2006) *World Report on Violence against Children*, Geneva: United Nations.

Save the Children (2009) *What We Do in Nigeria* (available online at http://www.savethe-children.org.uk/sites/default/files/docs/Nigeria_CB_2008.pdf) (accessed on 27 March 2013).

Smith, D. (2001) 'Ritual killing, 419 and fast wealth: inequality and the popular imagination in southeastern Nigeria', *American Ethnologist*, 28 (4): 803–26.

Transparency International (2011) *Global Corruption Barometer* (available online at http://gcb.transparency.org/gcb201011/results/) (accessed on 26 March 2013).

UNICEF (2007) *Information Sheet – The Child Rights Act* (available online at http://www.unicef.org/wcaro/WCARO_Nigeria_Factsheets_CRA.pdf) (accessed on 26 March 2013).

UNICEF (2010) *Water, Sanitation and Hygiene in Nigeria* (available online at http://www.unicef.org/nigeria/ng_media_WASH_fact_sheet_Apr_2010.pdf) (accessed on 27 March 2013).

United Nations Committee on the Rights of the Child (2010) *Concluding Observations: Nigeria* (available online at http://www2.ohchr.org/english/bodies/crc/crcs54.htm) (accessed on 26 March 2013).

United Nations Development Programme (2006) *Niger Delta Human Development Report*, Abuja: United Nations Development Programme.

United Nations Development Programme (2009) *Human Development Report – Nigeria 2008-2009: Achieving Growth with Equity*, Abuja: United Nations Development Programme.

12 Progressing street children's rights and participation in policy

Evidence from South Africa

Lorraine van Blerk

Introduction

Street children[1] – those who live their lives connected to the street in one or more ways – are perhaps one of the most visible groups of marginalized young people that require specific attention when discussing children's rights and the progress of the Convention on the Rights of the Child (CRC) since its drafting almost 25 years ago. Despite their emergence on the international stage around the same time, as a group, street children are consistently failed in terms of being able to access their rights. This is not least in terms of fulfilling basic needs such as shelter, food, play, and family life, but also in relation to more abstract umbrella rights such as 'the best interests of a child' and 'participation'. This chapter examines how street children's rights and participation have been accounted for in policy in the African context, and drawing on evidence from South Africa, offers a more progressive understanding for realizing these rights.

Over the last 30 years research has been undertaken which has investigated many aspects of street children's lives. Initially, attention focused on numbers and definitions and whether there was a Latin American (and latterly an African) model of street children's lives (Boyden and Ennew, 1997). Progressing beyond these discussions, research began to identify that young people who are connected to the streets spend much of their daily life creatively using the city for survival, fluidly working, sleeping, and engaging recreationally in the city. A diverse body of literature has developed exploring the daily minutiae of street children's lives, including their lifestyles, reasons for being on the streets, survival strategies, subcultures, and identity (Aptekar, 1988; Hecht, 1998; Beazley, 2002, 2003; van Blerk, 2006). In addition a number of scholars have detailed the experiences of street children in African cities (for example, Swart, 1990; Young, 2003; Evans, 2006; Abebe, 2009; van Blerk, 2012).

The academic framing of street children also shifted attention during this time. Researchers began to move away from utilizing assumptions based on Western conceptualizations of childhood as a period of innocence, where the protection of children was paramount and firmly located within family settings.

This conceptualization was coupled with the idea that any experience outside this was considered deviant (Boyden, 1990). Instead attention turned to understandings of street children's agency and abilities. From an academic perspective, this shift towards celebrating street children's agency emerged through a renewed theoretical focus on the sociology of childhood in the 1990s, conceptualizing children as active agents and childhood as socially constructed (Jamieson and Milne, 2012), coupled with international attention on the child rights agenda through the CRC. The result has been a move towards more focused detailed qualitative studies. However, much research has taken place at the micro-scale, exploring the creativity of street life from children's perspectives, celebrating their resourcefulness, but resulting in a limited focus on the impacts of their exclusion, rarely drawing connections between street children's lives and wider society. Yet street children are intricately connected to wider society, their public existence and visible profile impacting on the public image of cities; the international image of nations; and subsequently the way in which urban places are managed and policed (van Blerk, 2012). Further, celebrating agency does not necessarily mean freedom on the streets (Bordonaro, 2012) where agency for street children is often 'thin' agency (Klocker, 2007); their ability to act freely in making decisions and choices is only enabled within a highly restrictive context. Therefore thirty years after street children first received international attention, violent tactics continue to be used to reduce street children's presence: this contravenes their rights, exacerbates experiences of violence, and alienates them and their families (Thomas de Benitez, 2007). They are still on the streets and in many cases not accessing or experiencing their full set of rights.

This chapter aims to explore the ways in which street children are represented in policy and how this relates to their ability to access rights, as expressed in the CRC. In this chapter I focus on the participation articles (12 and 13) in the CRC which outline that (street) children have the right to express their views in all matters affecting their lives and that they have freedom of expression. As this chapter discusses, these articles are especially pertinent to street children as their existence outside idealized conceptualizations of childhood means they are often not afforded participation rights. The chapter progresses by examining how street children are represented in policy documents before moving on to demonstrate how they have fallen through the gap. The remainder of the chapter then draws on participatory philosophy and considers ways in which street children might be better facilitated to express their views and offer meaningful input into the (re)drafting of policy and practice. Evidence from South Africa is presented to support the ideas put forward.

Representing street children in policy

Street children began to receive international attention in the 1970s and 1980s and were the visible presence of the harsh realities faced by many children in the Global South. Although initially presented as a 'Latin American problem', it was quickly realized that street children were also one of the visible faces of poverty in cities across Africa and Asia. By 1989, at the same time as the drafting of the CRC, UNICEF was estimating that 100 million children were growing up on the streets of large cities across the world (Campos *et al.*, 1994), and attention was beginning to incorporate a focus on African cities, where rapid processes of urbanization, high levels of poverty and inequality, the emergence of the AIDS pandemic, and pockets of civil insurgency were resulting in the reporting of an African street children problem (Young, 2003). For example, in Uganda in the 1990s children aged as young as 8 years old were moving into Kampala, the capital city, from the surrounding rural areas due to poverty, parental death (fuelled by the onset of AIDS), and, particularly in the case of those coming from the north of the country, rebel activity by the Lord's Resistance Army which included child abduction (Young, 2003).

Reports of large numbers of children living on the streets of African cities fuelled the desire for agencies and governments to intensify their efforts to work towards changing children's lives. This was achieved, at least partly, through the drafting, and ratifying of the CRC from 1990 and other policies and conventions such as the African Charter on the Rights and Welfare of the Child. Although principally to protect children, the Charter does also make mention of children having the right to express their opinions. It does not however, make mention of such views being taken into account in all matters affecting their lives only in relation to legal and administrative proceedings, significantly diverging from the CRC. Yet the commitment of African states to the principles of the CRC and children's rights more generally, is witnessed by the widespread ratification of such instruments across the continent and the subsequent development of national legislation to back it up (for example the Children's Act (Amended), 2005, South Africa; the Children's Act 1998, Ghana; and the Children Statute 1996, Uganda). Yet, Mulinge (2002) points out, having the laws and even the political will to implement them is often hampered by the difficult socioeconomic and political contexts of many nations where the magnitude of poverty means policies are often poorly implemented due to lack of resources. Children continue to live in conditions characterized by poor access to health care, sanitation, clean water, education, and other services. Therefore, although street children emerged as one of the first visible faces of child poverty, 25 years later they still suffer from violation of their rights in many respects (Thomas de Benitez, 2007).

Street children's participation and the policy gap

Some contextualization of the emergence of these policies is important for understanding how street children have, to some extent, managed to fall through the net. International legislation in the 1990s was derived from Western conceptualizations of childhood which prioritized protection of childhood innocence (Boyden, 1990), and placed children firmly within a family context. Street children, who often fell outside this understanding of the ideal childhood, and were considered out of place on the streets (Ennew, 1994), sat uncomfortably on the boundary between innocent and deviant conceptualizations.

For example, Ghana was one of the first African countries to ratify the CRC and subsequently began drafting its own policy on child welfare (Oduro, 2012). Yet, the Children Act 1998 makes little provision for children that do not neatly fit into the protected model of childhood. According to the Act, the principles of protection and family life emerge as central. With respect to street children, the Act serves to limit their legal ability to survival on the streets. The Act makes it illegal for children to engage in work below the age of 15 (13 in the case of light work) and officializes their place within family settings. Street children are not specifically mentioned in the Act but provision for the care of children who are outside a family setting is evident. It states: 'A child is in need of care and protection if the child… is wandering and has no home or settled place of abode or visible means of subsistence' (1998: 9). The response is for a probation or social welfare worker to remove the child to a place of safety and then place the child in a residential home, or in the home of a parent or guardian.

Similarly in Uganda, the Children Statute 1996 was drawn up and implemented into policy in 1996 as Uganda's commitment to ratification of the CRC. The Statute focuses on the rights of the child, but again these are predominately the protection rights of children, focusing on the right to family life, education, and protected from harm, work, and discrimination (1996: 10). Children's agency and their ability to participate in decisions that affect their lives are not mentioned. It also states that children are the responsibility of parents from the moment of birth and this cannot be renounced except through formal adoption (1996: 7). Although street children are not specifically mentioned in the Statute, the section on criminal offences lists many activities that street children participate in to be crimes that they can be tried for (once they are above the age of 12 years) (Young, 2004). These include prostitution in a public place, begging, playing cards for money, using a disability or wound to beg, stealing, trespass, malicious damage, and assault (Children's Statute, 1996: 50–1).

Subsequent to the Children's Statute, Kampala City Council produced an action plan for street children (1997–2000) developed through the international funding of a non-governmental organization (NGO) network. The plan was a major step forward at the time as it sought to bring attention to street children and their rights within the policy process. However, the protectionist discourse presented offered little room for street children to exercise agency and participate in the decisions around implementation of support. The plan had two goals: to reduce the number of street children and to prevent children coming to the streets. It sought to achieve this over the three-year period by 'rehabilitating 600 children' through resettling them with their families and where necessary providing alternative placement, and improving the socioeconomic conditions of families (Kampala City Council, 1997). Here the protectionist discourse of rights overshadows the participation of children in decision-making. As Cheney (2012) notes, Judith Ennew, the social anthropologist and street children advocate, has pointed out the 3P hierarchy of children's rights in the CRC has resulted in the provision and protection agendas taking precedence in national policies to the detriment of participation.

Street children then, appear to have fallen through the policy gap and governments are poorly resourced to update the initial policies drafted under the momentum of the CRC (Mulinge, 2002). I would like to draw out two interconnected reasons for this discrepancy for street children which also relate to their lack of participation in decisions affecting their lives and in developing policy that best represents them. First, their lack of formal representation as a group places street children outside the arena of policy development and, secondly, their independent status places them outside recognized channels of protection.

Street children's lack of formal representation

Despite the history of children's rights and their implementation in the policy arena, street children have proved elusive in many respects. They are still on the streets and often experience violation of their rights. Ray *et al.* (2011) in a major study for Plan International, point out that street children are seldom specifically mentioned in policies, and their rights and issues are not specifically addressed except in some national legislation or localized policy. They state that this is partly because there is no legal definition of street children and their elusiveness as a group makes them difficult to develop legal policy for. Ennew (1994, 2003) has further argued that the clear failure to support street children properly is related to terminology, stating that without proper definitions, it is not possible to estimate the extent to which children are connected to the street and therefore provide appropriate support. This issue of 'who is a street child' is particularly problematic because, unlike other groups that require specific attention, they are not defined by their status (e.g. orphans, children living with disabilities) or the particular activities they are undertaking (e.g. sex work, begging) but rather by a relational process: being connected to the streets. The nature of street life is fluid and changing over time; adapted and adapting those young people with connections to the street (van Blerk, 2012). This suggests that the term 'street children' is socially constructed and as such their experiences will vary socially and temporally from child to child influenced and shaped by their individual strategies (Thomas de Benitez, 2011).

Therefore, despite attempts to pin down 'who street children are', models and continuums – such as that produced by UNICEF in the 1990s which distinguished children *on* the street (working and spending time there) from children *of* the street (homeless children who stayed on the streets without parental contacts) – have been critiqued as wholly unsatisfactory. For instance, although widely used in policy and academic writings, this categorization has largely been discredited, in part at least for not accounting for the fluidity of children to move between and beyond these neatly defined categories temporally and spatially (Conticini, 2004).

It is this positioning of street children that is key to their elusiveness. The inability to neatly categorize street children has resulted in their demise on the international agenda almost as soon as they arrived. Poretti *et al.* (2013: 12) discuss this in detail pointing out that street children were rapidly replaced on the international agenda by child victims of violence. In relation to child rights advocates, they state:

> Notwithstanding the general consensus around the CRC, they often face strong opposing forces in either efforts to promote the rights of the child. As disputes, disagreements and internal divisions threaten their capacity to mobilize resources and political will on behalf of children, consensual issues tend to be prioritised.

Therefore, although street children need to see many of the articles in the CRC realized in their lives, and connect to many of the optional protocols such as sale of children, prostitution, and children in armed conflict, there is no specific mention of children living on the streets and no general comment related to street children specifically (Ray *et al.*, 2011). Poretti *et al.* (2013) give two reasons for this. At the ontological level, it is much easier to mobilize the alarming statistics of violence produced by UNICEF in advocacy than the vague estimation of the number of street children and, at the axiological level, the child victim of violence embodies better than the street child the protectionist discourse of rights. Street children are both victims and perpetrators of crime and, therefore, less well situated than the victim of violence to mobilize shared representations of the vulnerable child. The prioritization of the protection of the body over systemic forms of abuse such as social inequalities and exclusion is far easier to account for.

Street children's independent status

This links neatly to the second reason for street children falling through the policy gap – their independent status which positions them outside the continued prevailing discourse of a protected childhood where children are situated within families and under adult supervision. Cheney (2012) using the example of orphans and vulnerable children (OVC) in Kenya makes this point well. Although Cheney draws on the case of an orphan, street children (whether orphaned or not) are often placed within the OVC categorization. The over-representation of children as vulnerable makes it difficult for those outside adult protection to access help and support. Although an OVC cash transfer scheme was established to support children in Kenya, Cheney (2012) gives the example of Margaret, an orphan, who was unable to access the scheme because as a child she required an adult to apply for her (see also Cheney, this volume). Here the *protection* rights of children, as defined in the CRC, supersedes the *participation* rights; the less-than-competent status being favoured in current rhetoric over empowerment agendas which seek to include young people's meaningful participation. For street children this is particularly problematic as they are often positioned as vulnerable yet living outside adult protection. Their agency is suppressed by the way adults have positioned them as in need of protection.

Implementing street children's rights through participation: evidence from South Africa

The process of falling through the gap based on the elusive categorization of street children and the rhetoric of street-connected children as vulnerable, have been, and continue to be, problematic concerns among non-governmental agencies and policy-makers in terms of how to approach street children's rights. They are viewed simultaneously as either victims or delinquents, resulting in the persistence of strategies of removal from the streets (for public safety), reintegrated into families, and placed within residential settings (for their protection). I now want to draw on the reflective experiences of three young people from research I conducted in Cape Town, South Africa in 2006–7 to demonstrate how street children's (non)participation in policy and practice has resulted in many unhelpful strategies being put in place. The research employed a street ethnographic approach which was participatory in nature and included narratives and discussions with over 50 street children over an extended period of time on the streets. The first two examples explore the often difficult situations children face at home and explore some of the reasons why returning to such settings may be problematic. The final example, from Angela, further demonstrates that parental responsibilities can be fulfilled on the streets and how policies of blanket removal may disrupt caring family settings.

Wes (17) describes why he left home at the age of 9. Being at home was resulting in a violation of Wes' rights. A policy of reintegrating Wes into the family may be appropriate but not without his consultation:

> I used to stay with my parents and from there I run away from home. Ok it was... I liked it there but due to some circumstances... how can I say... my father was an abuser and it was like he had more love for my sister than me so I decided to run away. Ok I didn't get along well with him. He used to beat me and if my sister did something wrong I got the blows,

like if there was some money missing at home I get a hiding... I like my mother... she'd listen to my problems but when it came to my father it was like she was afraid of him.

However, family and community life are sometimes so problematic for young people that it results in a permanent decision to leave the home. The following extract reveals why three boys chose to leave their homes and also highlights the relative safety of the streets in Berg-en-See.[2] In this example, the danger of being drawn into gang activity resulted in their decisions to go to the streets in the first place. Yet, for some, such a decision means renouncing family connections which may place them in more danger should they return at a later point. For Martin, Mikey, and Sker, policies of family reintegration could result in significant violence towards them from relatives attached to gangs in their communities:

Martin (15):	They shoot you with a gun. Gangsters there... you stand by your gate then they shoot you.
Mikey (16):	The lifestyle of the people in that White Sands is just stealing, smoking buttons, drinking and they die on a Friday night.
Mikey (16):	They get killed by brothers [gang members]. There's a tavern, every Friday there's a gun shooting or a knife stabbing, then someone dies.
Martin (15):	Every Friday. It's horrible there now. We don't want to go there every Friday, come rather to Berg-en-See.
Sker (16):	You see here is Berg-en-See, the gangsters don't come to you and tell you, you must stand for [support] this gangster and that gangster and that gangster.

The situation was slightly different for Angela, but positioning children on the streets as vulnerable and implementing policies of placing those under 18 in residential settings created a significant challenge for maintaining contact with her young son. The following extract demonstrates Angela's commitment of care for her child yet juxtaposes this against global models of what 'the best interests of the child' mean.

Angela (20) talks about having a child on the streets. She describes how she took care of her baby, making sure he was warm and dry at night and how she provided food from him. However, following her boyfriend's incarceration, Angela had to find other means of support. First she found a new boyfriend and later she had to send her child away in order to stop him being taken from her. Angela's son stayed with his great-aunt and Angela was able to see him regularly:

We didn't do much because I was sleeping with him most of the time. I was always prepare the bed at 7 o'clock already, so he can sleep ... but I could cover us nice with banana boxes, I close us so the wind can't come in, we had mattress, we had a mat and we had blankets that I get by people, so we was always warm. I bought me a stove for R30 so I can boil water for his milk, I can make food for him to eat, even for me to eat. I spend less money than if I am going to buy takeaways, and so I saved the money, but at the moment we can't park cars anymore... My ex-boy-friend go to jail. I couldn't take it anymore because every time he leave me with the baby, he go to jail, I must look after the child. I must run up and down for cops, scared the cops is going to take my baby. So I looked for another boyfriend who would take me and my child... Two years he [the baby] stayed on the street with me. Then the cops wanted to take him, so I had to send him to someone.

These examples highlight two issues related to the problem with conceptualizing street children as only requiring protection. First, home and family are not always the most appropriate settings for children and, secondly, being without a home does not necessarily mean without the care of a loving parent. Yet, as these examples demonstrate, children are rarely consulted about the effectiveness of these particular approaches and in many circumstances reintegration to 'family life' may directly contravene street children's rights and place them into the same abusive situations that resulted in their going to the streets (van Blerk, 2013). In addition, the participation articles suggest that we must also recognize the capabilities of street children and their creative adaptability to survive in often hostile, dangerous, and lonely city environments, while recognizing that basic needs can be fulfilled in many diverse ways that break with traditional (Western) conceptions of shelter, family, and other basic survival needs, as Angela showed. This is not to suggest that street children are comfortable on the streets or that they are not desperately requiring support and attention but merely that they have immense capacity to lead their own lives productively if given the opportunity to participate in decisions that may affect them. Yet there is still a significant gap in the ways in which street children are enabled to participate, not least because many organizations would like to do more to ensure child participation but are unsure where to start.

South Africa is a useful example to focus on in order to explore the ways in which street children need to be afforded participation rights more readily in policy and practice. Unlike many other African states, where policies developed 15 years ago are still in place, South Africa has updated legislation and now has particularly progressive policies related to children's rights and their participation. Specifically, since the mid-2000s, new and amended legislation has been produced that actively incorporates street children's participation as a right. The Children's Act 38 of 2005 has the most substantive provision for children's rights, stating that every child has the right to participate in matters concerning that child and that their views should be given due consideration (Viviers and Lombard, 2013). Here we see national legislation appropriately taking account of the CRC participation articles. In addition, in 2008 South Africa produced a strategy and guide-lines for children living and working in the streets. This is a particularly important piece of legislation to highlight because of the progressive way in which participation is included. The strategy documentation offers two principles for an approach to street children within a rights-based frame-work. These are protection and participation, where street children are positioned as being experts on their own lives and needs and therefore their views must be accounted for in the design and development of any intervention (p. 17). Further, it does not seek to offer a prescriptive frame-work for working with street children, thereby reducing the need for a definitive categorization or definition. Instead it seeks to offer guidelines to enable stakeholders at national, provincial, and local levels to develop their own programmes, in consultation with children. Although reintegration into residential settings and rehabilitation are highlighted as a key strategy for children permanently on the streets, the policy progressively also makes reference to supporting young people on the streets to reach adulthood safely by developing and supporting their survival strategies on the streets (p. 9). A shortfall of the strategy is that it does not offer guidelines for how to include street children through meaningful participation. The final sec-tion explores some ways for achieving this.

Facilitating participation: lessons from research

Some momentum is emerging from international advocacy and policy groups around street children's rights and two major studies have been com-missioned: the Plan International study *Still on the Streets: Still Short of Rights* (Ray *et al.*, 2011) and the UNOHCHR (2012) study, *Protecting and Promoting of the Rights of Children Working and/or Living on the Streets*. These documents both recommend that street children be consulted on, and participate in, the drafting and design of policies, interventions, and services that impact on them. They articulate that policy development should be based on research evidence and that research should be participatory. This would facilitate street children's participation. This final section explores how street chil-dren's participation can be facilitated and draws on lessons from participa-tory research in three key areas: engaging with street children; techniques to facilitate participation; and participation as a process.

Engaging with street children

In general, participation entails engaging *with* street children, rather than extracting *from* them and treats them not as objects but active agents in their own lives (Cahill, 2004; Beazley and Ennew, 2006). This includes using a critical in-depth approach, most radically, rooted in the work of Paulo Freire (1972), which at best aims to increase participants' awareness of their circumstances in order to effect change in their lives and transform the world through action and reflection (Pain and Francis, 2003). Participatory philosophy is therefore a process involving commitment to on-going information sharing, dialogue, trust, reflection, and action whereby participants lead and control the process from initiating interventions and policy through to analysis and implementation (O'Kane, 2004). In practice, levels of participation vary greatly and the deepest levels of participation are rarely actualized. Hart's (1997) 'ladder of participation' describes a spectrum of ways of involving young people in decision-making, and although the most basic may be tokenistic and even exploitative, participation at the highest level is not always beneficial to participants or actually desired. Indeed, street children may prefer not to participate at all; hence it is most appropriate to work with children on their own terms (O'Kane, 2004). This is pertinent to street children where their agency and ability to participate are often highly constrained within cultural practice including street culture and hierarchies (Abebe, 2009; Bordonaro, 2012). However, engaging in implementing interventions without significant discussion with street children of the entire process has been widely criticized (Boyden and Ennew, 1997). As Mark Connolly (1990) states street children are their own experts: they know what issues are important to them and how they understand their future. Participation then should be engaged in on an equal basis with street children; on their terms and in their spaces. Hunger, lack of sleep, lack of available time, loss of earnings, and mobility are issues which require careful integration into the ways in which street children are able to participate. The timing and placing of participatory evidence gathering must therefore be on their terms. This may involve working at a variety of times and places in order to suit the needs of children, their daily work patterns, and levels of mobility. Further, gender is an important consideration particularly where girls may find that they are severely restricted in their freedom to spend time engaged in research. For example, girls engaged in commercial sex work may be subject to varying working patterns with those located in red-light districts potentially having very little freedom, their time often highly structured and accounted for (van Blerk, 2008). However, remembering the context of street children's situations and the relationships they are part of can be helpful in negotiating time to participate in dialogue when it is convenient for all parties. This may not be a quick process but it is one which needs to work within significant constraints, and where participation can be developed over time through trusted relationships with those specifically involved in developing and designing interventions.

Methods of facilitating participation

In thinking through how participation can be facilitated, there are some useful lessons to draw from research. Most importantly, the evidence-base required for designing and implementing policy should be research-based

(Ray *et al.*, 2011; UNOHCHR, 2012). Therefore the process of engaging street children in research has much to offer for the process of collecting an evidence-base for policy in a participatory manner.

Ansell *et al.* (2012) make the distinction that participation in research does not necessarily mean utilizing participatory techniques. For street children, participation is about participating in the decision-making processes around the research and adapting tools and techniques for facilitating the design of interventions rather than using specific participatory tools per se (Young and Barrett, 2001). It is not the techniques themselves that make the process participatory, but rather the way the policy and/or programme is produced through the social relations that take place between street children and policy-makers. Yet, those researching with street children advocate participatory techniques, for both ethical and practical reasons. Participatory techniques are understood to shift power relations, giving children greater control over their involvement in the research, and similarly in any evidence-based policy formation. Moreover, children's insights into their own lives are said to be most readily expressed when they are facilitated through self-directed activities (Young and Barrett, 2001). Different children prefer or require different techniques (Punch, 2002), so a multi-method approach enables most to contribute (Morrow, 2008) and seeks to include the experiences of the hardest to reach groups, usually those whose rights have been violated the most. The techniques employed by researchers are equally ones that can be used with street children in designing solutions to particular problems or issues. Visual techniques such as mapping, photography, drawing, and video, and active techniques such as drama and role-play have been shown to work well with street children as strategies for thinking through solutions and appropriate responses (Young and Barrett, 2001). The active process of these techniques coupled with their non-written format are especially useful for street children who may have very low levels of literacy and struggle with attention if they have previously or currently engaged in drug-use. They also help to reduce uneven power relations through using visual materials as a focus for subsequent discussion, minimizing any power hierarchies between participants and practitioners. Exploring possibilities for children facilitating their own participation and that of their peers can also be empowering as long as appropriate ethical and practical training is provided to all facilitators.

Participation as a process

Finally, when considering the participation of street children it is important to reflect on participation as a process. The point that is most useful to make here is that participation is not just important in evidence gathering but that street children have the right to be listened to in every aspect of policy development. This means participation in deciding what the problems are that require attention, the best ways to provide support and also the outcomes and recommendations put forward into policy. The process should also be iterative, enabling street children to comment, through appropriate means, on all aspects of the process.

However, the process of empowerment through participation can be an uncomfortable space. It is important therefore to consider the ethical implications of including street children in the policy process. This means that because children are active participants throughout the process and their agency recognized, we should not overlook the complex ways in which their lives are shaped by events and situations beyond their control. The numerous ways in which street life affects children's abilities to engage in particular types of activity should be carefully considered. Participating in any relational process can raise challenges. An ethical process needs to ensure that it does not violate young people's rights and can in fact offer some empowerment through engaging in the process, with appropriate debriefing. This is particularly important when children have experienced traumatic events in their lives. This is more often the case when exploring street experiences, which have the potential to be emotionally harmful. Often the narratives presented by street children will raise numerous concerns regarding life on the streets covering both negative issues in children's personal lives and their involvement in illegal activities. In many instances this may be the first time they openly disclose such detailed information on their past and present lives. Putting in place practical strategies of debriefing and follow-up counselling/life coaching can result in improvements in self-confidence and self-worth among those that participate (van Blerk, 2011).

Conclusion: progressing participation rights for street children

This chapter has highlighted that street children's access to rights is fundamentally linked to their participation rights. Understanding children's experiences of street-connectedness can have critical implications for policy regarding current and future well-being, and how best to protect their rights, particularly where they have been violated through the negative outcomes of street life. Additionally, as children's agency is now a widely regarded given, their participation in the process is essential. Participatory research is now being recognized as one of the more successful ways in which street children's voices are beginning to be heard and this can be utilized to offer advice for the inclusion of street children in decision-making. As this chapter has shown, despite the political commitment of African governments to ratify the UN convention, the transportation of a (Western) global childhood ideal has not always been in the best interests of street children. Their particular circumstances which often locate them outside formal family structures, coupled with a positioning of children as vulnerable and needing protection, make it difficult for street children to access their rights without the support of adults. Further the need for formal documentation on street children may help to expedite this process. Ray *et al.* (2011: 21) state:

Given the paucity of specific references to street involved children in international human rights instruments, it is recommended that the Committee on the CRC develops a General Comment on 'Non-discrimination and Street Children' in order to provide more detailed guidance to States Parties. It is proposed that the General Comment contain guidance on prevention and how the economic, social and cultural rights of children should be respected, protected and fulfilled. It should also include guidance on how the autonomy of children to react to their circumstances can be reconciled with their right to protection.

Such a comment may enable governments to see street children as meaningful autonomous people with much to say about their own lives, and move away from classifying street children with all children under the same banner, recognizing that child protection should take different forms depending on the contextual experiences of children.

Policies designed to support street children have, then, not always taken account of the specific negative experiences of family life many such children have chosen to leave behind. More recent policies, as discussed, are now recognizing the importance of street children's participation in decisions which affect them and, as is now the case in South Africa, are making provision in legislation for this; a model that could be used as an exemplar for other states. Similarly, international documents (UNOHCHR, 2012) are calling for participatory research to become part of the policy process where street children's voices are at least heard and included in the evidence-base from which policy is developed. However, the extent to which African governments are able to fully incorporate street children's voices in a fully participatory process remains a challenge.

Notes

1 The problematic nature of the term 'street children' and by association 'street youth' is acknowledged: it locates young people in the street, which is static, excluding the capacity of young people to move between different social and spatial environments, and it associates the negative characteristics of street environments to childhood (Conticini, 2004; see Connolly and Ennew (1996), Young (2003), for a discussion of street children's 'out of placeness' in the city through their use of marginal locations and illegal activities). The definition of street children has been widely debated since their emergence on the international stage, and remains a hotly contested and debated term. However, it is now acknowledged that street children is a socially constructed term that varies over time and place, often referring to a variety of groups of children with different connections to the street. The term is used here to highlight the particular circumstances of young people who are in one or more ways significantly connected to the streets, living and working in the streets.

2 This extract was previously published in van Blerk (2012).

References

Abebe, T. (2009) 'Multiple methods, complex dilemmas: negotiating socio-ethical spaces in participatory research with disadvantaged children', *Children's Geographies*, 7: 451–66.

Ansell, N., Robson, E., Hajdu, F., and van Blerk, L. (2012) 'Learning from young people about their lives: using participatory methods to research the impacts of AIDS in southern Africa', *Children's Geographies*, 10: 169–86.

Aptekar, L. (1988) *Street Children of Cali*, Durham, NC: Duke University Press.

Beazley, H. (2002) '"Vagrants wearing make-up": negotiating spaces on the streets of Yogyakarta, Indonesia,' *Urban Studies*, 39 (9): 1665–83.

Beazley, H. (2003) 'Voices from the margins: street children's subcultures in Indonesia', *Children's Geographies*, 1 (2): 181–200.

Beazley, H. and Ennew, J. (2006) 'Participatory methods and approaches: tackling the two tyrannies', in V. Desai and R. Potter (eds) *Doing Development Research*, London: Sage.

Bordonaro, L. (2012) 'Agency does not mean freedom. Cape Verdean street children and the politics of children's agency', *Children's Geographies*, 10: 413–26.

Boyden, J. (1990) 'Childhood and the policy makers: a comparative perspective on the globalization of childhood', in A. James and A. Prout (eds) *Constructing and Reconstructing Childhood: Contemporary Issues in the Sociological Study of Childhood*, Basingstoke: Falmer.

Boyden, J. and Ennew, J. (1997) *Children in Focus – A Manual for Participatory Action Research with Children*, Stockholm: Radda Barnen.

Cahill, C. (2004) 'Defying gravity? raising consciousness through collective research', *Children's Geographies*, 2 (2): 273–86.

Campos, R., Raffaelli, M., Ude, W., Greco, M., Ruff, A., Rolf, J., Antunes, C.M., Halsey, N., and Greco, D. (1994) 'Social networks and daily activities of street youth in Belo Horizonte, Brazil', *Child Development*, 65 (5): 319–30.

Cheney, K. (2012) 'Killing them softly? Using children's rights to empower Africa's orphans and vulnerable children', *International Social Work*, 56: 92–101.

Connolly, M. (1990) 'Adrift in the city: a comparative study of street children in Bogota, Colombia and Guatemala City', in N. Boxill (ed.) *Homeless Children: The Watchers and the Waiters*, London: The Hawthorn Press.

Connolly, M. and Ennew, J. (1996) 'Introduction: children out of place', *Childhood*, 3 (2): 131–45.

Conticini, A. (2004) 'We are the kings: managing, protecting and promoting livelihoods on the streets of Dhaka.' Paper presented at the 'Livelihoods on the margins' conference, SOAS, 8–9 July.

Department of Social Development (2009) *Strategy and Guidelines for Children Living and Working in the Streets*, Department of Social Development, Republic of South Africa.

Ennew, J. (1994) *Street and Working Children: A Guide to Planning. Development Manual 4*, London: Save the Children.

Ennew, J. (2003) 'Difficult circumstances: some reflections on "street children" in Africa', *Children, Youth and Environments*, 13 (1): 1–18.

Evans, R. (2006) 'Negotiating social identities: the influence of gender, age and ethnicity on young people's "street careers" in Tanzania', *Children's Geographies*, 4 (1): 109–28.

Freire, P. (1972) *Pedagogy of the Oppressed*, Harmondsworth: Penguin.

Hart, R. (1997) *Children's Participation: The Theory and Practice of Involving Young Citizens in Community Development and Environmental Care*, London: Earthscan.

Hecht, T. (1998) *At Home in the Street: Street-Children of North-East Brazil*, Cambridge: Cambridge University Press.

Holloway, S. and Valentine, G. (2000) *Children's Geographies: Playing, Living, Learning*, London: Routledge.

Jamieson, L. and Milne, S. (2012) 'Children and young people's relationships, relational processes and social change: reading across worlds', *Children's Geographies*, 10: 265–78.

Kampala City Council (1997) *Kampala City Council Network for Street Children Action Plan*, Kampala: KCC.

Klocker, N. (2007) 'An example of "thin" agency: child domestic workers in Tanzania', in E. Robson *et al.* (eds) *Young Rural Lives*, New York, NY: Taylor & Francis.

Morrow, V. (2008) 'Ethical dilemmas in research with children and young people about their social environments', *Children's Geographies*, 6 (1): 49–61.

Mulinge, M. (2002) 'Implementing the 1989 United Nations' Convention on the Rights of the Child in sub-Saharan Africa: the overlooked socioeconomic and political dilemmas', *Child Abuse and Neglect*, 26 (11): 1117–30.

Oduro, G. (2012) 'Children of the street: sexual citizenship and the unprotected lives of Ghanaian street youth', *Comparative Education*, 48: 41–56.

O'Kane, C. (2004) 'Responding to key challenges and ethical issues', in *Children and Young People as Citizens: Partners for Social Change*, Kathmandu: Save the Children Alliance.

Pain, R. and Francis, P. (2003) 'Reflections on participatory research', *Area*, 35: 46–54.

Poretti, M., Hanson, K., Darbellay, F., and Berchtold, A. (2013) 'The rise and fall of icons of "stolen childhood" since the adoption of the UN Convention on the Rights of the Child', *Childhood* (DOI: 10.1177/0907568213481816).

Punch, S. (2002) 'Research with children: the same or different from adults?' *Childhood*, 9: 321–41.

Ray, P., Davey, C., and Nolan, P. (2011) *Still on the Streets: Still Short of Rights*, London: Plan International.

Swart, J. (1990) *Malunde: The Street Children of Hillbrow, Johannesurg*, Johannesburg: Witwatersrand University Press.

Thomas de Benitez, S. (2007) *State of the World's Street Children: Violence*, London: Consortium for Street Children.

Thomas de Benitez, S. (2011) *State of the World's Street Children: Research*, London: Consortium for Street Children.

UNOHCHR (2012) *Protecting and Promoting the Rights of Children Working and/or Living on the Streets*, Geneva: United Nations.

van Blerk, L. (2006) 'Diversity and difference in the everyday lives of Ugandan street children', *Social Dynamics*, 32 (1): 47–74.

van Blerk, L. (2008) 'Poverty, migration and sex work: youth transitions in Ethiopia', *Area*, 40 (2): 245–53.

van Blerk, L. (2011) 'Researching street youth's life paths in Cape Town, South Africa.' Paper presented at the RGS-IBG International Conference, London, 1–3 September.

van Blerk, L. (2012) 'Berg-en-See street boys: merging street and family relationships in Cape Town, South Africa', *Children's Geographies* (special issue on family relationships), 10: 321–36.

van Blerk, L. (2013) 'New street geographies: the impact of urban governance on the mobilities of Cape Town's street youth', *Urban Studies*, 50: 556–73.

Viviers, A. and Lombard, A. (2013) 'The ethics of children's participation: fundamental to children's rights realisation in Africa', *International Social Work*, 56: 7–21.

Young, L. (2003) 'The place of street children in Kampala, Uganda: marginalisation, resistance and acceptance in the urban environment', *Environment and Planning D: Society and Space*, 21: 607–28.

Young, L. (2004) 'Journeys to the street: the complex migration geographies of Ugandan street children', *Geoforum*, 35: 471–88.

Young, L. and Barrett, H. (2001) 'Adapting visual methods: action research with Kampala street children', *Area*, 33: 141–52.

13 Making the case for a broader definition of child participation

Evidence from the Niger Delta
of Nigeria

Samuel Okyere and Afua Twum-Danso Imoh

Introduction

Children's participation rights have been much researched and theorized since they became one of the fundamental tenets of the 1989 United Nations Convention on the Rights of the Child (CRC). The Convention posits in Article 12 that children capable of expressing their views must be given space to do so in all matters that affect them. This demand enjoys significant support in principle. In practice, however, almost a quarter of a century after the Convention was approved and adopted by the UN General Assembly, children still face numerous obstacles in accessing their participation rights.

These difficulties are often attributed to long-held negative attitudes towards children and their position in diverse societies around the world. And indeed, the evidence suggests that attitudes towards children within their families and communities are severe obstacles to their ability to access their participatory rights as outlined in the Convention. However, while we do not disagree with the conventional definition of child participation or the explanations put forward for the limited implementation of participation rights, in this chapter, we raise certain questions about them. We explore the extent to which a substantial reason for the obstacles facing child participation may also be attributable to the way in which children's participation rights are conceptualized and implemented at the level of the international community.

In effect, the aim of the chapter is to show the extent to which the conventional definition of participation, in and of itself, can be a contributory factor in the limited implementation of so-called participatory rights. Drawing on evidence from fieldwork conducted in the Niger Delta area of Nigeria, the chapter will also suggest that the practice of children's participation rights could actually be more effective if greater attention were paid to the social and cultural context in which these rights are implemented, and importantly, to how communities themselves define, understand, and practise children's participatory rights. It will be seen later in the chapter that in societies such as the Niger Delta, where both adults and children owe obligations to each other, promotion of children's participatory rights may be greatly improved if the societal roles already assigned children are given their due recognition in dominant conceptualizations and discourses about child participation.

This chapter is based on a research study conducted by the University of Sheffield in collaboration with Stepping Stones Nigeria and funded by the University of Sheffield's Collaborative R&D Award as part of a knowledge transfer initiative. The focus of the study was on Akwa-Ibom, Cross River, and Rivers states in the Niger Delta area of Nigeria. The primary aims of the research were to explore the understanding of children's participation among non-governmental organizations (NGOs) which provide services to children in the region; whether these groups were incorporating children's participatory rights into their activities; how they were doing so if they were; and the obstacles they faced in the implementation of children's participation rights in their communities.

Organizations which participated comprised NGOs, orphanages, and educational institutions. A total of 75 staff from 40 of these organizations provided information at six focus group discussions which were organized in Akwa-Ibom and Cross River States. These adult participants and some of their colleagues who could not take part in the focus group discussions also completed 100 questionnaires to offer further information on the range of issues being explored in the research. Participatory workshops and group discussions involving games and artwork, as well as question-and-answer sessions, were organized to collect data from the 90 children who took part in the research. Semi-structured interviews and photo elicitation were used to collect more in-depth information from 24 of the children who attended the workshops. Finally, an art and essay competition was also organized within schools in the research setting inviting pupils to draw or write about the challenges facing children in their community and how these can be addressed. A total of 33 entries were received.

Both child and adult participants were asked about their understanding of children's participation rights and their views on the subject. They were also asked about the extent to which children were allowed, or were able, to voice their views and opinions in their environments, the conditions which aided or obstructed this process, and a wide range of other questions. As a precursor to these sets of questions, the participants discussed the conceptualization of childhood in their society, societal expectations of children in the Niger Delta, and the challenges children face in their communities.

At the end of the one-month fieldwork, the participants' responses were analysed thematically for the publication of a research report. The publication of the report was preceded by dissemination events held to inform the participants of the research findings. For reliability and validity records, it is useful to note that all who attended agreed with how the information they gave had been interpreted. Other outputs of the study included a documentary showcasing children's views about a broad range of issues in their society and a cartoon sketch highlighting the challenges children face in the Niger

Delta. The winning art entry was also developed into a poster aimed at promoting the rights of children in this part of Nigeria.

Children's participation rights: a brief overview

Almost a quarter of a century after the CRC declared participation to be one of children's fundamental rights, many children continue to be denied involvement in the discussion of issues which concern them. Nevertheless, we are in agreement with Lansdown (2002) that the prevailing situation can still be considered as a significant departure from what transpired prior to the Convention. Further optimism can also be drawn from Woodhead's (2010) observation that while the implementation of children's participation rights faces challenges, the idea or principle of child participation itself is increasingly and widely being accepted across the globe. This observation is wholly supported by our own research – at least at the level of NGO acceptance and support for the concept. Of the 75 NGO workers who participated in the focus group discussions and the 100 questionnaire respondents, only one person answered in the negative when asked whether children should be included in participatory activities and programmes.

This intuitive support among some sectors of the population in various countries for the principle of child participation is partly attributable to transformations in certain assumptions about childhood and attitudes towards children (Mayall, 2000). Many scholars now agree that children can play meaningful roles in their own lives, and should be given space to do so (Iversen, 2002; Bastia, 2005, Punch, 2007; Thorne, 2008). As James and Prout (1997: 23) put it in their seminal text, children are not merely 'cultural dopes of socialization theory'; rather, they are active in the construction of their own lives. This understanding of children and childhood had actually begun gathering momentum in the period leading up to the adoption of the CRC (see Holt, 1974). Hence, children's exclusion from decision-making, particularly about their own lives, was increasingly called into question (Sinclair, 2004).

From the above, it can be deduced that the understanding that children possess agency was a key deciding factor in the decision by children's rights policy-makers to make children bearers of rights. The CRC is, therefore, the 'most significant legal response' or representation of the idea that children themselves have roles to play in transforming their lives (Simpson, 1997: 111). However, another important consideration also influenced the elevation of participation rights as one of the CRC's four cardinal principles (UNICEF, 2005). During the development of the CRC, policy-makers recognized that in spite of all the provisions intended for children in the new Convention, they could still be open to abuse and exploitation because they did not have a voice (Buchanan, 2006). As Willow (2002) also adds, this voicelessness or lack of representation potentially undermined all other rights being considered for children. The introduction of participation rights into the new legislation was, therefore, also intended to empower children themselves 'to challenge abuses or neglect of their rights and to take action to promote and protect those rights' (Lansdown, 2001: 2).

In effect, the case for the implementation of children's participation rights can first be made on the basis that, as members of society, they also have a right to be heard. Support for implementation can also be garnered on the basis that when given a voice, children will themselves be legally able to 'advocate for their own cause and transform their situations' (Reddy and Ratna, 2002: 7). These two core positions have been echoed by many who have explored the subject (see, for example, Shier, 2001; Hill *et al.*, 2004; Sinclair, 2004; Partridge, 2005; Hart, 2007; Rimmer, 2012). However, as discussed in the next section, and indeed as our own study found, this consensus begins to falter when the meaning and scope of children's participation rights, and how they are to be implemented, are subjected to deeper scrutiny.

Child participation: a term in search of a definition and scope?

Child participation, according to the UN Committee on the Rights of the Child (2009: 5), principally implies the involvement of children in dialogue. The committee defines the term as:

> ongoing processes, which include information-sharing and dialogue between children and adults based on mutual respect, and in which children can learn how their views and those of adults are taken into account and shape the outcome of such processes.

This point is re-echoed by Lansdown (2002: 273), for whom children participate when they are given a say in 'processes, decisions, and activities that affect them, in order to achieve greater respect for their rights'. Chawla (2001: 1) makes a similar argument because she sees participation as 'a process in which children and youth engage with other people around issues that concern their individual and collective life conditions'. Dialogue is also the focus of Hart's study (1992: 5) in which he defines participation as 'the process of sharing decisions which affect one's life and the life of the community in which one lives'.

There clearly is substantial support for the conceptualization of children's participation rights in terms of dialogue. However, a number of concerns have also been raised about it. As Lundy (2007) makes clear, those who have expressed disquiet about the dominant explanation of participation do not doubt or disagree that children should be allowed to express their opinions about issues that affect them. Contrarily, as seen in Hill *et al.* (2006), the outcome of children's involvement in decision-making, or rather the lack of outcome, is the concern. Contributors to Hill *et al.* (2006) argue that children are 'consulted', rather than allowed to 'participate' when their views are sought without any feedback or impact. As such, participatory discourses and practices must emphasize the fact that once children's voices and opinions have been elicited, they must also be offered responses or feedback for their views.

Bird (1999) and Liebel (2002) go even further, as they question whether having a voice alone necessarily addresses certain challenges and denials of rights faced by some children. It is instructive to note that this point has also been highlighted by children themselves. In the work of Karunan (2005), Save the Children (2008), van den Berge (2007), and van Beers (2011), we are introduced to groups of working children from South America, Asia, and Africa who express the anxiety that children's participation rights are not being thought through or practised in the fuller or broader sense that they should. Similar concerns about the understanding and scope of children's participation rights also came up among the poignant issues in our own research in the Niger Delta. The chapter focuses on this issue in more detail shortly. Specifically, we will draw attention to how the children who participated in this study make sense of their participation rights and the manner in which they participate or think they should participate in their environments.

Linked to the above, one of the most important findings emerging from our study is that children's participation rights are ultimately given meaning and value by the society within which they are being implemented. This is a point Reddy and Ratna (2002: 4) also highlight when they argue that 'the understanding of participation and the way it is translated into action varies and seems to be defined by the sociocultural context of the child and the ideological frame surrounding this understanding'. Another important finding emerging from our study is that children's participation rights are ultimately given meaning and value by the society within which they are being implemented.

CRC-defined child participation rights in the Niger Delta: understandings and implementation

Key among the research objectives was to explore the understanding of children's participation rights among the adults and children who participated in the study. It was found that many of the adult participants were knowledgeable about the meaning of child participation as defined by the Convention. The definitions presented by some were quite similar to those found within the dominant literature on the subject. For instance, compare two commonly cited definitions within the literature:

> a process in which children and youth engage with other people around issues that concern their individual and collective life conditions. (Chawla, 2001: 1)

the process of sharing decisions which affect one's life and the life of the community in which one lives. (Hart, 1992: 5)

with the following which were offered by some of the NGO workers during the focus group discussions:

Child participation is when a child is involved in decision-making or given a degree of consent. (FGD participant in Eket)

Child participation is when children's voices are heard and their opinions count at home, at school, and the environment in which they find themselves. (FGD participant in Eket)

Child participation means encouraging and enabling a childto take part in matters concerning him or her. (FGD participant in Calabar)

That some NGO workers understood child participation in the sense intended by the Convention was somewhat anticipated. Their explanations confirmed a presumption that as children's rights practitioners and advocates, they would have found the need to scrutinize certain provisions of the CRC in the course of their work. We also saw the adult participants' explanations as an illustration of the CRC's progressive influence on the understanding and operations of not only international NGOs, but also local NGOs. This assumption was lent further credence when the reflections of some of the child participants confirmed that they were given the chance to take part in decisions and discourses in various areas of their community:

Last year, me and my brother and my mother we were moving from the place we stay. So my mother now call us and say we are going to change school so what school do we like. I say my own idea and my brother also say his own and we all agree, but when we went to the new school we were not comfortable there. We told my mother again and she ask us if we want to go to our old school and we now say yes. Now we are there again. (Bassey, 13)

And at church, if erm… when… erm rules are to be made in the choir, everybody is erm… required to speak to say what they think. Also, even at school, we have clubs for children, for the students, and if we think that there is something wrong with the rules that have been made, we say whether we… tell principal. (Otomoye, 11)

When my mum is making a decision, she will call my elder sister and I and say that what do you think about this, what should we do?… and we will bring our own suggestion and it will be accepted by her. (Chidima, 15)

The above exemplifies our view that in line with Article 12 of the CRC, some children in the research setting were offered space to air their opinions in matters which had implications for their education, recreation, religion, family, and other aspects of their lives. Although these children participated in diverse areas of their community including in NGO projects, most of the examples they cited were drawn from discussions and events in their homes. A conclusion we drew from this, which was also confirmed in an interview with Edidong (13), was that participatory opportunities for children in the research setting were more likely to be available at home than in other spheres of their society:

Interviewer:	Where do you participate most... at home, at church, in the wider community or at school?
Edidong:	At home.
Interviewer:	Why do you say so?
Edidong:	Because when decisions are being made, I'm involved, I'm included.
Interviewer:	Can you give me an example of a time that you have been included in the decision-making?
Edidong:	When I was to change school, I was being consulted that do you want to change and said yes I want to change.
Interviewer:	Was this taken into account?
Edidong:	Yes it was.
Interviewer:	So how did this make you feel... the fact that you were taken into account... how did that make you feel?
Edidong:	Happy because I was being involved in decision-making.

Edidong's feeling of contentment and his assurance that his views count is another of the positive outcomes which have been linked with participation (Woodhead and Faulkner, 2000).

However, our study equally found that on the whole, there was substantial room for improvement relating to the extent to which children's voices were being solicited and considered in the research setting. We have already highlighted the fact that children actually had limited participatory opportunities in other places besides the home. Indeed, even within the home itself, a range of challenges hampered the extent to which children could participate. The following section will discuss these and other constraints found by the study, but it is worth noting beforehand that a number of the challenges we found are not necessarily unique to the Niger Delta. A review of existing literature and research on children's participation generally shows that challenges similar to those we found also hamper the implementation of children's participation rights in diverse societies around the world (Willow, 1999; Thomas, 2000; Walker, 2001; Twum-Danso, 2009, 2010; Vis et al., 2012).

Obstacles to the implementation of children's participation rights in the Niger Delta

Although some of the children who were involved in this study are able to access their participatory rights to an extent – at least in the context of the family – the broader picture is that the majority of the 90 child participants were not being given the space to participate in the manner stipulated by the CRC. Together with the adult research participants, the children highlighted a myriad factors to explain why they and other children are denied the chance of being involved in dialogue within the contexts of the family and community – even on issues affecting themselves. Many of the challenges they highlighted support Cole's (1996) assertion that attitudes towards children and their position in society have a significant impact on the implementation of their rights. Notable among the points raised by the participants was children's subservience in society; their status demands that they listen to what their parents and other adults say and obey without question. Owing to this expectation, the very idea of child participation instinctively troubles some adults, as our data show:

> Like my Uncle for example, he will tell me that because he is the one who take care of me, he must decide everything for me so I should only keep quiet and listen. (Ida, 11)

> Here in Eket, our traditional norms and values do not emphasize on children's participation in terms of what the UNCRC Article 12 states. We believe that children must be subservient and listen to what they are told. Therefore, they are allowed to participate but this is only through work. (FGD participant in Eket)

> Because people here believe that whenever a family issue or matter is being discussed, a child is not supposed to be there to hear or take part in what they are saying. A child should hide while their parents or relatives are there having their meeting. A child is not supposed to be in there. (Chidima, 15)

Children's position of subservience in the Niger Delta, like many other communities elsewhere, is first because they are dependent on adults. In addition to this, or indeed because of their reliance on adults, there is also the expectation that they show courtesy and respect to their seniors (Dei, 1994). The idea of courtesy and respect for adults or any other person can be deemed virtuous. However, our study found that the expectation that children show 'unqualified respect and obedience to those who are older than them', as Ndofirepi and Ndofirepi (2012: 21) have described the situation, can also have negative ramifications for children's participation rights. In particular, many adults are wary that when children are permitted to voice their own opinions, they may question or contradict what adults say, and as such, dis-respect adults:

> Like if we try to air out our views... we just say this thing is not right, it should be changed. Then they say we are not respecting them so we get punished sometimes. Flogging or being made to work or weeding. (Edidong, 13)

> Here in our Eket, children who try to get their views across are said to be disrespectful by many adults, he or she will be told to shut up and sit down. (FGD participant in Eket)

Numerous authors have conclusively undermined the passive child para-digm and the perception that children's voices have no value (James *et al.*, 1998; Alderson, 2000; Kellett *et al.*, 2004; Bourdillon, 2006; Wells, 2009; Tisdall and Punch, 2012). However, these ideas prevail, for this study found such attitudes towards children to be another major reason why they are excluded from discussions by some adults. As Odey (14) lamented in an interview, he and his peers are often underestimated and denied their par-ticipation rights by adults who feel that children cannot make any useful contributions to discussions:

> Because the community, they view children as, you know, irrelevant... they are like... because children are always playing and they are also engaging in other activities that children do... the adults don't think that children are matured enough to say something that matters. (Odey, 14)

Similar views were expressed by two other child participants in interviews conducted for this study:

> In Cross River here, children are being looked at like people who don't deserve to be involved in decision-making, they are not active in most things that are going on in the society, they just look at them like they are helpless individuals. (Edidong, 13)

> If a decision is being made in this family, children are being sent out, then the elder ones are being kept to make decisions, they don't involve the children. Most of the times, the decisions taken, the children don't really play any role in it. The parents think they are too small to make decisions. (Nse, 10)

This last assertion by 10-year-old Nse was further corroborated during interactions with adult research participants. It was suggested that due to assumptions about children's maturity and capacity, some adults feel that involving them in discussions is simply a waste of time: 'Many adults consider children to be too young and ignorant to make informed choices or contribute in any way, therefore involving them will be a waste of time' (FGD participant in Eket).

Further, although children's best chances of participation are mostly in the home, they are still likely to be excluded from household discussions when issues of a sensitive nature are being discussed. This is for fear that children are incapable of keeping certain family secrets to themselves:

> Because they think that children don't understand the main reason for what they are saying we may go and say it outside to our friends... we may go and say it to somebody, something that was supposed to be a secret that we are not supposed to tell anybody, we will go and tell our friends that this is what happened and the secret will not really be a secret. Everybody will hear about it. (Chidima, 15)

> Many adults, particularly parents are concerned that children may leak family secrets if they are made aware of these. (FGD participant in Calabar)

It is evident thus far that many of the obstacles to children's participation are due to societal attitudes to children and expectations from them, especially by adults. The irony of the fact that significant opposition to children's participation comes from adults, as a participant in Calabar observed, is that many are also keen for their own children to play active roles in society:

> What my colleagues have said is true, but it is also ironic that most parents want their children to be bold, confident, and take part in public displays such as school plays, church dramas, and cultural expos and so on. (FGD participant in Calabar)

Nevertheless, children's position in society was not the only issue which served as an impediment to their participation rights. Numerous studies in the Global South have underscored the crucial role poverty plays in the inability of children to access numerous provisions guaranteed them by the CRC (Bonnet, 1993; Basu and Van, 1998; Admassie, 2002; Schmitz *et al.*, 2004; Emerson and Knabb, 2006). This argument is supported by this study as poverty was found to be another serious obstacle to children's access to many of their rights including participation in the Niger Delta and Nigeria as a whole. Indeed, the causal chain between poverty and the denial of various aspects of children's rights has also been established by some of the child participants themselves, as can be noted in 15-year-old

Bassey's statement and the interview with Edim (12), both of which are presented below:

Interviewer: What are some of the problems children face in your community?
Edim: Like street hawking, parents do not have enough money to send their children to school so they send them to hawk. Child labour, child pawning[1]...
Interviewer: What do you think are the causes of these problems?
Edim: Poverty because poverty in turn give way for malnutrition. Child labour and child pawning because of inadequate money, parents do not have money to buy food for everybody. (extract from interview with Edim, 12)

> Some people... some children that have these rights, maybe they came from a good family, that the family are, are well did [wealthy/well off], they have money, but some [children], their father or mother does not have enough money to send his or her child to school so they give the child oranges to hawk or any foodstuff. (Bassey, 15)

The obstacles caused by poverty to children's rights to participate are perhaps equally daunting as those caused by cultural norms or opposition from adults. The linkage between poverty and participation is also very broad because it extends to other aspects of life in the Niger Delta. Whole families and communities are living in poverty because they are not permitted to participate in decisions and discussions about their natural resources (UNDP, 2006; Amnesty International, 2009). This poverty caused by exclusion from participation partly fuelled the militancy and youth violence for which the region has become known (Joab-Peterside, 2007). As many participants in this study also argued, poverty or financial distress equally accounts for a multitude of instances where parents in particular have denied their children permission to express themselves:

> Poverty and lack of adequate resources also makes it difficult for some parents to seek children's views even where they may be willing. This is because they may not be able to meet the demands the children make. (FGD participant in Calabar)

> From my experience living in a communal house, I can say that many adults do not speak with the children because they cannot provide what the children ask. For everybody's peace of mind, they just shut them down and do what they can afford. (questionnaire respondent)

This study also found poverty to be equally responsible for the social exclusion present in communities across the Niger Delta. Children from deprived parts of the community are not able to join with their peers from affluent neighbourhoods when events are being organized. The clearest manifestation of this, according to the research participants, are the children's parliaments in Cross River and Akwa-Ibom States. These children's parliaments were instituted as a model for the promotion of children's participation rights; yet, children from poor backgrounds and other constrained circumstances are excluded from the parliamentary sessions:

> We have talked about how everything around us is being politicized; like the issue of using children for 'show making'.[2] I also want to add that even then, those children are not picked randomly. They are still the children of elites such as state functionaries and executives, so they will just bring them... the other man like the senator will have two or three of his daughters at the so-called children's parliament and the commissioner will have the same. (FGD participant Calabar)

> Though a children's parliament exists in Akwa-Ibom State, it is a very exclusive club because only a handful of children from affluent, educated, and well-connected backgrounds are able to participate. The ordinary child, street children, and others are excluded. (FGD participant in Eket)

The exclusion of disadvantaged children from participating in the wider society is an issue which concerns UNICEF too, as evidenced by the point below taken from the web page of UNICEF Nigeria:

> The Federal Government inaugurated the Children's Parliament in 2003 to enhance children's participation. Since then, 26 States have inaugurated children's parliaments. The main challenge is to make these Parliaments truly representative of the broad categories of Nigerian children, including the most vulnerable and disadvantaged. (UNICEF, 2007)

This concern corroborates Edim's (12) view that poverty and the social exclusion it has created in their society do not bode well for the participation of some children:

> Erm... for an instance... a community are made up of let's say... ok ok ok like rich people when they see poor people, erm. It's like the rich people are separated from the poor people and the poor people cannot attend the rich people part or meeting so this becomes a problem.

Indeed, even when invitations are issued to children from poor backgrounds to participate in participatory or leadership development events, the lack of funds still makes it impossible for many to take up the opportunity:

> There is also the case that many families or children in this community do not have the finances to attend programmes and events aimed at

helping children to boost their outlook and ability to engage in communal activities. (FGD participant in Calabar)

The examples above illustrate the significance of poverty and its effects when children's inability to access their participation rights in the Niger Delta is being considered. However, it is also important to highlight 17-year-old Enobong's point that the poverty argument also risks being overstated at times:

> The main thing people look at is poverty, but it's not really poverty, I think it will be ignorance and illiteracy... when parents are ignorant, some of them might be rich but they are ignorant of the fact that their children have rights that it needs to be this particular thing... I'm going to... another thing like their emotional... talking about the emotional aspect of the child and some parents do not know that emotionally, they abuse their child when they do not go close to the child to know their problems. They make them sad... instead of asking the children [about their problems] they shout them down. And just like hugging a child and telling a child I love you. So I think it's ignorance and illiteracy that makes some children to suffer all this. Children whose parents are ignorant suffer this abuse, but children that the parents are educated and they know that this is what my child needs, they enjoy it.

Thus with regards to the progress of children's participatory rights as defined by the Convention we can see that while there are indeed opportunities and understanding among some sectors of the population in the Niger Delta, on the whole the implementation is also limited by various challenges.

A case for broadening the concept of child participation: the views of children in the Niger Delta

In contrast to many of the adult research participants, the majority of the 90 children who participated in the study did not associate the concept of child participation with having a voice. Rather, they defined it in the common-sense understanding of the word 'participation' itself; or in 10-year old Ekpenyong's words 'child participation simply means the things in which a child participates'. Many of his peers expressed similar views:

> Child participation is when a child takes part in all activities. (Mary, 10)

> My idea is that participation means how a child participates in things like sports and reading of bible and books. (Child participant in group discussion)

Child participation refers to children's involvement in things in their community. (Child participant in group discussion)

This contrast in the definition of child participation between some adults and all the children is accounted for by the fact that the latter did not have the same need to scrutinize the CRC and other children's rights legislation in the same way as the NGO workers who needed to do so for their work. Indeed, the participatory workshops organized during the fieldwork were the first time some of the children had been given the opportunity to discuss children's rights and the idea of child participation in any detail. It was certainly the first time the majority had been asked to reflect on their status as children or what it means to be a child in their society. And yet, it was not only the children who explained participation in this manner; some NGO workers also came up with the same explanations:

> It means when a child participates in every activity in the home, in the church, and everything in the society at large. (FGD participant in Eket)

> Child participation is the process whereby a child participates in home activities such as cleaning the house, sweeping, and even ideas. (FGD participant in Eket)

> It is when a child participates in things like sports, athletics competitions, and things in the church. (FGD participant in Calabar)

> Child participation means what a child needs to do, like attending lesson or helping the parents. (FGD participant in Eket)

To ensure that all participants were answering questions about the same idea of participation, they were told about Article 12 of the Convention and how participation is commonly explained in the literature. And yet, even after they had been told that children's participation rights mainly implies – at least within the context of the Convention – freedom to express their views and opinions and for these to be taken into account, many of the children still referred to other activities, especially work, when talking about their participation. The researcher's initial reaction to this was that they had not understood the conventional explanation offered them. However, after further explanations and pointers by way of reading exercises and games, the trend did not change. The conclusion drawn from this was that while the children did not disagree with the dominant explanation, they were keen to draw the researcher's attention to the ways in which they already saw themselves as 'participating' in their households and wider society:

> In the house, I participate in sweeping, washing the plates, obeying my parents. In the church, I participate in sweeping the floor... I take part in

> singing in the church and in the children rally, while in the school, I take
> part as a school prefect... I take part in keeping the surrounding cleanse,
> keeping our classroom cleanse, leading the devotion and teaching other
> classes. (Mary, 10)

> I participate in washing the plates, sweeping the surroundings, washing
> the clothes, and washing the plates. (Ime, 11)

Considered from the perspective of the Convention and the dominant
discourse, these examples do not reflect participation. However, we urge
caution against this dismissal. To put our argument in context, in the
place where the children live, everybody has a role to play in society and
duties to each other. A similar finding by Hashim (2005) in Ghana suggests that it is this reciprocal expectation which fuels the informal social
security system in many African communities. The duty of adults is to
care for the young, protect them, and cater for their various needs. In
turn, besides respecting adults as noted in the previous section, children
must support adults' endeavours, and a crucial part of this is to undertake
what are considered to be light domestic tasks. This norm and expectation were evident in the accounts of both adult and child research participants. In the adults' focus group discussions, it was stressed that such
contributions by children are highly valued and partly inform attitudes to
children:

> It is very much valued in our community, it is in practice, and they help
> us to do the farm work. I have seen children clean village streets where
> parents do not have a chance to do so [when parents do not have time to
> sweep the streets themselves]. Those who do not do it are classified as
> bad or lazy children and nobody likes them. (FGD participant in Eket)

The children, who had themselves come to recognize these chores as part of
their duties, also suggested that they were quite happy to perform them as
long as these tasks are not overly taxing: 'Weeding the roadside is for the
older ones that is why I like it when they ask me to go and fetch the water'
(Mary, 10).

Indeed, when they were asked to take pictures to show the things that
make them happy in their society, many of the children, such as 10-year-old
Nse, came back with images which featured them sweeping, cooking, cleaning, and performing other household chores:

Interviewer: Among the pictures you took, which one makes you happy?

Nse (he shows a picture of himself sweeping):   This one makes me happy... this
is how I'm sweeping and this one make me happy because this is the job they
give to me. I like this job... this job is not too hard for me.

The research established that the children cook for their families, do the laundry, take care of their siblings, clean the church, the school compound, and overgrown communal pathways, activities which are not prohibited by policy-makers. Discussions with both adult and child participants established that these activities are integral to what it means to be a child in the research setting and also partly served as the means through which children stake their claim in society. It is for this reason that the children persistently pointed to their work contributions when talking about their participation. To them and to their communities, such contributions are integral elements of participation; yet, policy guidance seems to point to the contrary. We argue that because children's work contributions offer them recognition, they also present an opportunity to advocate for children's participation in decision-making or family and communal discourse.

For this opportunity to be fully exploited, however, a more holistic view of participation must be adopted. Children's participation rights may arguably be improved if thought through in a manner similar to that demonstrated by the children in this research. That is to say, the concept must embrace the opportunities children currently have and the contributions they presently make, rather than dismiss them. An approach which explicitly recognizes the ways in which children currently 'participate' may make it easier to advocate for them to be given other participatory opportunities besides work. Further, in view of the social importance attached to the contributions the children enumerated in their examples, giving them due recognition, rather than brushing them aside, may also help to avoid the antagonistic response from local communities who feel that their own values are being undermined.

Conclusion

This chapter has shown that the implementation of children's participatory rights, as articulated by the Convention, has certainly faced severe obstacles in the Niger Delta due to a number of reasons that have often been put forward by other commentators in relation to other societies – for example, culture, tradition, the attitude of adults, and poverty. However, this chapter has gone further and argued that the way the Convention defines participatory rights may actually present a further significant obstacle to the full implementation of this right in Nigeria and, in fact, elsewhere, as it does not take into account how children and their communities define, understand, and, indeed, 'live' the concept of child participation within their contexts. This is not to devalue the Convention's definition of participation. Certainly, many of the children who participated in the study showed some support for the concept once they were told about it as they felt that children's views could add value to their families and communities, especially on issues concerning them. Rather, what we are suggesting is that this definition needs to go beyond a focus on children's ability to express their views and participate in decision-making and instead, take into account not only the lived experiences of children in relation to participation, but also, and importantly, the ways they want to participate in their families and communities which, ultimately, may include expressing views as well as sweeping, cooking, and fetching water. This more holistic, and indeed, meaningful, approach to the concept of child participation may lead to a situation whereby we may begin to see a more effective implementation of children's participatory rights in countries around the world.

Notes

1 Child pawning is a practice whereby children are used as collateral for loans and for other favours (see Coe, 2012).
2 The participant's explanation of the term 'show making' refers to Hart's (2002) ladder of participation and suggests the decorative, manipulative, or deceptive use of the children involved in the youth parliament.

References

Admassie, A. (2002) 'Explaining the high incidence of child labour in sub-Saharan Africa', *African Development Review*, 14 (2): 251–75.
Alderson, P. (2000) 'Children as researchers: the effects of participation rights on research methodology', in P. Christensen and A. James (eds) *Research with Children: Perspectives and Practices*, London: Falmer Press.
Amnesty International (2009) *Petroleum, Pollution and Poverty in the Niger Delta* (available online at http://goo.gl/2Zbxy) (accessed on 20 December 2012).
Archard, D. (1993) *Children: Rights and Childhood*, London: Routledge.
Bastia, T. (2005) 'Child trafficking or teenage migration? Bolivian migrants in Argentina', *International Migration*, 43 (4): 57–87.
Basu, K. and Van, P. (1998) 'The economics of child labour', *American Economic Review*, 88 (3): 412–27.
Beers, V.H. (1995) *Participation of Children in Programming*, Stockholm: Rädda Barnen.
Bird, S. (1999) *Child Protagonism: Training Children to be Catalysts for Social Change. Capstone Collection* paper 585.
Bonnet, M. (1993) 'Child labour in Africa', *International Labour Review*, 132 (3): 371–89.
Bourdillon, M. (2006) 'Children and work: a review of current literature and debates', *Development and Change*, 37 (6): 1201–6.
Boyden, J. and Ennew, J. (eds) (1997) *Children in Focus: A Manual for Experiential Learning in Participatory Research with Children*, Stockholm: Rädda Barnen.
Buchanan, L. (2006) 'The child's right to be heard in Northern Ireland: human right or token gesture?' *Human Rights Law Commentary*, 2: 65–87.
Chawla, L. (2001) 'Evaluating children's participation: seeking areas of consensus', *PLA Notes*, 42 (October): 9–13 (available online at http://goo.gl/vQkRe) (accessed on 1 May 2012).
Coe, C. (2012) 'How debt became care: child pawning and its transformations in Akuapem, the Gold Coast, 1874–1929', *Africa: The Journal of the International African Institute*, 82 (2): 287–311.
Cole, M. (1996) *Cultural Psychology: A Once and Future Discipline*, Cambridge, MA: Harvard University Press.

Dei, G.J.S. (1994) 'Afrocentricity: a cornerstone of pedagogy', *Anthropology and Education Quarterly*, 25 (1): 3–28.

Emerson, P.M. and Knabb, S.D. (2006) 'Opportunity, inequality and the intergenerational transmission of child labour', *Economica*, 73 (291): 413–34.

Hart, J. (2007) 'Empowerment or frustration? Participatory programming with young Palestinians', *Children, Youth, and Environments*, 17 (3): 1–23.

Hart, R. (1992) *Children's Participation: From Tokenism to Citizenship*, Florence: UNICEF Innocenti Research Centre.

Hashim, I. (2005) *Exploring the Linkages between Children's Independent Migration and Education: Evidence from Ghana. Migration DRC Working Paper* WP-T12. Brighton: Migration DRC, University of Sussex.

Higgins, K. (2007) *Regional Inequality and the Niger Delta. Background Papers for the World Development Report 2009* Issue 5 (available online at http://goo.gl/8PyTh) (accessed on 23 December 2009).

Hill, M., Davis, J., Prout, A., and Tisdall, K. (eds) (2004) 'Special issue: children, young people and participation', *Children and Society*, 18 (2): 77–176.

Hill, M., Turner, K., Walker, M., Stafford, A., and Seaman, P. (2006) 'Children's perspectives on social exclusion and resilience in disadvantaged urban communities', in E.K.M. Tisdall *et al.* (eds) *Children, Young People and Social Inclusion: Participation for What?*, Bristol: The Policy Press.

Holt, J. (1974) *Escape from Childhood*, New York, NY: Dutton.

Ikejiaku, B.V. (2009) 'The relationship between poverty, conflict and development', *Journal of Sustainable Development*, 2 (1): 15–28.

Iversen, V. (2002) 'Autonomy in child labour migrants', *World Development*, 30 (5): 817–34.

James, A., Jenks, C., and Prout, A. (1998) *Theorising Childhood*, Cambridge: Polity Press.

James, A. and Prout, A. (1997) *Constructing and Reconstructing Childhood: Contemporary Issues in the Sociological Study of Childhood*, London: Falmer Press.

Joab-Peterside, S. (2007) On the Militarisation of Nigeria's Niger Delta: The Genesis of Ethnic Militia in Rivers State, Nigeria. Niger Delta Economies of Violence Working Papers no. 21: 1–21.

Karunan, V. (2005) 'Working children as change makers: perspectives from the South', in B.H. Weston (ed.) *Child Labor and Human Rights: Making Children Matter*, Boulder, CO and London: Lynne Rienner.

Kellett, M., Forrest, R., Dent, N., and Ward, S. (2004) '"Just teach us the skills please, we'll do the rest": empowering ten-year-olds as active researchers', *Children and Society*, 18 (5): 329–43.

Lansdown, G. (2001) *Promoting Children's Participation in Democratic Decision-Making. Innocenti Insight* 6 (available online at http://goo.gl/lQihC) (accessed on 4 March 2012).

Lansdown, G. (2002) 'The participation of children', in H. Montgomery *et al.* (eds) *Changing Childhoods*, Milton Keynes: Open University Press.

Liebel, M. (2002) 'Child labour and the contribution of working children's organisations in the Third World', *International Review of Education*, 48 (3–4): 265–70.

Lundy, L. (2007) '"Voice" is not enough: conceptualising Article 12 of the United Nations Convention on the Rights of the Child', *British Educational Research Journal*, 33 (6): 927–47.

Matthews, H. (2001) *Children and Community Regeneration: Creating Better Neighbourhoods*, London: Save the Children's Fund (available online at http://goo.gl/zwnQh).

Mayall, B. (2000) 'The sociology of childhood in relation to children's rights', *International Journal of Children's Rights*, 8 (3): 243–59.

Moses, S. (2008) 'Children and participation in South Africa: an overview,' *International Journal of Children's Rights*, 16 (3): 327–42.

Muyila, W.J. (2006) *African Values and the Problem of the Rights of the Child: A Search for Explanations*, Copenhagen: Danish Institute for Human Rights.

Ndofirepi, A.P. and Ndofirepi, E.S. (2012) '"(E)ducation or (e)ducation in traditional African societies?" A philosophical insight study of tribes', *Tribals*, 10 (1): 13–28.

Partridge, A. (2005) 'Children and young people's inclusion in public decision making,' *Support for Learning*, 20 (4): 181–9.

Plan International (2007) *Mid-Term Review of the African Common Position on Children* (available online at http://goo.gl/CZg5d) (accessed on 5 November 2012).

Punch, S. (2007) 'Negotiating migrant identities: young people in Bolivia and Argentina', *Children's Geographies*, 5 (1): 95–112.

Reddy, N. and Ratna, K. (2002) *A Journey in Children's Participation, Vimanapura: The Concerned for Working Children* (available online at http://goo.gl/bQOQw) (accessed on 4 July 2012).

Rimmer, M. (2012) 'The participation and decision making of "at risk" youth in community music projects: an exploration of three case studies', *Journal of Youth Studies*, 15 (3): 329–50.

Sala-i-Martin, X. and Subramanian, A. (2003) *Addressing the Natural Resource Curse: An Illustration from Nigeria. IMF Working Paper* WP/03/159.

Save the Children (2008) *An Analysis of Children's Participation Working Methods and Materials within Save the Children Sweden*, Stockholm: Save the Children.

Schmitz, C.L., Elizabeth, T., Kim, J., and Larson, D. (2004) 'Introduction', in C.L. Schmitz et al. (eds) *Child Labor: A Global View*, Westport, CT: Greenwood Press.

Shier, H. (2001) 'Pathways to participation: openings, opportunities and obligations: a new model for enhancing children's participation in decision-making, in line with Article 12.1 of the United Nations Convention on the Rights of the Child,' *Children and Society*, 15 (2): 107–17.

Simpson, B. (1997) 'Towards the participation of children and young people in urban planning and design,' *Urban Studies*, 34 (5/6): 907–25.

Sinclair, R. (2004) 'Participation in practice: making it meaningful, effective and sustainable,' *Children and Society*, 18 (2): 106–18.

Sinclair, R. and Franklin, A. (2000) *Young People's Participation. Quality Protects Research Briefing 3*. London: Department of Health.

Snapps, O.J. (2011) 'Dynamics of poverty among Niger Delta women: an empirical assessment,' *American Review of Political Economy*, 9 (1): 33–44.

Thomas, N. (2000) *Children, Family and the State: Decision-Making and Child Participation*, Bristol: Policy Press.

Thorne, B. (2008) 'Editorial: what's in an age name?' *Childhood*, 15 (4): 435–9.

Tisdall, E.K.M. and Punch, S. (2012) 'Not so "new"? Looking critically at childhood studies', *Children's Geographies*, 10 (3): 249–64.

Treseder, P. (1997) *Empowering Children and Young People: Training Manual*, London: Save the Children.

Twum-Danso, A. (2009) 'Reciprocity, respect and responsibility: the 3Rs underlying parent–child relationships in Ghana and the implications for children's rights', *International Journal of Children's Rights*, 17 (3): 415–32.

Twum-Danso, A. (2010) 'The construction of childhood and the socialization of children: the implications for the implementation of Article 12 of the Convention on the Rights of the Child in Ghana', in N. Thomas and B. Percy-Smith (eds) *The Handbook of Children's Participation*, Abingdon: Routledge.

UN Committee on the Rights of the Child (2009) General Comment no. 12, 'The right of the child to be heard', New York, NY: UNICEF (available online at http://bit.ly/9zkjP5) (accessed on 14 March 2013).

UNDP (2006) *Niger Delta Human Development Report, 2006*, Abuja: UNDP (available online at http://goo.gl/Uu9uu) (accessed on 5 January 2012).

UNICEF (2005) *Convention on the Rights of the Child*, New York, NY: UNICEF (available online at http://www.unicef.org/crc/) (accessed on 4 March 2013).

UNICEF (2007) *Child Rights and Participation*, Abuja: UNICEF (available online at http://www.unicef.org/nigeria/children_1938.html) (accessed on 4 March 2013).

Van Beers, H. (2011) *Children's Participation* (Internet blog) (available online at http://goo.gl/QGLKA) (accessed on 4 March 2013).

Van den Berge, M. (2007) *Working Children's Movements in Peru*, Amsterdam: IREWOC.

Vis, S.A., Holtan, A., and Thomas, N. (2012) 'Obstacles for child participation in care and protection cases – why Norwegian social workers find it difficult', *Child Abuse Review*, 21 (1): 7–23.

Walker, S. (2001) 'Consulting with children and young people', *International Journal of Children's Rights*, 9 (1): 45–6.

Wells, K. (2009) *Childhood in a Global Perspective*, Bristol: Policy Press.

Willow, C. (1997) *Hear! Hear! Promoting Children and Young People's Democratic Participation in Local Government*, London: Local Government Information Unit.

Willow, C. (1999) *It's Not Fair: Young People's Reflections on Children's Rights*, London: Children's Society.

Willow, C. (2002) *Participation in Practice: Children and Young People as Partners in Change*, London: The Children's Society.

Woodhead, M. (1998) 'Quality in early childhood programmes: a contextually appropriate approach', *International Journal of Early Years Education*, 6 (1): 5–17.

Woodhead, M. (2010) 'Foreword', in B. Percy-Smith and N. Thomas (eds) *A Handbook of Children and Young People's Participation*, London: Routledge.

Woodhead, M. and Faulkner, D. (2000) 'Subjects, objects or participants? Dilemmas of psychological research with children', in P. Christensen and A. James (eds) *Research with Children: Perspectives and Practices*, London: Falmer.

14 The Convention on the Rights of the Child

Advancing social justice for African children?

Nicola Ansell

Introduction

It is very apparent from the chapters in this volume that the idea of universal children's rights, and in particular the specific rights children are deemed entitled to, are neither universally applied nor universally valued. Some of the chapters have demonstrated a lack of progress in implementing the Convention on the Rights of the Child (CRC) in particular contexts or among certain groups of young people. This failure is sometimes attributed to extrinsic factors such as lack of enthusiasm or capacity on the part of the state (as McAlpine charts in relation to Tanzania); at other times to the inadequacy of measures adopted to implement rights (Secker, for instance, recounts how people in Nigeria remain unaware of the legal protections introduced). Some groups of children (notably those with special needs, as illustrated by O'Riordan *et al.*, or street children, as explored by van Blerk) have been relatively neglected in the implementation of rights, and progress for these has been particularly slow.

In other contexts, however, rights discourse has deeply penetrated society, transforming both laws and practices. Norman describes the extensive transformations to policy and practice in South Africa that have permeated intergenerational relationships. Similarly Abebe and Tefera describe how rights-based approaches infuse local government, government, and donor-driven non-governmental organizations (NGOs) in Ethiopia, in the process reshaping ideas about the nature of childhood and child–family relations. André and Godin demonstrate how rights discourse has wrought changes in subjectivities and relationships in the Democratic Republic of Congo (DRC), particularly among the middle classes. These transformations have not happened quietly; they have been produced through tensions and controversies and their impacts on children's wellbeing have not been wholly positive. As Bourdillon and Musvosvi point out, it is important to question not only the effectiveness of the CRC in Africa, but the appropriateness of its clauses and their interpretations to children's contexts.

In this concluding chapter I explore five broad areas of tension arising from the CRC which, the foregoing chapters suggest, strongly affect how it shapes African children's lives. Given that the rights enshrined in the CRC are contested, and accused by some of harming impoverished children, I apply an alternative normative framing. Specifically, I consider how these five aspects of the CRC affect whether it advances social justice for African children.

I begin with a discussion of three approaches to understanding children's interests. First, I consider liberal rights discourse, exploring why this is problematic and accounts for some of the less positive outcomes of the CRC. I then move on to social justice, which like rights is a complex, contested, and diversely defined notion. I introduce the liberal notion of distributive justice, and explain why this is of limited value in relation to children. Finally I explore Iris Marion Young's 'politics of difference' (1990) and her 'social connection' model of responsibility for justice (2006), arguing that these offer a more useful approach to social justice in relation to children.

Framing children's interests: rights or justice? Equality or difference?

Liberal rights: the autonomous, individual, universal child in the service of neoliberalism?

Liberal rights rest on principles of autonomy, individualism, and universalism, all of which are theoretically and practically problematic. During the European Enlightenment of the eighteenth century, ideas of individual freedom acquired a particular moral authority. Civil and political rights were avidly promoted, founded on the assumption that human beings are capable of making rational autonomous decisions and should therefore be left to lead their own lives as they see fit. The liberalism advocated by writers such as J.S. Mill considered individuals to be the best judges of their own interests, and to have a God-given right to pursue those interests, provided their actions do not interfere with the freedom of others.

The challenges of relating an abstract notion of rights (and of people as individual autonomous rights bearers) to a 'real world' in which all individuals were not actually deemed capable of making rational decisions in their own interests, and in which allowing them to do so would seriously challenge the social order, led to a paradoxical situation in which 'universal' rights were thought of as applicable only to certain types of subject, not, for instance, women or slaves. Slave ownership remained legal in the USA long after the nation's founding 'Declaration of Independence' announced that it was 'self-evident' that 'all men are created equal, that they are endowed by their Creator with certain unalienable Rights'. The notion of rights did, nonetheless, prove valuable in challenging both slavery and gender discrimination (viz. Wollstonecraft, 1792).

The idea that rights are an individual property is also challenged by the fact that rights inevitably imply an obligation or duty on others. Moreover, contestations over rights and lack of agreement, particularly cross-culturally, as to the rights a person should possess undermine the assumption that they are universal and natural.

While liberal rights discourse was always problematic, the application of liberal rights to children proved particularly challenging. Both the explanation, and the solution, lay partly in the separation of children from adults associated with modernization and the rise of capitalist economy from the seventeenth century onwards (Aries, 1962; Aitken, 2001). The gradual disappearance of (respectable) children from the workplace and public sphere, and their seclusion in home and school, both reflected and (re)produced a view that children differ fundamentally from adults. Like women and slaves (also largely invisible in the public sphere), Western society deemed children poor judges of their own interests and incapable of exercising autonomous agency.

The separation of children from adults allowed liberalism to deal with children's challenge to rights discourse by holding that rights only apply within the public sphere. It also later allowed children to be thought of in relation to an alternative type of rights that did not assume an autonomous rights-bearer. In the early twentieth century, rights discourse expanded beyond liberal notions of freedom to also encompass rights to welfare (Levine-Clark, 2010). This gave momentum to the Declarations of the Rights of the Child in 1924 and 1959 which inscribe children's rights to provision and protection, but not to autonomy.

In the 1980s, however, the social construction of children as merely passive beneficiaries of welfare rights was increasingly questioned. The drafting of the CRC took place in parallel with the development of a new paradigm in the social sciences which became known as the 'new social studies of childhood'. A groundswell of research recognized children to be social actors, exercising agency over their lives, and explored how institutional environments contributed to the construction of childhood experience. Reflecting this new perspective, and while maintaining that children are distinct from adults, the CRC offers some autonomy rights to children.

Many critiques of children's autonomy or participation rights focus on characteristics of liberal rights discourse. Children, particularly very young children, are not fully autonomous agents. Ruddick (2007) explains how the discourse of children's rights underlies acts of ventriloquism in which the law purports to speak for children, even those unborn. Through rights discourse, she argues, the child approaches but does not attain 'personhood' and is actually silenced in the process. The fact that political projects are mobilized in the name of children's rights by neoliberal and neo-conservative groups that claim to speak for children reveals the limits of the liberal construction of the subject as an autonomous individual. Others, including Norman and Abebe and Terefa in this volume, are critical of the focus on the individual within liberal rights discourse, and the corresponding neglect of children's relationships with others. This, they argue, limits the analysis of structural constraints (see also Grugel, 2013).

Rights, then, particularly in their liberal conception, prove a theoretical challenge when applied to children. As a consequence, a rights-based approach can be confined to limited areas of children's lives or may be hijacked by groups with particular agendas and consequently fail to serve children's interests.

Liberal justice: a case for redistribution in favour of children?

If rights overemphasize the individual, to the neglect of societal conditions and structural constraints, what of social justice? Much writing on the subject of justice has focused on the distribution of advantage and disadvantage between individuals. Many scholars draw on Rawls' (1971) argument that a just society would be one that all members would collectively negotiate if unaware in advance of the position they would take in it. It is assumed that in such a scenario rational people would organize society such that the distribution of goods and burdens is relatively equal.

Little research relating to children has engaged with issues of justice. A small number of scholars have applied liberal ideas of distributive justice to children, focusing both on distribution between adults and children and distribution among children. Bojer (2002), for instance, argues that Rawls' theory of justice should be applied to children in understanding how resources should be allocated across the life course. She argues that from an abstract, rational position, income should be distributed so as to ensure reasonable comfort and happiness in childhood for everyone – partly because childhood years are important in their own right and partly because wellbeing in adult life depends on wellbeing in childhood. On this basis, every child should have a minimum level of access to primary goods such as nutrition, health care, education, and a caring environment. Bojer further argues that failure to secure this will increase future inequality between adults.

In practical terms, however, while the resources available to some children can be compared with those available to others, it is difficult to envisage exactly what a fair distribution of resources between children and adults might mean. Like rights, the idea of distributional justice subscribes to a liberal worldview that assumes formal equality, and unitary moral subjectivity. Moreover, Rawls envisaged justice to be concerned with the distribution of rights and liberties, not just wealth (underlining an overlap between the concepts). When viewed as impartial, definitive, and mechanistic, justice, like rights, is based on claims to liberal autonomy (Aitken, 2001). The ideal of impartiality denies difference, suggesting the same rules must apply in all situations (Young, 1990). Children, again, pose a challenge, hence a liberal concept of justice relies on conceptually distinguishing children from adults (Aitken, 2001).

The distributional paradigm is critiqued by Young (1990) for being individualist and pattern-oriented, based on the experience of liberal capitalist societies, while pretending to be universal. Perhaps more significantly, Young points to the limits to the logic of distribution. Distribution cannot meaning-fully be extended beyond the material – power, for instance, cannot be redis-tributed. Social relations and processes are fundamental to everyday notions of justice, hence the constitution of decision-making structures is more sig-nificant than the distribution of decision-making powers.

Thus focusing on social justice draws attention to relationships between individuals and points to the structural processes that shape wellbeing. However, although the liberal distributional paradigm offers a lens on to the dramatic differences in wellbeing between children worldwide, notions of equity and impartiality are difficult to apply to relationships between chil-dren and adults.

Politicizing difference: an alternative social justice lens

Iris Marion Young (1990) proposes a broader conceptualization of social jus-tice that is not reduced to distributional justice. Rather than a universal, abstract 'theory of justice', Young argues for a perspective that examines what happens in society and why, and who benefits and who is harmed as a result of these processes. Within a society, injustices are not identified through objective calculations, but are recognized in cries of suffering or distress. Young is critical of the assumption that society is homogenous, recognizing that claims for justice often arise from specific social groups. Although chil-dren are not among the groups she explicitly considers, her focus on social difference makes her ideas highly relevant to understanding what social jus-tice might mean for children. They are also valuable in seeking to understand ways in which the CRC does or does not advance social justice for children.

Young's (1990) approach hinges on the existence of social groups, a term she gives to collectivities differentiated from other groups by cultural forms, practices, or way of life. Group members have an affinity because of this, and tend to associate more with one another than with those outside the group. Groups are not merely aggregates of individuals: they exist prior to individu-als and constitute identities (although these are fluid and shifting). However, a group may also be identified by outsiders without those identified having consciousness of themselves as a group.

Based on this description, children can certainly be understood as a social group. While the (conceptual, discursive, and physical) separation of children from adults has been critiqued by a number of scholars, Young argues that being defined as a social group, with distinct interests, is only problematic if the group is (systematically) subjected to social injustice. Rather than the dis-tribution of goods and burdens, Young (1990: 38) understands injustice to operate through processes of domination and oppression, wherein:

> Oppression consists in systematic institutional processes which prevent some people from learning and using satisfying and expansive skills in

socially recognized settings, or institutionalized social processes which inhibit people's ability to play and communicate with others or to express their feelings and perspective on social life in contexts where others can listen... Domination consists in institutional conditions which inhibit or prevent people from participating in determining their actions or the conditions of their actions. Persons live within structures of domination if other persons or groups can determine without reciprocation the conditions of their action, either directly or by virtue of the structural consequences of their actions.

A social group is deemed to be oppressed if it is subject to one or more of five conditions: exploitation (being expected to work for the benefit of others), marginalization (exclusion from 'useful participation in social life'), powerlessness, cultural imperialism (being both rendered invisible and stereotyped by the dominant in society), and violence (particularly the social context that makes acts of violence possible and even acceptable). It is not difficult to see that most societies subject children to many of these processes, and that poor children are systematically subjected to most of them.

To address such injustice does not require measures aimed at formal equality in the way envisaged by liberal conceptions of rights or justice:

> The politics of difference sometimes implies overriding a principle of equal treatment with the principle that group differences should be acknowledged in public policy and in the policies and procedures of economic institutions, in order to reduce actual or potential oppression... sometimes recognising particular rights for groups is the only way to promote their full participation. (Young, 1990: 11)

Another valuable area of Young's (2006) work is her 'social connection' model of responsibility for justice which posits that obligations of justice exist between persons as a result of the social processes that connect them. These processes are complex, sometimes global in extent, difficult to trace directly, and extended over varied periods of time (which makes the concept particularly pertinent in relation to obligations towards children). While individuals who are privileged through certain social processes might not be considered personally 'liable' when those processes oppress distant others, they do bear responsibility to seek to change the structures that produce injustice. As these social processes are distributed across a wide range of individuals, all involved have a responsibility, but this weighs more heavily on those more privileged, or with greater power to make a difference.

The CRC: five challenges for social justice

The CRC is not a straightforward unambiguous document: it contains ambiguities and tensions that play out differently in the diverse African contexts considered, and for particular groups of children, with differing implications for social justice. In the sections below I examine five areas of tension in the CRC.

Defining the subject of children's rights: entrenching separation?

The CRC offers children a set of rights that are distinct from those accorded to adults. Its existence both assumes and reinforces a distinction between children and adults. For some scholars (e.g. Burman, 1996; Aitken, 2001; White, 2002) this distinction is problematic. For White (2002), focusing on children as a separate category undermines recognition of their embeddedness in relationships that sustain them, relationships that are crucially important in shaping their lives. Burman (1996) points out that general statements about children such as those contained in the CRC assume a globally consistent separation of childhood and adulthood, implying that childhood is a natural rather than a social phenomenon.

So are there grounds for identifying children as a social group with their own interests? Young (1990) argues that while some see groups as invidious fictions that incite prejudices, stereotypes, and exclusions based on arbitrary attributes, in reality people identify with groups. Even in Africa, where the separation of children from adults is less entrenched than in Western society, young individuals certainly identify as children, at least for a few years, sharing attributes and cultural forms with other children, albeit not with all other children and not to the exclusion of other identities. Defining a group as different is not inherently defining them as inferior, homogeneous, or unconnected to others.

Moreover, irrespective of the existence of the CRC, children are systematically oppressed through a number of processes. One of these processes identified by Young (1990: 58–9) is 'cultural imperialism', which refers to 'how the dominant meanings of a society render the particular perspective of one's own group invisible at the same time as they stereotype one's group and mark it out as other'. The CRC does not invisibilize children in general: indeed it argues for greater attention to be paid to them. Certain groups of children, such as disabled or street children who do not conform to the expectations of childhood on which the CRC rests are, however, rendered invisible in and through it. Certainly the CRC marks children out as different from adults (although some would argue it offers them rights that were previously available only to adults), depicting them through a stereotype that has little resonance with the lives of many young people. From a 'politics of difference' perspective, mobilizing in the interests of a social group is necessary in the interests of social justice. Interestingly, Liebel (2012) argues that children's rights should be understood to come from children and their demands for justice. The CRC, however, is not itself based on children's own demands, although the participation articles could be deployed in a way that responds to children's own interests (see section below on identifying best interests).

The problematic issue identified by many authors of this volume is not that the CRC draws a distinction between children and adults, but that it defines a child as 'every human being below the age of eighteen years unless under the law applicable to the child, majority is attained earlier' (Article 1). For the African Charter on the Rights and Welfare of the Child 'a child means every human being below the age of 18 years' (Article 2). This rigid boundary between childhood and adulthood has been enshrined in much of the legislation that has enacted the CRC over the past quarter of a century, and has come to dominate policy and practice. However, as Abebe and Tefera point out, in Ethiopian communities, chronological age is seldom relevant and may not even be known. Social age is important, but childhood is traditionally understood in relation to other stages of the life course, as part of a gradual change in social position, rather than a separate identity.

From a social justice perspective, it is not defining children as a group that is problematic, but rather imposing an arbitrary definition that does not conform to individuals' own identification. By declaring a distinct set of rights for those aged under 18, the CRC effectively denies those externally defined as children access to many of the rights that are available to adults. This is problematic for young people who take on 'adult' roles sooner (those in employment, heading households, or parenting their siblings or their own offspring), since defining them as children means they cannot make use of their adult identity. As Cheney points out in relation to her research in Uganda, under the CRC children are stripped of any capacity to make direct claims on their rights. In effect, rights are operationalized in a way that is incommensurate with thinking of children as rights bearers. Rather, rights have to be claimed through an adult; as Norman suggests, it is often the perpetrators of children's oppression who are charged with securing their rights.

Declaring all humans under the age of 18 to be the subject of children's rights not only deprives these young people of access to 'adult' rights or the legal capacity to make their own claims, it also serves to homogenize. Clearly the needs and capacities of a 17-month-old child differ greatly from those of a 17-year-old, complicating the application of a uniform set of rights. The essentialist definition does not recognize the fluidity of group identification. Moreover, children's interests are not defined only by age. The CRC arguably imagines a particular type of child (Western, middle class, male, able bodied), and the more distant children's circumstances are from this norm, the less relevant the articles of the CRC. Thus, O'Riordan *et al.* argue that the rights of disabled children may be neglected. It has long been suggested that the rights in the CRC lack relevance to street children (Ennew, 2002a). Van Blerk suggests that the protection rights inscribed in the CRC make it harder for children to survive on the streets because, for instance, their employment is prohibited. It is easier to mobilize around 'types' of children that better match the imagined child of the CRC – those who are vulnerable and self-evidently in need of protection. Moreover, van Blerk argues that the neglect of street children is partly attributable to their lack of representation in the policy arena, and that they lack representation in part because they are hard to define: the social group to which they belong is not readily described by fixed parameters.

To summarize, a key difficulty with the CRC and its capacity to effect the advancement of social justice for children is its application to all aged under 18 and the assumptions it makes about this group. To recognize children as a social group with their own needs that derive in part from their subjection to systematic forms of oppression is valuable. The CRC seeks to address some of these forms of oppression. However, as Young (1990) argues, social groups are best understood as non-essentialist, relational, and fluid. While formal equality with adults is not a useful basis for action, nor is homogenizing all individuals aged under 18, and greater recognition of this in the implementation of the CRC would be beneficial.

Locating responsibility for securing children's rights

While the CRC offers a precise definition of children, it is ambiguous in the locus of responsibility for securing children's rights. Indeed, rights discourse seldom addresses questions of responsibility, whereas a justice framework interrogates issues of responsibility as well as entitlement.

The CRC is an international convention with global reach, but it does not clearly locate responsibility for implementation at the transnational level (Grugel, 2013). It is nation states that ratified the Convention, committing themselves to enact children's rights through legislative reform and, ultimately, national governments are held accountable by the Committee on the Rights of the Child. However, the preamble to the Convention locates children's rights within the family, and the primary responsibility of parents in relation to children is reiterated in numerous articles, particularly 5, 18, and 27. Article 27 (2), for instance, states 'The parent(s) or others responsible for the child have the primary responsibility to secure, within their abilities and financial capacities, the conditions of living necessary for the child's development' (United Nations, 1989). Moreover, the CRC is unusual among international conventions in involving intergovernmental and non-governmental organizations in securing children's rights (see Cohen, 1990; Türkelli and Vandenhole, 2012). Implementation of the CRC, then, is in some contexts altering the relationship and distribution of responsibilities between children, their families, the state, and a range of national and international actors, although not necessarily in consistent or even positive ways.

Society may hold families responsible for securing children's wellbeing in one of three ways: it may relinquish power to families, allowing them autonomy in raising children; it may impose particular expectations concerning how families raise children and seek to regulate them; or it may offer them support. The CRC is not wholly aligned with any single approach but tends towards imposing expectations, without fully ensuring families are supported.

Several contributors to this book are critical of the ways in which the CRC casts responsibility for securing children's rights on to families, without acknowledging that families often lack the necessary resources to fulfil the role. Abebe and Tefera, for instance, demonstrate how Ethiopian parents, unable to provide for the rights specified in the Convention, are cast as failures in policy and NGO discourse and may even be blamed by their children. Similarly, drawing on their research in the DRC, André and Godin reveal the stigmatizing effects of declaring parents responsible for ensuring their children attend school. Parents who allow their children to work are seen as exploiting them, although in practice they may have no alternative. McAlpine shows that the resources families require are not only economic but also emotional, and these may be lacking at times of stress. The emphasis on families is particularly inappropriate in relation to street children (van Blerk, this volume; see also Ennew, 2002a). It is perhaps ironic that the African Charter on the Rights and Welfare of the Child (ACRWC) focuses even more on family than the CRC, to the neglect of some of the most impoverished African children.

By contrast, drawing on her South African case study, Norman suggests that rights discourse emanating from the translation of the CRC into extensive national legislation and policy has left many parents feeling that they no longer have a decisive role in their children's upbringing. Parents resent their loss of autonomy, and feel disempowered by a lack of recourse to traditional means of socialization and discipline. Thus, rather than challenging their children's behaviour, many elect to abdicate responsibility to the state.

What then should be the role of the state vis-à-vis the family in securing social justice for children? Archard (2006) draws on Mill's view that the moral rule governing society should be practised in the family to argue that, if society espouses social justice, it should require families to be just. However, he also suggests that because children's experiences are shaped by broader social and economic conditions, not just their own families, families should not be held fully responsible for them. Social justice, he argues, demands that an individual should not be disadvantaged, or advantaged, in their pursuit of life choices by factors that are beyond their individual control but open to social influence. On this basis, states should intervene in families, for instance in regulating educational provision and inheritance. The role is not simply the provision of services for children. Given that social disadvantage is linked to parental abuse and neglect, the state has an obligation to address the former in order to protect children from the latter (Archard, 2006). However, wider concerns of social disadvantage are not directly addressed by the CRC; the specific roles of the state beyond protective legislation and basic service provision remain unclear.

Secker is also critical of the voluntaristic approach to securing children's rights that has characterized the implementation of the CRC. Her research in the Niger Delta suggests that the expectation that NGOs will secure children's rights ultimately absolves governments of responsibility. This is problematic because only governments can achieve the scale of systematic change that is needed if the rights enshrined in the CRC are to be delivered.

There are undoubtedly reasons why governments may be reluctant to take responsibility for children's rights. Many are seriously impoverished, capacity is often limited, and priorities lie elsewhere. Writing about Tanzania, McAlpine suggests that where the government's imperative is national development, a rights-based approach has little traction. She therefore argues that a macro-economic case must be made for investing in social security and child protection. Others argue for a stronger role for the international community, which currently casts responsibility on to states, without offering them support (Vandenhole, 2011).

Vandenhole (2011) suggests that the CRC may be seen to offer possibilities for framing children's rights as a transnational obligation. While Rawls envisaged his theory applying within political jurisdictions, distributive justice can also be framed in transnational terms, supporting redistribution. Young's (2006) 'social connection' model of responsibility for justice also supports a view that responsibility for securing children's wellbeing should not be vested in families and national governments alone, given that others across the world are implicated in social processes that currently limit the services that can be made available to children (through, for instance, structural adjustment programmes or allowing corporations to avoid paying tax in the countries in which they operate), as well as relying on the future labour of children in poor countries for their future prosperity.

In summary, while families, national governments, and international actors undoubtedly have different roles to play in relation to securing children's rights, the ambiguities and limitations of the CRC's text allow governments and the international community to cede much responsibility to families that are inadequately equipped to deliver social justice for African children.

Balancing rights to provision, protection, and participation

The CRC is said to embrace three types of rights: rights to provision, protection, and participation. Rights to provision (of, for instance, health care, education, social security, an adequate standard of living) and protection (from violence, sexual or economic exploitation) are similar to the rights that appeared in the earlier international declarations of children's rights. Rights to participation (the right to have a say in decisions concerning them, to freedom of expression, thought, conscience, and religion, and freedom of association) appear for the first time in the CRC. As Archard (2006) suggests, provision and (particularly) protection rights are based on an assumption that children require special rights (that acknowledge and respond to their difference from adults) and are fundamentally paternalistic. Participation rights, by contrast, reflect a view that adult rights should be extended to children. White (2002) describes this as the coming together of two dynamics – recognition (that children have particular distinctive needs and interests) and inclusion (challenging unthinking assumptions about children's difference from adults and the exclusion and exploitation that can arise from this). For Ennew (2002a), the CRC seeks to address two characteristics of modern childhood: dependency and powerlessness. It seeks to cater for one and to reverse the other. Significantly, based on Young's (1990) framing of social justice as a politics of difference, both approaches are arguably legitimate responses to injustice: one sensitive to the difference embodied in a relatively excluded social group, the other responding specifically to the powerlessness that is one dimension through which this group is oppressed.

Provision rights tend to inspire the least discussion; these are not foremost in people's minds when the subject of children's rights is raised. However, provision rights are highly significant in terms of social justice, promoting greater equity between children as well as responding to needs, but they have perhaps been the most breached. Provision of services and social security to children relies heavily on the state, but many children do not have access to schooling, social security, or an adequate standard of living. Moreover, the CRC fails to inscribe some very important provision rights such as children's right to food (Abebe and Tefera).

Rights to protection have proven more controversial. The chapters by Omoike, Okyere, and Bourdillon and Musvosvi illustrate how the protection of children from economic exploitation – the argument that they should not be involved in economic activities – may not serve children's interests. These chapters argue that protection from working is unlikely to improve wellbeing and can limit children's opportunities (see also Reynolds *et al.*, 2006). Bourdillon and Musvosvi question whether the protection articles of the CRC are principally concerned with avoiding deviation from the ideals of childhood set in high-income countries and communities wherein children do not work. Rather than focusing on what children are protected against, they advocate thinking about what protection is for. Drawing on research among working children in Zimbabwe, they argue that if the goal is to support children, then protection of opportunities (including opportunities to earn income) is as important as protection from risk and abuse, especially where opportunities are scarce. This might imply, for instance, recognizing the validity of working children's initiatives, in order that they have less need to depend on adults who exploit them.

In practical terms, there is also a tension between protection and participation rights. As Bourdillon and Musvosvi point out, measures to protect children often conflict with their rights to have some control over their lives. Both Cheney and van Blerk argue that by casting children as vulnerable, protection rights neglect the real lives of, respectively, orphans and street children, disempowering them and undermining their survival strategies. They advocate a stronger focus on children's participation rights that would allow children's voices to be heard and help them to protect their own interests. Okyere points out that being able to provide for themselves is particularly necessary when children lack access to the provision rights that are inscribed in the CRC. He suggests that this highlights the indivisibility of rights: protection rights are of little value where provision rights are not met.

It has long been argued that provision and protection take precedence over participation in national policies (Ennew, 2002b). Archard (2004) argues that while the 'caretaker' approach of the CRC's provision and protection articles is relatively uncontroversial, the 'liberationist' approach of the participation articles poses a greater challenge to society. In her chapter, Cheney makes the case that participation is not in fact very prominent in the CRC, with almost no direct mention of the concept. However, many donor-led NGOs have enthusiastically engaged children in participatory projects, as Abebe and Tefera highlight. Moreover, for governments the promotion of participation rights has low economic costs relative to securing provision or protection rights, particularly where parents or other institutions can be held responsible for listening to children's voices. Nonetheless, both governments and NGOs are reluctant to support genuine participation by children in the public sphere, beyond a very limited realm of issues and activities, as this is likely to challenge their priorities and ways of operating. Okyere, for instance, highlights how children's views are seldom elicited when the subject of child labour is discussed.

Defining meaningful participation is not straightforward. Children in any society participate in some ways. Indeed, Bourdillon and Musvosvi ask whether participation is what children do in the absence of their protection and provision rights being met. Children involved in the research Okyere and Twum-Danso Imoh undertook in the Niger Delta understood participation as something wider than the right to have a say. Their chapter argues we should take into account how children and their communities 'live' the concept of participation – as 'making a contribution' including through such activities as sweeping, cooking, and fetching water.

In summary, provision and protection rights respond to some of the five processes of oppression identified by Young (1990), notably exploitation and violence. However, the fact that children are singled out as requiring these rights to be defined and delivered by adults limits the extent to which the CRC can address other forms of oppression – and may even exacerbate these. For instance, they may serve to further marginalize children (excluding them from 'useful participation in social life') and subject them to cultural imperialism (stereotyping them, without allowing their own voices to be heard). Participation rights might have the power to overcome some of these forms of oppression, and also to address the fifth form of oppression – powerlessness – but the way in which these are implemented is often tokenistic and might not address all processes through which children are oppressed.

Identifying children's best interests

A related issue that tends to differentiate between caretaker and protectionist approaches is the identification of children's 'best interests'. For Archard (2006), the best interests principle is embedded in provision and protection rights and is fundamentally paternalistic. Parker (1994, cited in Burman, 1996: 49) claims that best interests can 'provide a convenient cloak for bias, paternalism, and capricious decision-making. Even worse, the open-endedness of the standard can legitimate practices in some cultures which are regarded in other cultures as positively harmful'.

Certainly, children's interests are usually seen as best determined by adults, a practice that is generally at odds with children's participation. While the CRC and national laws usually assume that economic participation is not in children's best interests, children often take a different view as Omoike's research with child domestic workers in Ghana and Nigeria suggests. There is a parallel here with Young's (1990) description of marginalization as exclusion from 'useful participation in social life': 'Marginals are people the system of labor cannot or will not use' (p. 53). Young argues that those marginalized are not just materially deprived as a consequence; even where welfare is provided, this deprives those dependent on it of freedoms (often confining them to institutions) and of the right to claim to know what's good for them. Young argues that dependency itself need not be oppressive – and is necessary at times – but justice requires that those who are dependent are accorded respect and are able to participate in decision-making and to make choices. Children's views of their best interests are, however, seldom taken into account in determining their best interests (Omoike). Abebe and Tefera also point to the lack of correspondence between the rights-based activities of NGOs and the needs that children define for themselves.

However, it is important to acknowledge that children – like adults – are not fully aware of their own best interests. White (2002) draws on Molyneux (1985) who argued that women have 'strategic gender interests' that they are unaware of to make the case that children do not necessarily recognize their own (structural) interests. Certainly, children's interests are not confined to sectors such as health and education that they are familiar with; macro-economic and foreign policy strongly affect children's welfare and equity (White, 2002). There is also a temporal dimension to the process: how should children's current needs be balanced against possible impacts on their future prospects? Moreover, a focus on children's best interests tends to draw attention to individual wellbeing, rather than to children as a social group.

Best interests cannot be objectively identified: outcomes of social processes are complex and never totally predictable, and, more significantly, interests always reflect the values of those defining them. Where values conflict, disagreements arise. At the same time, it is clear that some processes tend to have systematically problematic outcomes for children's present or future wellbeing. There is, therefore, value in systematic analysis. White (2002) puts forward a Marxist model developed by Oldman (1994) who saw adult–child relationships as a 'generational mode of production' for 'producing' human capital. If the relations of production are suboptimal for children while maximizing benefits to adults, this constitutes exploitation (echoing Young's (1990) discussion of processes of oppression).

Failure to consider children's perspectives on their own best interests, then, is arguably an injustice. However, the notion of best interests must not be confined to the self-defined wishes of individual children. Rather, children's rights should respond to analysis of systematic processes through which children are oppressed, taking account of the perspectives of children and relevant adults.

Connecting with alternative views of childhood

As Secker points out in her chapter, in the arena of children's rights there are considerable tensions between international and national provisions and local beliefs and practices. It is argued that lack of rights was externally defined as a problem for children by expert representatives of the 'global community' (White, 2007) rather than a 'cry of suffering' (Young, 1990) from children themselves. Consequently, the CRC is grounded in an idealized middle-class Western construction of childhood, characterized by innocence, dependence, and vulnerability. An outcome, Norman argues, is that the formal rights accorded to children in South Africa, which conform to the CRC, are out of tune with traditional constructions of proper childhood and children's roles within society. This perspective is echoed in many other chapters in this volume.

One of the key differences between the concept of childhood inscribed in the CRC and that prevailing in most African communities is the priority accorded to the individual. Rights discourse has historically been highly individualistic, yet in African communities, as Abebe and Tefera argue, it is often the need to sustain interdependent life that is prioritized. As indicated in the introduction, the situation of children cannot be understood separately from the social relations in which they are embedded; social relations may impose demands on them that render rights discourse problematic. André and Godin point out, for instance, that for children in the DRC there are strong continuities in social relations and divisions of labour between life in their families and in the artisanal mines in which they work. This makes it harder to condemn the mines as exploitative while praising the family as the proper place for children. Similarly, Bourdillon and Musvosvi make the point that younger children's wellbeing often depends on the economic activities of their older siblings, who may formally be regarded as children themselves.

In many parts of Africa, then, people seldom think about child-rearing from a rights-based perspective. Rather focusing on rights, the participants in the research that Abebe and Tefera undertook in southern Ethiopia adopted an investment-based approach. The way they raised their children reflected a concern with the future of the children and of their families, but children were understood to earn their rights through their role in 'reproducing the daily lives of family collectives' (this volume), rather than being entitled to them by virtue of citizenship of the nation state. As André and Godin make clear, the complexity of the reciprocal social relationships that shape children's lives is lost in a rights discourse in which children are portrayed as passive and their parents active. To a degree this reciprocity is reflected in the emphasis of the ACRWC on children's responsibilities as well as their rights and South Africa's 'Bill of Responsibilities' discussed by Norman.

In light of the fact that the CRC is centred on the figure of a child that is unfamiliar to many people, it is unsurprising that children's rights are often viewed as irrelevant or, as Abebe and Tefera suggest, an unnecessary luxury. If laws are not meaningful to people, it is very unlikely that they will be upheld; if they are not implemented they cannot advance social justice. Secker argues that when faced with practices such as witchcraft accusations, sexual abuse, and violence, that can cause harm to children, there is a need for dialogue. People cannot be forced to abandon their beliefs simply through legislation. Interestingly, it is not only adults that resist children's rights. Despite children's awareness of their rights in both South Africa and Ethiopia, the research by Norman and by Abebe and Tefera suggests that children do not simply seize all rights on offer and often remain deferential towards adults.

However, despite some resistance to embracing children's rights, the rights contained in the CRC, the laws that enact these, and the increasingly widespread discourse of rights are nonetheless reshaping many societies in diverse ways. André and Godin point to the ways in which children's rights are shaping subjectivities and intergenerational relationships in the DRC. Such changes are not always positive. Norman argues that the manner in which children's rights have been enacted in South Africa has caused inter-generational conflict, and the erosion of positive communication and rela-tionships. Effects differ between socioeconomic groups (Abebe and Tefera). André and Godin illustrate how, in the DRC, middle-class parents' social values are changing. As they adopt the NGO discourse of 'legal childhood' and 'dominant parent', in contrast to their less affluent peers, they increas-ingly view mining as child labour. Among middle-class children, however, increasingly individualistic values are pushing some to work in the mines in order to advance their personal interests. Valentin and Meinert (2009) argue elsewhere that NGOs have taken on a role as second guardian to children, cultivating 'proper' children and parents who can live up to the 'good child-hood' espoused in the CRC. This 'civilizing role' patronizes both children and parents and infantilizes nations in the South.

Some scholars, however, argue that the CRC is more diverse in its effects and more amenable to alternative uses. It does not offer a unitary discourse or prescription and can be interpreted and mobilized in diverse ways. Rights do not have to be seen in terms of abstract universalism (Reynolds *et al.*, 2006). The ILO, for instance, uses the CRC to argue for abolition of child labour; organizations of working children use it to argue for recognition of children's right to work in dignity (Reynolds *et al.*, 2006). It has the potential to be mobilized in ways that are more likely to advance social justice. Moreover, as Western ideas of childhood enter non-Western contexts through the CRC, they acquire new meanings; they are partially indigenized (Burman, 1996). Rights refracted through different contexts shape children's experiences in different ways (Reynolds *et al.*, 2006). Moreover, to assume that rights by definition are alien to Africa can be criticized as excluding Africa's children from access to rights (Reynolds *et al.*, 2006). Instead, as Abebe and Tefera (this volume) and White (2002) suggest, it is possible to use cultural resources and concepts to work in children's interests, recognizing the limits of a universalist approach but also critiquing local culture and recognizing that political economy plays a role in shaping this.

Neither culture nor political economy, however, are purely local (or even national) phenomena. The CRC is not simply a global prescription being implemented in local contexts. As de Berry (2001) points out, the implementation of CRC needs to be based in knowledge of the realities – local and global – that frame children's lives. Contexts are global as well as local, and cannot be addressed purely at nation-state level.

Recognition of the significance of context fits with a 'politics of difference' approach to social justice. As Young (1990: 5) points out: 'The call to "be just" is always situated in concrete social and political practices.' There are undoubtedly tensions that arise from the application of rights that were formulated in relation to one group of children in very different local contexts, and the apparent rigidity of some of the articles of the CRC is problematic. However, the CRC can be interpreted in locally meaningful ways. This flexibility is often overlooked or denied in the implementation of the CRC through the programmes and advocacy of NGOs and even by national governments. More consideration is needed of how locally meaningful interpretations may be realized through the implementation of the CRC in different contexts, if social justice for children is to be advanced.

Conclusion

An examination of the role played by the CRC in African contexts that differ from those familiar to most of the actors involved in drawing it up reveals much about both the Convention itself and children's rights more broadly. The particular conceptualization of rights within the CRC poses challenges for implementation in such settings, but also problems for children. There is a strong tendency in both the articles of the CRC and in its implementation to ignore, first, local conceptualizations (of both childhood and rights); secondly, local realities (particularly for the poor and other marginalized groups); and, thirdly, the influence of political economy. Additionally, the five areas of tension outlined above pose challenges for the beneficial implementation of the CRC, in Africa as elsewhere. Despite these difficulties, many scholars suggest a rights framework can serve children's interests. Burman (1996: 53), for example, considers 'a legal rights framework worth retaining even though there may be no coherent theory of child rights, so that rights legislation functions to define a minimum basis for moral codes of behaviour where interests clash'. The CRC has proved effective in mobilizing resources in children's interests as well as provoking (sometimes positive) cultural change. For Reynolds *et al.* (2006), not to declare and seek to implement rights could be harmful and neglect abuse or entrench the disregard of children's interests. As Bakker (2010: 159) suggests, 'human rights are not the solution but are rather a strategy for creating the context in which claims for social justice can be pursued'. Thus in implementing the CRC, it needs to be seen more as a strategic tool through which contextually appropriate policies and programmes might be constructed, rather than a 'solution' to be uniformly applied.

This chapter has interrogated how far claims rooted in the CRC are able to advance social justice for children in Africa. Applying Iris Marion Young's (1990) notion of a 'politics of difference' to issues raised in the chapters of this volume suggests a number of ways in which the CRC is failing to deliver social justice. In order to advance social justice through rights legislation, this should 1) address the contextually situated processes through which children are systematically oppressed (exploitation, marginalization, powerlessness, cultural imperialism, and violence); 2) allow for young people to identify/be identified as children in non-essentialist, relational, and fluid ways, rather than applying to all under-18s regardless of their circumstances; and 3) cast responsibility for securing children's rights in ways that recognize social connectedness and the power of diverse parties to make a difference. While the CRC will not be rewritten in the near future, governments, NGOs, and the Committee on the Rights of the Child could usefully attend to these considerations in its implementation and monitoring.

References

Aitken, S.C. (2001) 'Global crises of childhood: rights, justice and the unchildlike child', *Area*, 33: 119–27.

Archard, D. (2004) *Children: Rights and Childhood*, London: Routledge.

Archard, D. (2006) 'The moral and political status of children', *Public Policy Research*, 13: 6–12.

Aries, P. (1962) *Centuries of Childhood*, New York, NY: Vintage Books.

Bakker, K. (2010) *Privatizing Water: Governance Failure and the World's Urban Water Crisis*, Ithaca, NY: Cornell University.

Bojer, H. (2002) 'Children and theories of social justice', *Feminist Economics*, 6: 23–39.

Burman, E. (1996) 'Local, global or globalized? Child development and international child rights legislation', *Childhood*, 3: 45–66.

Cohen, C.P. (1990) 'The role of nongovernmental organizations in the drafting of the Convention on the Rights of the Child', *Human Rights Quarterly*, 12: 137–47.

De Berry, J. (2001) 'Child soldiers and the convention on the rights of the child', *Annals of the American Academy of Political and Social Science*, 575: 92–105.

Ennew, J. (2002a) 'Outside childhood: street children's rights', in B. Franklin (ed.) *The New Handbook of Children's Rights: Comparative Policy and Practice*, London: Routledge.

Ennew, J. (2002b) 'Future generations and global standards: children's rights at the start of the millennium', in J. MacClancy (ed.) *Exotic No More: Anthropology on the Front Lines*, Chicago, IL: University of Chicago Press.

Grugel, J. (2013) 'Children's rights and children's welfare after the Convention on the Rights of the Child', *Progress in Development Studies*, 13: 19–30.

Levine-Clark, M. (2010) 'From "relief" to "justice and protection": the maintenance of deserted wives, British masculinity and imperial citizenship, 1870–1920', *Gender and History*, 22: 302–21.

Liebel, M. (2012) *Children's Rights from Below: Cross-Cultural Perspectives*, Basingstoke: Palgrave Macmillan.

Rawls, J. (1971) *A Theory of Justice*, Cambridge, MA: Harvard University Press.

Reynolds, P., Nieuwenhuys, O., and Hanson, K. (2006) 'Refractions of children's rights in development practice: a view from anthropology – introduction', *Childhood*, 13: 291–302.

Ruddick, S. (2007) 'At the horizons of the subject: neo-liberalism, neo-conservatism and the rights of the child. Part one: from "knowing fetus" to "confused" child', *Gender, Place and Culture*, 14: 513–26.

Türkelli, G.E. and Vandenhole, W. (2012) 'The Convention on the Rights of the Child: repertoires of NGO participation', *Human Rights Law Review*, 12: 33–64.

United Nations (1989) *United Nations Convention on the Rights of the Child*, New York, NY: UN General Assembly.

Valentin, K. and Meinert, L. (2009) 'The adult North and the young South: reflections on the civilizing mission of children's rights', *Anthropology Today*, 25: 23–8.

Vandenhole, W. (2011) 'Children's rights in EU external action: beyond charity and protection, beyond instrumentalisation and conditionality', *International Journal of Children's Rights*, 19: 477–500.

White, S.C. (2002) 'Being, becoming and relationship: conceptual challenges of a child rights approach in development', *Journal of International Development*, 14: 1095–104.

White, S.C. (2007) 'Children's rights and the imagination of community in Bangladesh', *Childhood*, 14: 505–20.

Wollstonecraft, M. (1792/2004) *A Vindication of the Rights of Woman*, Harmondsworth: Penguin.

Young, I.M. (1990) *Justice and the Politics of Difference*, Princeton, NJ: Princeton University Press.

Young, I.M. (2006) 'Responsibility and global justice: a social connection model', *Social Philosophy and Policy*, 23: 102–30.

Index